D0881336

Prices, Cycles, and Growth

Studies in Dynamical Economic Science
Richard H. Day, editor

Richard H. Day, *Complex Economic Dynamics, Volume I:*
An Introduction to Dynamic Systems and Market Mechanisms, 1994

Hukukane Nikaido, *Prices, Cycles, and Growth,* 1996

Prices, Cycles, and Growth

Hukukane Nikaido

The MIT Press
Cambridge, Massachusetts
London, England

338.52
N69P

This book was set in Times Roman by Asco Trade Typesetting Ltd., Hong Kong and was printed and bound in the United States of America.

Library of Congress Cataloging-in-Publication Data

Nikaido, Hukukane, 1923–
  Prices, cycles, and growth / Hukukane [i.e. Hukukanee] Nikaido.
    p.   cm. — (Studies in dynamical economic science)
  Includes bibliographical references and index.
  ISBN 0-262-14059-4 (alk. paper)
  1. Prices—Mathematical models. 2. Business cycles—Mathematical models. 3. Economic growth—Mathematical models. I. Title. II. Series.
HB221.N542   1996
338.5′2—dc20   95-32646
                                                                      CIP

Contents

Series Foreword

Studies in Dynamical Economic Science is devoted to theoretical, mathematical, and empirical research concerning economic change and the forces causing it. It encompasses business cycles, economic growth, economic development, and the underlying microeconomic processes that govern individual, household, firm, market, and government behavior. It is eclectic as to theory and method, encompassing equilibrium, disequilibrium, optimizing, and adaptive evolutionary points of view. Theory and models that emphasize realistic assumptions and that are buttressed by an appeal to facts are especially encouraged. The ultimate goal of the series is to contribute to more effective policies for enhancing the benefits and ameliorating the costs of rapid change.

Foreword: Hukukane Nikaido, a Biographical Essay

Kazuo & Richard H.
Nishimura Day

Hukukane Nikaido received the B.S. and D.Sc. degrees in mathematics from the University of Tokyo. He taught himself economics, however, beginning with Karl Marx's *Das Kapital* in the German text, then absorbing modern, orthodox economics through Hicks's *Value and Capital* and Samuelson's *Foundations of Economic Analysis*. He began his own research career in economics at the Department of Mathematics, Tokyo College of Science, which was his first academic affiliation.

The output of his early efforts involved extensions to the von Neuman growth model (1954a, 1954b, 1955) and establishing the existence of competitive general equilibrium with many consumers and producers. The latter work, which was published in 1956, was first presented at the annual meeting of the Japan Association of Economics and Econometrics in the autumn of 1954, the same year that the existence proofs of McKenzie and Arrow and Debreu appeared. These achievements propelled him into the front ranks of mathematical economists and led to a visiting appointment at Stanford, 1955–1956, at the invitation of Kenneth Arrow. He was elected fellow of the Econometric Society in 1962.

On returning from Stanford Professor Nikaido joined the Institute of Social and Economic Research, Osaka University, headed by Michio Morishima. It was there that he turned his efforts to an investigation of the stability of general equilibria, his work culminating in studies published in the period 1959–1964. Osaka was a very active intellectual center in those days and welcomed many eminent economists from abroad. John Hicks was one who shared an interest in the turnpike theorem of multisector economic growth. Turnpike theorems had been proved by Morishima (1961) and Radner (1961). Radner's theorem was heightened into a strong turnpike theorem by Nikaido (1964). He worked with David Gale, a visiting professor at the institute in 1961, and coauthored a classic paper (Gale and Nikaido 1965) on the uniqueness of solutions of nonlinear simultaneous equations, a result generally known as the Gale–Nikaido Theorem. In his later years in Osaka, his previous research was integrated and published in 1968 as the book *Convex Structures and Economic Theory*. Widely regarded as a masterpiece in mathematical economics, the book has served widely as a text and reference, and has been read by students and researchers around the world.

In 1969, Nikaido moved from Osaka to Hitotsubashi University in Tokyo. During this period, his stay was interrupted by visiting professorships at the University of Minnesota and the University of California,

Berkeley. He began to work on general equilibrium involving monopolistic competition. In this theory of an imperfectly competitive market, each firm decides its own supply based on a perceived demand function. Nikaido recognized, however, that the demand function, a partial equilibrium theoretic construction, involves inconsistencies in a general equilibrium situation. He introduced the concept of "objective demand functions," which are free from the inconsistencies. Using this idea, he was able to explore the existence of monopolistically competitive equilibria. The results (appraised by Arrow as a highly original model of pricing and allocation) culminated in the 1974 paper and the 1975 book *Monopolistic Competition and Effective Demand*.

Subsequently, Nikaido developed a dynamization of this theory, which was originally presented at the Symposium on Adaptive Economics at the University of Wisconsin in 1974 and published subsequently in Nikaido 1975. From this time on, he concentrated on developing dynamic economic theory of out-of-equilibrium adjustments. The present volume (which contains in part I the early essays on the stability of general equilibrium) is primarily devoted to these studies, which include work undertaken during sabbatical periods at the University of Southern California in 1976–1977 and in several subsequent years.

Part II shifts attention to the stability analysis of monopolistic competition in explicit models of pricing and adjustments but within an intersectoral framework with Leontief technology. The essays of part III investigate various issues of stability, income distribution, and factor substitution in von Neuman, Solow, and Keynesian frameworks. Part IV contains Nikaido's reconsideration of Marxian issues using the rigorous tools of dynamic analysis developed in his earlier work.

Readers of this book will discover why Nikaido is known for his impeccably high standards of model construction and analysis, and for his concentration on the truly fundamental aspects of the subject. Despite his distinguished career and pioneering achievements, he is equally known for his quiet and gentle demeanor and for the friendly modesty that characterizes those who achieve much and gain wisdom along the way.

Kazuo Nishimura
Richard H. Day

References

Gale, D., and H. Nikaido (1965): The Jacobian Matrix and Global Univalence of Mappings. *Mathematische Annalen* 159.

Morishima, M. (1961): Proof of a Turnpike Theorem: The "No Joint Production Case," *Review of Economic Studies* 28.

Nikaido, H. (1954a): Note on the General Economic Equilibrium for Nonlinear Production Functions. *Econometrica* 22.

————. (1954b): On von Neumann's Minimax Theorem. *Pacific Journal of Mathematics* 4.

————. (1955): New Aspects of von Neumann's Model with Special Regard to Computational Problems. *Annals of the Institute of Statistical Mathematics* 6.

————. (1956): On the Classical Multilateral Exchange Problem. *Metroeconomica* 8.

————. (1964): Persistence of Continual Growth near the von Neumann Ray: A Strong Version of the Radner Turnpike Theorem. *Econometrica* 32. Reprinted as chapter 7 in this book.

————. (1974): What Is an Objective Demand Function? *Zeitschrift für Nationalökonomie* 34.

————. (1975): Economic Adjustments under Noncompetitive Pricing, R. H. Day and T. Groves, eds. *Adaptive Economic Models.* New York: Academic Press. Reprinted as chapter 3 in this book.

Radner, R. (1961): Paths of Economic Growth that Are Optimal with Regard Only to Final States, a Turnpike Theorem. *Review of Economic Studies* 28.

NA

Part I

I developed a deep concern for economics when I was still a mathematics student in the early 1950s. From that early time on, I concentrated on the theory of the economy as a whole beginning with the Walrasian system. Even at this initial stage I seriously doubted the workability of the Walrasian concept of capitalism, based as it was on the counting of unknowns and equations. This motivated my initial inquiry into the existence of competitive equilibrium. In spite of my reservations, I had hopes for its prospects based on my success during this period in proving certain existence theorems in game theory (1954, 1955). These hopes were realized in my proof of the existence of competitive equilibrium published in 1956. I then turned to dynamic aspects of the subject, which were preoccupying the then contemporary mainstream of mathematical economics in its concern with the asymptotic stability of Walrasian tâtonnement. This led to the works published in chapters 1 and 2.

An Overview along Heretical Lines

These early results dealt with statics and dynamics within the Hicksian week of a generic Walrasian, Arrow–Debreu economy, one that is solely composed of production, exchange and consumption but devoid of capital formation, credit, and money. In my view, such models describe ideal resource allocation in an institutional framework of complete private ownership, rather than the working of the market economy in the real world. They are best thought of as normative, rather than positive, constructions.

Economics is not only a social science but a social thought, a product of society itself that reflects a need for coherent images or portraits by which its members can comprehend what is going on and better guide their actions within the system as a whole. It is the economist's brush that provides these economic self-portraits. From the 1970s on, while casting a sidelong glance at the still ongoing construction of ever more sophisticated works in mathematical economics, I have been more and more captivated by the inquiry into manifold features of the working of the economy, dynamic as well as static but in distinction from its idealized working.

The principal view, which drives me most, is that the working of the real world capitalist economy can better be elucidated along the lines suggested by Keynes (1936) in his criticism of the Classical school rather than along the lines currently pursued by the rational expectationists and new Classicals as descendants of the old Classicals. It is especially his grand vision that the economy is unstable and can be ill-behaved that seems most important.

Being more concerned with the problems of instability than with those of equilibrium, I have been exploring directions suggested by him, although I am not completely committed to any specific school, neither the old, the new, or the left-wing post Keynesians, nor others, whereas I have indeed learned much from them. The essays in parts II–IV are primarily the products of the inquiry that these thoughts possessed me to undertake in the 1970s and 1980s. These studies can be seen from three key viewpoints, namely, *disequilibrium, economy-wide noncompetition* and the *socioeconomic role played by pricing in income distribution.*

Disequilibrium means that markets do not generally clear, yet nonetheless transactions are carried out. In dynamics perspective, this disequilibrium situation not only persists but evolves over time, while transactions are executed at non-equilibrium prices, which, too, change over time.

Economy-wide noncompetition means that generally, and even in a short-run situation, more or less noncompetitive forces, such as monopoly, monopolistic competition and so forth, are operative in the economy as a whole. The problem is how to conceptualize the noncompetitive working of the economy as a whole, not merely that of a single market.

Political economic or socioeconomic light is shed on the income distribution that ensues from pricing, dynamic as well as static, in the economy as a whole to elucidate certain socioeconomic aspects of the function of price mechanism.

Finally, but not least, in addition to the key viewpoints, *Say's law* is often referred to below as a very important concept by which to examine, more specifically, to characterize, the performance of the economy in question.

Having already described the background of my essays that are reprinted in parts II–IV, I turn to reflections on them by part.

Part II

Prices are set by a producer who adjusts quantities toward dissolution of the discrepancies between demand and supply. In case the dissolution is perfect in the short-run, objective demand functions can be defined so that the resulting equilibrium quantities can be thought of as outcome of monopolistic decisions to determine prices. Using this concept, I reconsidered general equilibrium with noncompetitive behavior both in a multisector context (1975) and for a macromodel (1974), labor being fully employed in the former, underemployed in the latter.

Chapters 3 and 5 are the dynamic versions of these two studies in which discrepancies persist and changes in price-making emerge over time. Chapters 4 and 6 are devoted to the elucidation of certain political economic or socioeconomic aspects of the role played by pricing in income distribution. In the former attention is focused on the trade-off between profits and wages that drives a wage-price spiral in a multisector model of the Leontief–Sraffa type. The purpose of the latter is to show how income distribution is regulated by pricing and vice versa in a multisector model of income distribution, attention being focused on both static and dynamic aspects.

Part III

The contents of part III are classified into two portions, according to how growth and cycles are dealt with. Chapters 7 and 8 treat growth when Say's law holds, while ignoring cycles. Contrariwise, chapters 9–12 come to grips with both growth and cycles when the economy is in disequilibrium and Say's law is presumed not to obtain, and show how the two are interdependent. Chapter 7 is my earlier work done completely along the mainstream of study of growth in the early 1960s as a process of efficient capital accumulation. It is a treatise on idealized resource allocation over time, so that it is normative-oriented, not just because of optimality as a target, but because of the very ways of problem-posing and model-building.

The primary objective of chapter 8, which works out a Solovian neoclassical growth model (Solow 1956) under monopolist's price-making, is to introduce the conceptualization of economy-wide noncompetition in a dynamic setting. At each moment the volume of full employment and the resulting level of output are determined by the monopolist's choice of the real wage. Given the applicability of Say's law, the resulting level of income creates an amount of demand equal to the level of output, which implies the existence of a well-formulated, objective demand function. On the basis of such a function, the monopolist's behavior determines a temporary equilibrium. The long-run steady state and the implied balanced growth paths, which are generated by weaving these temporary equilibria, are examined.

Solow's model, which establishes the dissolution in the long-run of the discrepancies between the warranted and natural rates of growth under smooth factor substitution, is often misinterpreted as dissolving Harrod's knife-edge. At each moment a temporary equilibrium with full employment of capital and labor is achieved by way of the automatic equality of savings to investment, that is, under Say's law implicitly assumed. These temporary equilibria form an asymptotically stable growth process, which rules out at the outset any possibility for the economy to slip off the growth path. Harrod's perception that the economy is balanced at a knife-edge is, however, of disequilibrium dynamics nature, and persists even under flexible factor substitution. Chapters 9 and 10 examine this perception by re-examining Solow's growth process when it is embedded in a disequilibrium dynamics process where Say's law does not pertain. Markets do not generally clear, but transactions are carried out on the short-side principle. The economy grows in a Keynesian way.

Chapter 11, which takes into explicit consideration the monetary side, introduces two additional variables, the price level and the rate of interest. The rate of interest is adjusted so as to equate the demand for money to its supply growing steadily. The growth rate of intended investment depends on the captial/labor ratio and the rate of profit net of real rate of interest. As to the mode of change in price level over time, the rate of inflation is shown to be the difference between intended and actual rate of capital accumulation in real terms, a result that follows from the supposition that intended investment is always realized in money terms.

The working thus formulated leads to a system of three differential equations of three variables, namely, the capital/labor ratio, the rate of intended capital accumulation, and the rate of interest. In a typical case the system generates a cyclical growth path, which has major cycles of long-term in the first variable accompanied by minor cycles of short-term in the other two variables. Specifically, minor cycles emerge only in up-swing phases of major cycles, while no minor cycle appears in downswing phases. The movement of the economy along the growth path in this mode is so complex that no state is recurrent in the three dimensional state space.

The model in chapter 12 is essentially the same as that in chapter 11 except that the monetary side has been deleted so that the dynamics occurs in two dimensions. The two-variable system of differential equations generates growth paths which are eventually enclosed in a bounded region, which includes an unstable critical point corresponding to a steady growth state with underemployed labor, by virtue of the constraint origi-nating in the supply side. Application of the Poincaré–Bendixon theorem implies the existence of a limit cycle.

Part IV

My concern for Marxian economics dates as far back as my youthful wandering through social and economic thoughts in the late 1940s, but had been suspended until almost thirty years later and in isolation from the lines of study among contemporary Classicals working in the Ricardo –Marx tradition, I took up the old classical conjecture of the equalization of profit rates through capital movement across sectors, while on leave at the University of Southern California in Los Angeles.

Initially distributed in Nikaido 1977, my results were published after further work subsequently in two papers here reproduced in chapters 13 and 14. In these models changes in prices take place toward dissolution of discrepancies between demand and supply in such a way as affects materi-alization of intended investment in nominal terms to sustain the relation between money and real capitals over time, as in chapter 11. Changes in quantities emerge as savings ensuing at the current prices. Naturally, the changes in both monetary and real variables are intertwined.

Throughout chapter 14 and section 8 in chapter 13 Say's law is assumed to hold in the sense that the entire profit income is intended to be spent on consumption and investment. Nonetheless, labor is generally under-employed. It is well known that Marx was very critical of the law, though he works out his scheme of reproduction by assuming its validity (cf. Morishima 1973). On the other hand, in chapter 13, except for section 8, the law is not assumed.

Because of their explicit treatment of Marx's conception of capitalist competition and because they show that the classical conjecture does not hold in general, these pages seem to have stimulated an accelerating effort in model-building along these lines as indicated, for example, in Flaschel and Semmler 1987.

Epilog

I shall conclude this brief summary with some additional remarks on the collection as a whole. They have two special features in the ways of approach. One is the lack of microeconomic foundations for the macroeconomic behavioral equations investigated. I admit the ad hoc nature of the model-building in this respect. This misdeed might originate in my underlying view that microeconomic underpinning is not the sine qua non for the construction of a macroeconomic image of the capitalist economy in the real world.

The other is that they ignore inventories. In the treatment of capital accumulation I could not bear to presume materialization of investment exceeding savings by pulling down inventories implicitly assumed to exist without taking inventories and inventory investment into explicit consideration. Instead of dealing with inventories explicitly, therefore, in chapters 11 and 12, I formulated gorwth and cycles in their mutual interaction within the supply potential originating in the existing capital stock and labor force. The disequilibrium dynamics growth process in chapters 9 and 10, too, are formulated in the same way.

In my building and analyzing the models in most works in parts III and IV, I owe much to what I learned in the spirit of nonlinear economic dynamics, though not in any specific ways of approach relevant to them, to literature on the subject matter. In this respect, Goodwin, whose works on this topic were collected and published in 1982, is a prominent figure.

References

Flaschel, P., and W. Semmler (1987): Classical and Neoclassical Competitive Adjustment Processes. In *The Manchester School*, 55.

Goodwin, R. (1982): *Essays in Economic Dynamics*. London: Macmillan.

Keynes, J. M. (1936): *General Theory of Employment, Money and Interest*. London: Macmillan.

Morishima, M. (1973): *Marx's Economics, A Dual Theory of Value and Growth*. Cambridge: Cambridge University Press.

Nikaido, H. (1954): On von Neumann's Minimax Theorem. *Pacific Journal of Mathematics* 4.

Nikaido, H., and K. Isoda (1955): Note on Noncooperative Convex Games. *Pacific Journal of Mathematics* 5, Supplement 1.

Nikaido, H. (1956): On the Classical Multilateral Exchange Problem. *Metroeconomica*, 8.

———. (1974): What Is an Objective Demand Function? *Zeitschrift für Nationalökonomie* 34.

———. (1975): *Monopolistic Competition and Effective Demand*. Princeton: Princeton University Press.

———. (1977): Refutation of the Dynamic Equalization of Profit Rates in Marx's Scheme of Reproduction. Mimeo, University of Southern California.

I Walrasian Tâtonnements

1 Stability of Equilibrium by the Brown–von Neumann Differential Equation

1 Introduction

Much Interest has recently been taken in the problem of the global stability of competitive equilibrium (Arrow and Hurwicz 1958; Arrow, Block, and Hurwicz 1959; Morishima 1958; Uzawa 1959), but either special or little attention has been focused upon the nonnegativity of relevant variables. The present article offers some results regarding this problem for a new type of price adjustment process. Speical attention will be given to the nonnegativity of price systems as well as to the economically important requirement that excess demand functions are defined only for nonnegative values of variables.

In order to meet the difficulties that arise from paying special attention to this nonnegativity requirement, the orthodox pattern of price adjustment is slightly modified yet no serious harm is done to its economic significance. It will be shown that the competitive market admits global stability along with the nonnegativity requirement provided that the tâtonnement process is *one-sidedly flexible* in the following sense: The price of each commodity is sensitive only to its positive excess demand, but insensitive to its positive excess supply. This will be achieved by transforming the primal dynamic system to a tâtonnement system described by the Brown–von Neumann differential equation. This equation was originally designed to solve zero-sum two-person games, and was also used by this writer to solve the orthodox utility maximization problem (Nikaido 1958). The proof of stability will be achieved by carrying further the idea of Brown and von Neumann (1950) so that it covers not only the case of competitive equilibrium but also generalizes the Brown–von Neumann result. A substantial portion of the proof will be carried out with a local behavioral assumption on excess demand functions, though it will later be shown that this assumption must entail a similar global relation and, therefore, the uniqueness of equilibrium.[1]

2 The One-sidedly Flexible Process of Price Adjustment

2.1 As an appropriate set of assumptions about the competitive market, the following conditions are imposed:

From *Econometrica* 27 (October 1959): 654–671. Reprinted by permission.

There are n commodities whose prices are denoted by $p_i \geqq 0$, respectively, and a price system denoted by a nonnegative vector $p = (p_1, p_2, \ldots, p_n) \geq 0$, where $\geq$ has the meaning that each component is ≥ 0 but not all components $= 0$. p is said to be *normalized*, if its components add up to unity, $\sum_{t=1}^{n} p_i = 1$; otherwise p is said to be *nonnormalized*.

(1)   The excess demand for the ith commodity is a single-valued continuous function $E_i(p)$ of $p \geq 0$, $(i = 1, 2, \ldots, n)$, and furthermore, each of them fulfills the Lipschitz condition for *normalized*[2] price systems, that is, there exists a set of positive numbers M_{ij} such that $|E_i(p) - E_i(q)| \leqq \sum_{j=1}^{n} M_{ij} |p_j - q_j|$, $(i = 1, 2, \ldots, n)$ for all normalized price systems p and q.

(2)   Each of the $E_i(p)$ is homogeneous of degree zero.

(3) $\sum_{i=1}^{n} p_i E_i(p) = 0$ is true identically for all price systems p, that is, the Walras law prevails.

(4) $\sum_{i=1}^{n} \Delta p_i \Delta E_i(p) < 0$ for $\sum_{i=1}^{n} |\Delta p_i| > 0$ is valid *locally* on the set S of all *normalized* price systems.

The force of condition (4) will be explained below. Let p and q denote two normalized price systems. Condition (4) then means that each normalized price system p has some sufficiently small neighborhood $U(p)$ within S such that $\sum_{i=1}^{n} (q_i - p_i) (E_i(q) - E_i(p)) < 0$ for $q \in U(p)$ provided q is distinct from p. Roughly speaking, if sufficiently small displacements take place within normalized price systems, then (4) holds. As will be shown later, the local validity of assumption (4) necessarily implies its global validity. Since, however, no advantage will be taken of the latter until the fourth paragraph of Section 3, we shall for the time being ignore this point so as to bring the crucial part of the proof into relief.

2.2   The market is said to be in equilibrium for a price system $\hat{p}$, if

$$E_i(\hat{p}) \leqq 0 \quad (i = 1, 2, \ldots, n), \tag{5}$$

$$E_i(\hat{p}) = 0 \quad \text{for } i \text{ such that } \hat{p}_i > 0. \tag{6}$$

It is now well known that the Walras law and the continuity of the $E_i(p)$'s already suffice to assure the existence of such an equilibrium price system (Arrow and Debreu 1954, Gale 1955, McKenzie 1954, Nikaido 1956). It should be noted, however, that the present approach to stability need not assume the existence of equilibrium, but, on the contrary, provides us with another proof of the existence of equilibrium, in a dynamic version, of this special competitive market. This corresponds to one of the basic ideas underlying the Brown–von Neumann article. But this point is not of major importance in the present article.

2.3 In discussing the stability of price adjustment processes, we here consider the differential rather than the difference equation version. Let us begin by considering an orthodox system of price adjustment for the *nonnormalized* price system $q = (q_1, q_2, \ldots, q_n) \geq 0$:

$$\frac{dq_i}{dt} = E_i(q) \quad (i = 1, 2, \ldots, n). \tag{7}$$

In the market described by (7) the price of each commodity is two-sidedly flexible in the sense that it rises or falls depending upon whether the excess demand for the commodity is positive or negative. If a given initial price system is strictly positive, (7) may have a solution defined in a small interval of time $[0, \sigma]$. The study of global stability is concerned with the long-run behavior of the solution and, therefore, assumes that this local solution can be continued to all $t \geq 0$. It is generally very doubtful, however, whether this continuation is possible,[3] unless the $E_i(p)$'s are assumed to be defined for some negative values of the q_i's. But this contradicts the condition required by the economic viewpoint that the $E_i(q)$'s are defined only for $q \geq 0$.

There is another difficulty in system (7). In the market studied here the equilibrium state is given by inequalities (5) and (6) rather than by equalities. If the excess supply of some commodity is positive at equilibrium, its price must be zero by (5) and (6). If the price adjustment is described by system (7), there might appear the unreal tendency for the price of a commodity with positive excess supply to be lowered below zero even in equilibrium. This also motivates a modification of system (7).

There are several solutions to these difficulties. As a possible one, we here pay special attention to the following modified system. We sacrifice two-sided flexibility and replace it by the one-sided flexibility of price change. In our new system the price of each commodity is only sensitive to its positive excess demand, whereas it is insensitive to negative excess demand. This may correspond to the well known Keynesian lower rigidity of the money wage, and may therefore still bear some connection with reality. But this one-sidedness is more apparent than real. If the excess supply of a commodity is positive, and if the market is *not* as yet *in equilibrium*, then there are one or more other commodities with positive excess demands. The nominal prices of the latter commodities must therefore rise by virtue of the upper-flexibility, so that the price of the former will certainly fall *in relation to* the prices of the latter.

Analytically, the new tâtonnement process may be represented by the differential equation for the *nonnormalized* price system

$$\frac{dq_i}{dt} = \theta_i(q) \quad (i = 1, 2, \ldots, n), \tag{8}$$

where

$$\theta_i(q) = \max[E_i(q), 0] \quad (i = 1, 2, \ldots, n). \tag{9}$$

Under the assumption that each $E_i(q)$ is continuous[4] and homogeneous of degree zero for $q \geq 0$, equation (8) has a solution $q(t)$ for $t \geq 0$ starting from any prescribed initial price system. Therefore, corresponding to the heuristic discussions above concerning system (8), there is a mathematical formulation that makes sense and whose properties we wish to investigate below. The proof of these results can almost be worked out along the customary lines of an existence proof. Its outline will be given at the end of the final section.

It is obvious that critical points of (8), namely those which make $\theta_i(q)$ on the right-hand side of (8) vanish, correspond to equilibrium price systems given by (5) and (6). Inasmuch as prices are not normalized in system (8), what is important is not the behavior of the solution $q(t) \geq 0$ of (8) itself, but that of the corresponding normalized system $q(t)/\sum_{i=1}^{n} q_i(t)$. System (8) is defined as *asymptotically globally stable* if the normalized price system of any solution of (8) converges to *some* equilibrium price system as time t tends to infinity.

The main thesis of this study is summarized in the

THEOREM   Under assumptions (1), (2), (3) and (4), system (8) is asymptotically globally stable.

As the first step towards the proof of this thesis we shall investigate the relation between system (8) and a system described by the Brown–von Neumann differential equation. For this purpose we define a transformation function for time. A nonnegative numerical function $\alpha(t)$ defined for

$t \geq 0$ will be called a *transformation function* if $\alpha(0) = 0$, $d\alpha/dt > 0$, and $\lim_{t \to +\infty} \alpha(t) = +\infty$

PROPOSITION 1[5]   For any solution $q(t)$ of (8) there is a transformation function $\alpha(t)$ such that the normalized price system

$$p(t) = q(\alpha(t)) \Big/ \sum_{i=1}^{n} q_i(\alpha(t))$$

satisfies

$$\frac{dp_i}{dt} = \theta_i(p) - \zeta(p)p_i \quad (i = 1, 2, \ldots, n), \tag{10}$$

where

$$\theta_i(p) = \max[E_i(p), 0] \quad (i = 1, 2, \ldots, n), \tag{11}$$

$$\zeta(p) = \sum_{i=1}^{n} \theta_i(p). \tag{12}$$

Proof   We obtain an $\alpha(t)$ as a solution of an auxiliary differential equation. Let $q(t)$ be a solution of (8). Consider the differential equation for an unknown function $\alpha(t)$, $t \geq 0$,

$$\frac{d\alpha}{dt} = \sum_{i=1}^{n} q_i(\alpha), \quad \alpha(0) = 0. \tag{13}$$

By (8),

$$\sum_{i=1}^{n} q_i(\alpha) \geq \sum_{i=1}^{n} q_i(0) > 0, \quad \text{for } \alpha \geq 0,$$

and fulfills the Lipschitz condition for all $\alpha \geq 0$, because the $\theta_i(q)$'s appearing on the right-hand side of (8) are bounded owing to the zero degree homogeneity of the $E_i(q)$'s. Therefore, a solution $\alpha(t)$ of (13) can be shown to exist over all $t \geq 0$ by a customary method of proof. Furthermore,

$$d\alpha/dt = \sum_{i=1}^{n} q_i(\alpha(t)) \geq \sum_{i=1}^{n} q_i(\alpha(0)) = \delta > 0.$$

This result also implies the inequality $\alpha(t) \geq \delta t$, which gives $\lim_{t \to +\infty} \alpha(t) = +\infty$. $\alpha(t)$ is therefore a transformation function. Now construct the normalized system $p(t) = (p_1(t), p_2(t), \ldots, p_n(t))$ of the transformed solution

$q(\alpha(t))$, where

$$p_i(t) = q_i(\alpha(t)) \Big/ \sum_{j=1}^{n} q_j(\alpha(t)).$$

The proof will be complete if it is shown that $p(t)$ fulfills equation (10). This can be done by a simple formal computation. In fact, from definition, it immediately follows that

$$p_i(t) \sum_{j=1}^{n} q_j(\alpha(t)) = q_i(\alpha(t)).$$

Upon differentiation[6] we get at once

$$\dot{p}_i(t) \sum_{j=1}^{n} q_j[\alpha(t)] + \dot{\alpha}(t)p_i(t) \sum_{j=1}^{n} \dot{q}_j[\alpha(t)] = \dot{\alpha}(t)\dot{q}_t[\alpha(t)]. \tag{14}$$

But $\dot{q}_t(\alpha(t)) = \theta_i[q(\alpha(t))]$ by (8), which in turn is equal to $\theta_i(p(t))$ by virtue of the zero order homogeneity of the $E_i(q)$'s. In view of equation (13), relation (14) reduces to

$$\dot{\alpha}\dot{p}_i = \dot{\alpha}\left[\theta_i(p) - p_i \sum_{j=1}^{n} \theta_j(p) \right]. \tag{15}$$

As was seen above, $\dot{\alpha}(t) > 0$ identically. Hence, dividing (15) by $\dot{\alpha}(t)$ gives equation (10). This completes the proof.

These results lead to the study of equation (10).

2.4   Equation (10) was originally devised and studied by Brown and von Neumann to solve game problems. In their case, the functions $E_i(p)$ are linear functions with skew symmetric coefficients, explicitly,

$$E_i(p) = \sum_{j=1}^{n} a_{ij} p_j, \quad \text{with } a_{ij} = -a_{ji}.$$

They proved for this special case that any solution remains nonnegative and normalized over time and that $\sum_{i=1}^{n} [\theta_i(p)]^2 \to 0$ as $t \to +\infty$. But their result can not apply to the present case because the assumptions on $E_i(p)$ are too stringent. This calls for a generalization of their result. If the $E_i(p)$'s are linear functions with skew-symmetric coefficients, then clearly

$$\sum_{i=1}^{n} p_i E_i(p) = \sum_{t,j=1}^{n} a_{ij} p_i p_j = 0 \quad \text{and} \quad \sum_{i=1}^{n} \Delta p_i \Delta E_i(p) = \sum_{t,j=1}^{n} a_{ij} \Delta p_i \Delta p_j = 0.$$

The former relation implies condition (3) whereas the latter implies that

$$\sum_{i=1}^{n} \Delta p_i \Delta E_i(p) \leq 0 \qquad (4')$$

is valid locally on S, which is weaker than condition (4). Condition (1) is obviously fulfilled.

This suggests a generalization of the Brown–von Neumann result in the following direction:

PROPOSITION 2   Let the $E_i(p)$'s satisfy condition (1). Then, for any given normalized price system p^0, there exists one and only one solution of (10) starting from p^0 and being defined for all $t \geq 0$. This solution remains normalized over time.

PROPOSITION 3   Suppose the $E_i(p)$'s fulfill conditions (1), (3) and (4'). Then, for any solution, $p(t)$, of (10),

$$\sum_{i=1}^{n} [\theta_i(p(t))]^2 \to 0 \quad (t \to +\infty).$$

PROPOSITION 4   Under conditions (1), (3) and (4), any solution, $p(t)$, of (10) converges to a unique normalized equilibrium price system, as t tends to infinity.

Propositions 3 and 4 will be proved in the following section and Proposition 2 in the final section.

The theorem in question regarding the asymptotic global stability of system (8) is an immediate consequence of these propositions. In fact, by propositions 1 and 4, $q[\alpha(t)]/\sum_{i=1}^{n} q_i[\alpha(t)]$ converges to a unique equilibrium price system. But, in view of the properties of $\alpha(t)$, the *nontransformed* $q(t)/\sum_{i=1}^{n} q_i(t)$ also converges to the same equilibrium price system.

2.5   There is another point to be mentioned. In system (10) coefficients giving the speed of adjustment do not appear or, in other words, their values are taken to be unity. But this is not important. It is possible to incorporate these coefficients into the system without causing any essential modification of the method of analysis.

Let

$$k_i \frac{dq_i}{dt} = E_i(q) \quad (i = 1, 2, \ldots, n) \qquad (16)$$

be a classical orthodox system of price change, where $k_i > 0$ are these coefficients. Then, in analogy with (10), the corresponding nonnegative system

$$k_i \frac{dq_i}{dt} = \theta_i(q) \quad (i = 1, 2, \ldots, n) \tag{17}$$

is conceivable. The normalized system of a suitably transformed solution of (17) satisfies the corresponding Brown–von Neumann equation

$$\frac{dp_i}{dt} = \theta_i(p)/k_i - \zeta(p)p_i \quad (i = 1, 2, \ldots, n) \tag{18}$$

where $\theta_i(p)$ is defined by (11), and

$\zeta(p)$ by $\xi(p) = \sum\limits_{i=1}^{n} \theta_i(p)/k_i$

instead of by (12). Asymptotic global stability can also be proved for system (17) by showing in the same way as in the case just discussed that

$$\sum_{i=1}^{n} [\theta_i(p(t))]^2/k_i \to 0, \quad \text{as } t \to +\infty.$$

2.6   In the discussion above the process of price adjustment described by (8) was converted to that described by the Brown–von Neumann equation (10) for the normalized price system. It is here noted that the tâtonnement process given by (10) is still in some agreement with the orthodox version. This proces is such that if $E_i(p) \leq 0$, $\zeta(p) > 0$, then $dp_i/dt < 0$ or $dp_i/dt = 0$ according as $p_i > 0$ or $p_i = 0$; i.e., if the market is not as yet in equilibrium, and if the excess supply of the ith commodity is currently nonnegative, then its price is lowered or remains unchanged depending upon whether the current price is positive or zero. Thus, the price of any commodity with positive excess demand is increased or remains unchanged relative to the prices of commodities whose excess demand is nonpositive and the amount and direction of price change are determined by the current values of the price of the commodity concerned and the excess demands of all commodities.

It is easily seen that the critical points of equation (10), i.e., the points which make the right-hand side of (10) vanish completely, correspond to equilibrium price systems. In fact, multiplying $\theta_i(p) - \zeta(p)p_i = 0$ by $E_i(p)$ and summing for $i = 1, 2, \ldots, n$ gives

$$\sum_{i=1}^{n} \theta_i(p)E_i(p) = \zeta(p) \sum_{i=1}^{n} p_i E_i(p) = 0$$

by (3). In view of the relation $\theta_i(p)E_i(p) = [\theta_i(p)]^2$, this reduces to $\sum_{i=1}^{n} [\theta_i(p)]^2 = 0$, which implies $E_i(p) \leq \theta_i(p) = 0$ for all i. Condition (6) is an immediate consequence of (3) and (5). Also, the converse is almost obvious.

Finally, attention should be called to the fact that condition (2) of homogeneity plays no essential role in studying the Brown–von Neumann equation. Accordingly, this condition does not appear in any of Propositions 2–4.

3   Global Stability by the B–N Equation

It this section we shall prove Propositions 3 and 4. As was remarked, Proposition 3 generalizes the result obtained by Brown and von Neumann, but the proof here is more complicated than theirs because much weaker assumptions are adopted. It must be emphasized that during the proof we rely heavily on Proposition 2 (to be proved later), especially on the fact that the solution $p(t)$ of (10) fulfills $p_i(t) \geq 0$ and $\sum_{i=1}^{n} p_i(t) = 1$ over time.

3.1   We begin by proving

LEMMA 1   Let $x = (x_1, x_2, \ldots, x_n)$, $y = (y_1, y_2, \ldots, y_n)$ stand for n-vectors, and furthermore let the function $w(x)$ be defined by the formula

$$w(x) = \sum_{i=1}^{n} [\max(x_i, 0)]^2. \tag{19}$$

Then, for any x and y, the important inequality

$$w(y) - w(x) \leq 2 \sum_{i=1}^{n} (y_i - x_i) \max(y_i, 0) \tag{20}$$

is true.

Proof   It is readily seen that $w(x)$ is a continuously differentiable function of x with the partial derivatives $\partial w/\partial x_i = 2 \max(x_i, 0)$. On the other hand, $w(x)$ is a convex function of x so that the function $F(s) = w[x + s(y - x)]$ is also convex with respect to the real variable s. Hence $F'(s)$ is a nondecreasing function of s. By the theorem of the mean in elementary calculus, $w(y) - w(x) = F(1) - F(0) = F'(s)$ for some s, $0 < s < 1$. In view of the nondecreasing nature of F' we have $w(y) - w(x) \leqq F'(1)$. Upon differentiation, we get

$$F'(1) = 2 \sum_{i=1}^{n} (y_i - x_i) \max(y_i, 0).$$

These relations, combined together, prove (20). We now proceed to prove Proposition 3.

3.2 *Proof of Proposition 3*   Let

$$\Phi(p) = \sum_{i=1}^{n} [\theta_i(p)]^2, \tag{21}$$

where $\theta_i(p)$ is given by (11). For any solution $p(t)$ of (10) let $\psi(t) = \Phi(p(t))$, $t \geqq 0$. Then Proposition 3 asserts $\lim_{t \to +\infty} \psi(t) = 0$.

We denote by S the set of all normalized price systems as in the foregoing section. It is unnecessary to say that we have only to deal with the case where $\psi(t)$ does not vanish at any time point.

Consider any fixed time point t and choose a neighborhood $U[p(t)]$ of $p(t)$ within S where (4') is true. Since $p(t)$ is naturally continuous, $p(t + \Delta t) \in U[p(t)]$ for a sufficiently small increment $\Delta t > 0$.

Now, for convenience, let $q_i(t) = p_i(t + \Delta t) = p_i(t) + \Delta p_i$ and $E_i(q(t)) = E_i(p(t)) + \Delta E_i(p(t))$. For simplicity, we occasionally abbreviate $p_i(t)$, $q_i(t)$ to p_i, q_i, etc. $\psi(t)$ can be written in terms of $w(x)$ in Lemma 1 as $\psi(t) = \Phi(p(t)) = w[E(p(t))]$. Therefore, in view of (20), we have

$$\tfrac{1}{2}[\psi(t + \Delta t) - \psi(t)] = \tfrac{1}{2}[w(E(q(t))) - w(E(p(t)))]$$

$$\leqq \sum_{i=1}^{n} \Delta E_i(p(t)) \max[E_i(q(t)), 0]$$

$$= \sum_{i=1}^{n} \theta_t(q(t)) \Delta E_t(p(t)). \tag{22}$$

Substituting $\dot{q}_i + \zeta(q)q_i$ for $\theta_i(q)$ based on (10) at period $t + \Delta t$, we obtain

$$\tfrac{1}{2}[\psi(t + \Delta t) - \psi(t)] \leqq \sum_{i=1}^{n} [\dot{q}_i + \zeta(q)q_i] \Delta E_i(p). \tag{23}$$

The right-hand side of (23) can be rearranged as follows:

$$\sum_{i=1}^{n} \left[\dot{p}_i(t + \Delta t) - \frac{\Delta p_i}{\Delta t} \right] \Delta E_i(p) + \frac{1}{\Delta t} \sum_{i=1}^{n} \Delta p_i \Delta E_i(p)$$

$$+ \zeta(q) \sum_{i=1}^{n} q_i \Delta E_i(p). \tag{24}$$

The second term in (24) is nonpositive for sufficiently small $\Delta t > 0$ by (4′) so that

$$\tfrac{1}{2}[\psi(t + \Delta t) - \psi(t)] \leqq \sum_{i=1}^{n} \left[\dot{p}_i(t + \Delta t) - \frac{\Delta p_i}{\Delta t} \right] \Delta E_i(p)$$

$$+ \zeta(q) \sum_{i=1}^{n} q_i \Delta E_i(p) \tag{25}$$

for small $\Delta t > 0$.

By virtue of the Walras law (3), we always have

$$\sum_{i=1}^{n} p_i E_i(p) = \sum_{i=1}^{n} q_i E_i(q) = 0.$$

Hence, $\sum (p_i - q_i) E_i(p) = \sum q_i (E_i(q) - E_i(p))$, i.e.,

$$- \sum_{i=1}^{n} \Delta p_i E_i(p) = \sum_{i=1}^{n} q_i \Delta E_i(p). \tag{26}$$

Combining (25) with (26), and dividing by $\Delta t > 0$ yields

$$\frac{1}{2\Delta t}[\psi(t + \Delta t) - \psi(t)] \leqq \sum_{i=1}^{n} \left[\dot{p}_i(t + \Delta t) - \frac{\Delta p_i}{\Delta t} \right] \frac{\Delta E_i}{\Delta t}$$

$$- \zeta(q) \sum_{i=1}^{n} \frac{\Delta p_i}{\Delta t} E_i(p) \tag{27}$$

for small $\Delta t > 0$.

We shall next show that the right hand side of (27) tends to $-\zeta(p(t))\psi(t)$ as $\Delta t \to 0$.

To accomplish this, it suffices to prove:

(i)   The first term tends to zero as $\Delta t \to 0$.

(ii)   The second term tends to $-\zeta(p(t))\psi(t)$ as $\Delta t \to 0$.

Proof of (i)   Since $p(t)$ as well as $q(t) = p(t + \Delta t)$ is always normalized, the Lipschitz condition assumed in (1) works very well so that

$$\left|\frac{\Delta E_i}{\Delta t}\right| \leq \sum_{j=1}^{n} M_{ij} \left|\frac{\Delta p_j}{\Delta t}\right| \to \sum M_{ij}|\dot{p}_j(t)| \quad (\Delta t \to 0).$$

On the other hand, as, by (10), $\dot{p}_i(t)$ is continuous with respect to t for each i, $\lim_{\Delta t \to 0} \dot{p}_i(t + \Delta t) = \dot{p}_i(t)$. In view of $\lim_{\Delta t \to 0} \Delta p_i / \Delta t = \dot{p}_i(t)$, we see that

$$\left|\sum_{i=1}^{n} \left[\dot{p}_i(t + \Delta t) - \frac{\Delta p_i}{\Delta t}\right] \frac{\Delta E_i}{\Delta t}\right| \leq \sum_{i=1}^{n} \left|\dot{p}_i(t + \Delta t) - \frac{\Delta p_i}{\Delta t}\right|$$

$$\sum_{j=1}^{n} M_{ij} \left|\frac{\Delta p_j}{\Delta t}\right| \to 0 \quad (\Delta t \to 0).$$

Proof of (ii)   As $q \to p$ $(\Delta t \to 0)$, so by continuity the second term converges to

$$-\zeta(p) \sum_{i=1}^{n} \dot{p}_i E_i(p).$$

Substituting $\theta_i(p) - \zeta(p)p_i$ for $\dot{p}_i$, by (10), we get

$$-\zeta(p) \sum_{i=1}^{n} \dot{p}_i E_i(p) = -\zeta(p) \sum_{i=1}^{n} \theta_i(p)E_i(p) + \zeta(p)^2 \sum_{i=1}^{n} p_i E_i(p).$$

But,

$$-\zeta(p) \sum_{i=1}^{n} \theta_i(p)E_i(p) = -\zeta(p)\Phi(p) = -\zeta(p)\psi(t),$$

since $\theta_i(p)E_i(p) = [\theta_i(p_i)]^2$ by virtue of definition (11). Also,

$$\zeta(p)^2 \sum_{i=1}^{n} p_i E_i(p) = 0$$

by the Walras law (3). This proves (ii).

Now, on the basis of the results established above, (27) can be written as follows:

$$\frac{1}{\Delta t}[\psi(t + \Delta t) - \psi(t)] \leq \varepsilon(t, \Delta t) - 2\zeta(p(t))\psi(t) \tag{28}$$

for sufficiently small $\Delta t > 0$; and $\lim_{\Delta t \to 0} \varepsilon(t, \Delta t) = 0$.

Because $\zeta(p(t)\psi(t) > 0$, we have $\varepsilon(t, \Delta t) \leq \zeta(p(t))\psi(t)$ for small $\Delta t > 0$. Accordingly, we get

$$\frac{1}{\Delta t}[\psi(t + \Delta t) - \psi(t)] \leqq -\zeta[p(t)]\psi(t) \tag{29}$$

for small $\Delta t > 0$.

As $\zeta(p)^2 = \left[\sum_{i=1}^{n} \theta_i(p)\right]^2 \geqq \sum_{i=1}^{n} [\theta_i(p)]^2 = \Phi(p)$,

we see that $-\zeta(p)\psi(t) \leqq -\psi(t)^{3/2}$. Therefore,

$$\frac{1}{\Delta t}[\psi(t + \Delta t) - \psi(t)] \leqq -\psi(t)^{3/2} \tag{30}$$

for small $\Delta t > 0$.

It is needless to say that the bounds for the Δt's assuring (30) can not be uniform with respect to t, but may change with t.

The proof will be complete, if we show that (30) implies $\lim_{t \to +\infty} \psi(t) = 0$. To this end, we could proceed in a less constructive way. We shall achieve the aim here, however, by establishing more explicitly the majorizing relation

$$\psi(t) \leqq \psi(0)/(1 + \psi(0)^{1/2}t/2)^2, \quad (t \geqq 0), \tag{31}$$

which obviously implies, in view of $\psi(t) \geqq 0$, that $\psi(t) \to 0$ as $t \to +\infty$. This majorant function is nothing other than the solution with the initial value $\psi(0)$ of the differential equation

$$\frac{d\lambda}{dt} = -\lambda^{3/2}, \quad \lambda(0) = \psi(0). \tag{32}$$

Let $\lambda(t)$ be the solution of (32). It will be proved that $\psi(\sigma) \leqq \lambda(\sigma)$ at each arbitrary fixed time point $\sigma > 0$. Consider in the closed interval $[0, \sigma]$ the subset $F = \{t \mid 0 \leqq t \leqq \sigma, \psi(t) \leqq \lambda(t)\}$. F is not empty because $0 \in F$. Since $\psi(t)$ as well as $\lambda(t)$ is continuous, F is closed in $[0, \sigma]$. Hence F contains a maximum ω. The assertion is proved if $\omega = \sigma$. Suppose $\omega \neq \sigma$; then $0 \leqq \omega < \sigma$. The way of choosing ω and the continuity of $\psi(t)$ and $\lambda(t)$ imply $\psi(\omega) = \lambda(\omega)$ and $\psi(t) > \lambda(t)$ for t with $\omega < t \leqq \sigma$. Hence

$$\frac{\psi(t) - \psi(\omega)}{t - \omega} > \frac{\lambda(t) - \lambda(\omega)}{t - \omega}$$

for these t.

By virtue of the theorem of the mean, the right-hand side of the above inequality reduces to $\dot{\lambda}(s)$ for an s with $\omega < s < t$, which is equal to $-\lambda(s)^{3/2}$ by (32). On the other hand, if t is sufficiently close to ω, the left-hand side is majorized by $-\psi(\omega)^{3/2}$ by (30). Furthermore, we certainly have $\psi(s) \leq \psi(\omega)$ also by (30) because s is closer to ω than t. These relations altogether imply $\psi(s)^{3/2} < \lambda(s)^{3/2}$, that is, $\psi(s) < \lambda(s)$ for an s between ω and σ. This result contradicts the way of choosing ω. Accordingly $\omega = \sigma$ and $\sigma \in F$, i.e., $\psi(\sigma) \leq \lambda(\sigma)$. As the selection of $\sigma > 0$ was arbitrary, this establishes the majorization $\psi(t) \leq \lambda(t)$. The explicit solution of (32) can be easily obtained by direct integration. The proof of Proposition 3 is thereby complete. It is finally noted that the convergence of $\psi(t)$ to zero is uniform with respect to initial conditons, since (31) implies $\psi(t) \leq 4/t^2$ for $t > 0$.

3.3 In the case where $E_i(p)$ is continuously differntiable, $\psi(t)$ is also continuously differentiable with respect to time. Hence, by putting $\Delta t \to 0$ directly into (28) it can be shown that $\psi(t)$ satisfies

$$\frac{d\psi}{dt} \leq -2\psi^{3/2}, \tag{30'}$$

which entails a better majorization $\psi(t) \leq \psi(0)/(1 + \psi(0)^{1/2}t)^2$. This majorization could also be obtained for this special case by directly differentiating $\psi(t)$ and taking into account the fact that

$$\sum_{i,j=1}^{n} \frac{\partial E_i}{\partial p_j} \dot{p}_i \dot{p}_j \leq 0,$$

which is an immediate consequence of assumption (4').

3.4 We now prove Proposition 4.[7] It should be borne in mind that condition (4) is assumed instead of (4') this time. To prove Proposition 4, however, it suffices to show that the local validity of (4) implies its global validity, which has been left untouched until now. Once this is checked, Proposition 4 is immediately derived from Proposition 3. We therefore proceed to

LEMMA 2 If condition (4) holds true locally, it must also hold true globally. Hence, there is at most one equilibrium price system, if any.

Proof For any distinct normalized price systems p, q let

$$p(t) = (1 - t)p + tq, \quad G(t) = \sum_{i=1}^{n} (q_i - p_i)(E_i(p(t)) - E_i(p)), \quad 1 \geq t \geq 0.$$

Then clearly $p(t) \in S$, and for s, t with $1 \geqq s > t \geqq 0$,

$$(s - t)(G(s) - G(t)) = \sum (p_i(s) - p_i(t))(E_i(p(s)) - E_i(p(t))). \tag{33}$$

By the local validity of (4) and the continuity of these functions it is seen that, given t with $1 > t \geqq 0$, (33) is negative for s sufficiently close to t, which gives $G(s) < G(t)$ for this s and t. On the basis of these results we first take a $\sigma \in (0, 1]$ with $G(\sigma) < G(0)$, then let $F = \{t | \sigma \leqq t \leqq 1, G(t) \leqq G(\sigma)\}$. It will be shown that supposing $1 > \tau = \sup t$ over all $t \in F$ leads to a contradiction. In fact, if $1 > \tau$, from the continuity of G and the definition of τ it follows that $G(\tau) = G(\sigma)$. But we have, $G(s) < G(\tau)$ for s with $1 \geqq s > \tau$, sufficiently close to τ, contradicting the definition of τ. Therefore $\tau = 1$. As F is closed in $[\sigma, 1]$, it contains τ. This gives $G(1) \leqq G(\sigma) < G(0)$, that is,

$$\sum_{i=1}^{n} (q_i - p_i)(E_i(q) - E_i(p)) = G(1) - G(0) < 0.$$

The first half of the proof is therefore complete.

It remains to determine whether the equilibrium is unique. It is a well established fact in economic literature that the global validity of (4) excludes the possibility of multiple equilibria, and it suffices to note that the customary proof of uniqueness also applies to the equilibrium defined by (5) and (6).

3.5 *Proof of Proposition 4*   First it should be noted that by Proposition 3, which is valid under (4'), weaker than (4), we have $\lim_{t \to +\infty} \Phi[p(t)] = 0$ for any solution $p(t)$ of (10). As $p(t) \in S$ over time by Proposition 2, and as S is compact, there is a subsequence $\{t_v\}$ tending to infinity such that $p(t_v)$ converges to some point $\hat{p}$ in S. Then, by continuity, $\Phi(\hat{p}) = \lim_{v \to +\infty} \Phi[p(t_v)] = 0$, which implies that $\theta_i(\hat{p}) = 0$ $(i = 1, 2, \ldots, n)$, that is $E_i(\hat{p}) \leqq \theta_i(\hat{p}) = 0$ $(i = 1, 2, \ldots, n)$. As was noted, (6) immediately follows from (3) and (5). Therefore $\hat{p}$ is an equilibrium price system.

Now take any small neighborhood $U(\hat{p})$ within S such that the complement M of $U(\hat{p})$ within S is not empty. By Lemma 2 there are no equilibrium price systems other than $\hat{p}$, and a fortiori M contains no such points. It follows that $\Phi(p)$ never vanishes and is always positive on M. As $\Phi(p)$ is a continuous function of p on M which is compact, it takes on a positive minimum ε there. But $\Phi(p(t)) \to 0$ as $t \to +\infty$. In consequence we can take a sufficiently large T such that $\Phi(p(t)) < \varepsilon$ for $t \geqq T$. This implies that $p(t)$

never belongs to M for $t \geq T$, and therefore $p(t)$ belongs to $U(\hat{p})$ for $t \geq T$. This proves $\lim_{t \to +\infty} p(t) = \hat{p}$.

3.6 Some Special Cases of Multiple Equilibria   In the preceding paragraph it was shown that under assumption (4) the unique equilibrium price system is globally stable. What can be said under assumption (4′)? It will be noted that Proposition 3 still reflects something of the stable character of the competitive market. Any solution of (10) approaches the compact *set L* of all equilibrium price systems. But it does not necessarily converge to a particular price system. The structure of L seems not to be simple except for some special cases, such as the original Brown–von Neumann case, though the global validity of (4′) is implied by its local validity. We can show, however, that the market enjoys global stability in the case of a finite number of equilibrium price systems; that is, we have

PROPOSITION 4′   If there are at most a finite number of equilibrium price systems, then under conditions (1), (3) and (4′) any solution $p(t)$ of (10) converges to some individual equilibrium price system, as t tends to infinity.

Proof   This proof is similar to, but somewhat more complicated than that for Proposition 4. Let $L = \{p^k | k = 1, 2, \ldots, m\}$, and take a neighborhood $U(p^k)$ within S such that

$$U(p^j) \cap U(p^k) = \text{empty set} \quad (j \neq k). \tag{34}$$

Then, by making use of the complement M of $\bigcup_{k=1}^{m} U(p^k)$ within S in the same way as in Proposition 4, we can take a sufficiently large T such that $p(t) \in \bigcup_{k=1}^{m} U(p^k)$ for $t \geq T$. $p(t)$ therefore continuously maps the half-interval $[T, +\infty)$, which is *connected*, into $\bigcup_{k=1}^{m} U(p^k)$. Hence the image lies entirely in a connected component, namely in one individual $U(p^k)$. We have therefore shown that

$$p(t) \in U(p^k) \quad \text{for } t \geq T. \tag{35}$$

Choose now any small neighborhood $V(p^k)$ such that $V(p^k) \subset U(p^k)$. Then, for exactly the same reason as above, there is a T' such that $p(t) \in V(p^k) \cup (\bigcup_{j \neq k} U(p^j))$ for $t \geq T'$. Then, $p(t)$ lies in the overlapping portion of this set with $U(p^k)$ for $t \geq \max(T, T')$. In view of (34), this implies $p(t) \in V(p^k)$ for $t \geq \max(T, T')$, which proves that $\lim_{t \to +\infty} p(t) = p^k$.

4 Final Mathematical Justification

4.1 In this section we shall present the proof of Proposition 2 as well as an assertion to the effect that equation (8) has a solution starting from any given price system. One may point out, in the light of Proposition 1 regarding the relation between the two systems (8) and (10), that the existence of a solution of (8) implies the first half of Proposition 2 provided that the $E_i(p)$'s are homogeneous of degree zero. But, in view of the fact that Proposition 2, which is of interest itself, does not premise any homogeneity, an independent proof will be provided.

4.2 *Proof of Proposition 2*   The problem of the existence of a solution is here a little more delicate to handle than that of the original Brown–von Neumann equation. For the right-hand side of (10) is defined only for *nonnegative vectors p other than* 0, whereas in the latter case the corresponding functions are defined for all vectors. Although the following proof will be modelled along the standard line, attention should be paid to the smoothness with which the difficulty of the restricted domain of definition for the relevant functions can be overcome.

Let $p = (p_1, p_2, \ldots, p_n)$ be the n-vector which is not necessarily nonnegative, and put $|p| = (|p_1|, |p_2|, \ldots, |p_n|)$, where $|p_i|$ is the absolute value of p_i. It is obvious that $|p| = p$ for $p \geq 0$, and $|p| \geq 0$ for $p \neq 0$. For simplicity, a modified version of the right-hand side of (10) will be denoted by

$$H_i(p) = \theta_i(|p|) - \zeta(|p|)p_i \quad (i = 1, 2, \ldots, n). \tag{36}$$

Since $E_i(p)$ is defined for all $p \geq 0$, the expression $H_i(p)$ certainly makes sense for $p \neq 0$. Now take an $\varepsilon > 0$ and let

$$N = \left\{ p \,\middle|\, \sum_{i=1}^{m} p_i = 1, |p_i - p_i^0| \leq \varepsilon \quad (i = 1, 2, \ldots, n) \right.$$

for some normalized price system p^0}. Then N is a nonempty convex compact set not containing 0. Accordingly, $H_i(p)$ is bounded on N so that we can choose $M > 0$ so large that $M > H_i(p)$ for all $p \in N$ $(i = 1, 2, \ldots, n)$. We shall first prove that equation (10) has a solution in $[0, \varepsilon/M]$ having the normalized initial price system p^0. To this end, following the customary procedure, let us consider the integral operator

$$q_i(t) = p_i^0 + \int_0^t H_i(p(s)) \, ds \quad (\varepsilon/M \geq t \geq 0) \quad (i = 1, 2, \ldots, n), \tag{37}$$

where $p^0 = (p_1^0, p_2^0, \ldots, p_n^0)$ is the given initial normalized price system. Denote by $N[0, \varepsilon/M]$ the set of all continuous vector functions $p(t)$ defined in $[0, \varepsilon/M]$ and having values in N such that $p(0) = p^0$. If $p(t) \in N[0, \varepsilon/M]$, we have in particular $p(t) \neq 0$ so that the operator is well-defined in $N[0, \varepsilon/M]$. Furthermore,

$$\sum_{i=1}^{n} q_i(t) = \sum_{i=1}^{n} p_i^0 + \int_0^t \left(\sum_{i=1}^{n} \theta_i(|p(s)|) - \zeta(|p(s)|) \right) ds = 1,$$

as

$$\sum_{i=1}^{n} p_i^0 = \sum_{i=1}^{n} p_i(t) = 1,$$

and

$$\zeta(|p(s)|) = \sum_{i=1}^{n} \theta_i(|p(s)|)$$

by definition.

Also,

$$|q_i(t) - p_i^0| \leq \int_0^t |H_i(p(s))| \, ds \leq M \cdot \varepsilon/M = \varepsilon.$$

That is, $q(t) \in N$. Hence the operator (37) maps $N[0, \varepsilon/M]$ into $N[0, \varepsilon/M]$. Therefore, the standard methods based on either the Cauchy–Peano existence theorem (Coddington and Levinson 1955, Chapter 1) or the Tychonoff fixed point theorem (Tychonoff 1935) work very well. By appealing to any of them it is seen that (37) has a fixed point, i.e., a function $p(t) \in N[0, \varepsilon/M]$ which is sent into itself under (37); namely,

$$p_i(t) = p_i^0 + \int_0^t H_i(p(s)) \, ds \quad (\varepsilon/M \geq t \geq 0) \quad (i = 1, 2, \ldots, n). \tag{38}$$

We next show that this $p(t)$ must be nonnegative. In fact, take any $\tau \in [0, \varepsilon/M]$ and let $F_i = \{t | \tau \geq t \geq 0, p_i(t) \geq 0\}$. As F_i contains 0, it is a nonempty compact subset of $[0, \tau]$. Suppose $\tau \neq \sigma = \max t$ over all $t \in F_i$. Then $\tau > \sigma$ and $p_i(\sigma) = 0$; and $p_i(t) < 0$, for $\tau \geq t > \sigma$. But, for $\tau \geq t > \sigma$ we have, by (38),

$$p_i(t) = p_i(t) - p_i(\sigma) = \int_\sigma^t (\theta_i(|p(s)|) - \zeta(|p(s)|)p_i(s)) \, ds \geq 0,$$

because the integrand is nonnegative in $(\sigma, \tau]$. This yields a contradiction. Therefore $\tau = \sigma \in F_i$, proving $p_i(\tau) \geq 0$.

As $p(t)$ is nonnegative, $|p(s)| = p(s)$ in (38). Accordingly, upon differentiation of (38) we get (10), that is,

$$\frac{dp_i}{dt} = \theta_i(p) - \zeta(p)p_i \quad (i = 1, 2, \ldots, n),$$

$$p_i(0) = p_i^0 \quad (i = 1, 2, \ldots, n),$$

$$(39)$$

for $\varepsilon/M \geq t \geq 0$.

We have thereby proved that for any initial normalized price system there is one solution of (39) in $[0, \varepsilon/M]$ such that it remains normalized over time. According to this result, and in view of the fact that M and ε can be independent of initial conditions, there is a solution $q(t)$ of (39) in $[0, \varepsilon/M]$ which also fulfills the normalization condition and has $p_i(\varepsilon/M)$ as imitial values. Then, defining $p_i(t) = q_i(t - \varepsilon/M)$ in $[\varepsilon/M, 2\varepsilon/M]$, $p(t)$ can be continued to $[0, 2\varepsilon/M]$. Proceeding in this way, $p(t)$ can be extended to $[0, +\infty)$ to get a solution for $t \geq 0$ fulfilling the normalization condition. The existence of a solution is thereby completely proved.

The proof of uniqueness remains. The standard proof of uniqueness is based on the Lipschitz condition. But, it is only assumed in condition (1) that $E_i(p)$ satisfies the Lipschitz condition for *normalized* price systems. It is therefore necessary to show that any solution of (10) automatically fulfills the condition of being normalized over time.[8] Indeed, let $p(t)$ be any solution of (10) starting from a normalized price system. We follow the procedure that has frequently been used in this note. Let $\sigma > 0$ be any fixed time point, and $F = \{t | \sigma \geq t \geq 0, \sum_{i=1}^{n} p_i(t) = 1\}$. F is a nonempty compact subset of $[0, \sigma]$. If $\sigma \neq \omega = \max t$ over all $t \in F$, we have $\sum_{i=1}^{n} p_i(\omega) = 1$; and either $\sum_{i=1}^{n} p_i(t) > 1$ for all $\sigma \geq t > \omega$ or $\sum_{i=1}^{n} p_i(t) < 1$ for all $\sigma \geq t > \omega$. The latter result is due to continuity. Summing up (10) and integrating, we have, for $\sigma \geq t > \omega$,

$$\sum_{i=1}^{n} p_i(t) - 1 = \sum_{i=1}^{n} p_i(t) - \sum_{i=1}^{n} p_i(\omega) = - \int_{\omega}^{t} \zeta(p(s)) \left(\sum_{i=1}^{n} p_i(s) - 1 \right) ds,$$

which excludes the possibility of $\sum_{i=1}^{n} p_i(t) - 1$ being either identically positive or identically negative in $(\omega, \sigma]$. Consequently, $\omega = \sigma$ and $\sigma \in F$, as asserted. According to this result, any solutions of (10) fulfill the normalization condition. The functions on the right-hand side of (10) satisfy the

Lipschitz condition for any solution, as is easily seen by (1). Thus, the proof of Proposition 2 is complete.

4.3 Finally, the proof of existence of a solution of (8) will be sketched briefly below. From the continuity and zero-order homogeneity of the $E_i(q)$'s, it follows that the $\theta_i(q)$'s are bounded over all $q \geq 0$. Take a large positive number M such that $M \geq \theta_i(q)$ for $q \geq 0$. Then a solution of (8) in the interval $[0, \varepsilon/M]$ can be obtained as a fixed point of the integral operator

$$q_i(t) \to q_i^0 + \int_0^t \theta_i(q(s))\,ds \quad (i = 1, 2, \ldots, n),$$

which maps any vector function $q(t)$ fulfilling $q(0) = q^0$, $q_i^0 \leq q_i(t) \leq q_i^0 + \varepsilon$ $(i = 1, 2, \ldots, n)$ in $[0, \varepsilon/M]$ into a vector function of the same category. Any such solution can be continued to $[\varepsilon/M, 2\varepsilon/M]$ in the same fashion as in the foregoing discussions. Thus, successive continuation will yield a solution defined for all $t \geq 0$.

Notes

1. This paper is written in memory of the late Professor J. von Neumann, to whose articles, books and communications the writer is indebted for much stimulation. Thanks are also due Professors K. J. Arrow and M. Morishima for invaluable criticism and suggestions. The earlier draft of this paper was circulated as ISER Discussion Paper No. 11, The Institute of Social and Economic Research, Osaka University.

2. The assumption that $E_i(q)$, which is homogeneous of degree zero, fulfills the Lipschitz condition for all price systems, entails its constancy.

3. For instance, the local solution $x = 1/(1 - t)$ $(1 > t \geq 0)$ of $dx/dt = x^2$ whose right-hand side is even analytic everywhere can not be continued beyond $t = 1$.

4. Cf. note 2.

5. This relation between the two systems (8) and (10) is heuristically suggested in a very interesting note in the Brown–von Neumann article (1950, p. 74). A rigorous discussion is presented here for the first time with the aid of transformation function $\alpha(t)$.

6. In the sequel a dot over a symbol implies differentiation with respect to time.

7. For $n = 2$, system (10) is always globally stable under assumptions (1) and (3). This can readily be seen by noting that if $\dot{p}_1(t)$ and $\dot{p}_2(t)$ do not simultaneously vanish at any finite time point, then either $\dot{p}_1(t) > 0$, $\dot{p}_2(t) < 0$ or $\dot{p}_1(t) < 0$, $\dot{p}_2(t) > 0$ are true over time by virtue of relation $p_1(t) + p_2(t) = 1$ and continuity.

8. The foregoing proof of existence can readily be adapted to the case where the $E_i(p)$'s are only defined for normalized price systems. In that case any solution, in order to be a solution, is required to satisfy the normalization condition at the outset so that an immediate appeal to the Lipschitz condition is possible.

References

Arrow, K. J. and G. Debreu (1954): Existence of an Equilibrium for a Competitive Economy, *Econometrica*, Vol. 22.

Arrow, K. J., H. D. Block and L. Hurwicz (1959): On the Stability of the Competitive Equilibrium, II, *Econometrica*, Vol. 27.

Arrow, K. J. and L. Hurwicz (1958): On the Stability of the Competitive Equilibrium I, *Econometrica*, Vol. 26.

Brown, G. W. and J. von Neumann (1950): Solution of Games by Differential Equation, *Annals of Mathematics Study*, No. 24.

Coddington, E. A. and N. Levinson (1955): *Theory of Ordinary Differential Equations*, New York: McGraw-Hill.

Gale, D. (1955): The Law of Supply and Demand. *Mathematica Scandinavica*, 3.

McKenzie, L. W. (1954): On Equilibrium in Graham's Model of World Trade and Other Competitive Systems, *Econometrica*, Vol. 22.

Morishima, M. (1958): *Gross Substitutability, Homogeneity and the Walras' Law* (Unpublished manuscript).

Nikaido, H. (1956): On the Classical Multilateral Exchange Problem, *Metroeconomica*, Vol. VIII, Fasc. II; A Supplementary Note, *Ibid.*, Vol. IX.

——— (1958): Solution of the Utility Maximization Problem by a Brown–von Neumann-type Differential Equation, *ISER Discussion Paper*, No. 10, The Institute of Social and Economic Research, Osaka University.

Tychonoff, A. (1935): Ein Fixpunktsatz, *Mathematische Annalen*, Vol. 111.

Uzawa, H. (1959): A Note on the Stability of Equilibrium, *Technical Report*, No. 44, Dept. of Economics, Stanford University.

2 Stability and Non-negativity in a Walrasian Tâtonnement Process

with Hirofumi Uzawa C62
Uzawa D51

1 Introduction

[1960]

Since some recent studies (Arrow and Debreu 1954; Gale 1955; McKenzie 1954, 1959; Nikaido 1956) thoroughly explored the static aspects of market mechanism by establishing the existence of competitive equilibrium, we have seen a revival of interest in the study of its dynamic aspects.[1] One problem of major importance centers around the derivation of the (mainly global) stability of competitive equilibrium from several conditions of economic significance imposed upon excess demand functions. Important results in this line were recently obtained by Arrow and Hurwicz (1958), Arrow, Block and Hurwicz (1959), Hahn (1958), McKenzie (1958) and Negishi (1958). However, except for the Arrow–Block–Hurwicz article and the result of McKenzie, little explicit attention seems to have been paid to the non-negativity of prices in these studies. As was already noted in the early thirties, negative prices are unjustifiable from the economic viewpoint, and the theory of general equilibrium should explicitly take into account the non-negativity of economic variables. This restriction led Wald (1936) and, in more recent times, several other authors Arrow, Debreu, Gale, McKenzie and Nikaido to investigate the existence of competitive equilibrium. The same restriction should also be relevant to the study of the dynamic aspects of a competitive market.

Working along this line, Nikaido (1959) attempted to offer some results on global stability with the non-negativity condition for a special type of competitive market described by the Brown–von Neumann differential equation. Uzawa (1957, 1958, 1959–60) also proposed and studied a non-negative price adjustment process which is formulated in terms of a difference equation and is in complete agreement with the classical law of competition. This process, as he proved, enjoys global stability in an approximate way, although it may fail to be stable in the ordinary sense. In this note we are concerned with a further study of this process, and ordinary non-negative global stability will be proved for a differential equation version of the process in which the weak axiom of revealed preference holds between any equilibrium price vector and any other price vector not proportional to the former.

With Hirofumi Uzawa. From *International Economic Review* 1, no. 1 (January 1960): 50–59. Reprinted by permission.

2 Summary of the Results

2.1 There are $n + 1$ goods denoted by $i = 0, 1, 2, \ldots, n$; their *nonnormalized* prices are denoted by $q_0, q_1, \ldots, q_n$. Let $q = (q_0, q_1, \ldots, q_n) \geq 0$, $\neq 0$ stand for the price vector.[2]

$E_i(q) = E_i(q_0, q_1, \ldots, q_n)$, the excess demand for the ith good, is assumed to fulfill the following conditions:

(a) $E_i(q)$ is single-valued and continuous for $q \geq 0$, $\neq 0$.

(b) $\sum_{i=0}^{n} q_i E_i(q) = 0$; i.e., Walras' law holds true.

The recent studies cited above have established, under assumptions (a) and (b), the existence of a competitive equilibrium price vector $\hat{q}$ such that

(i) $E_i(\hat{q}) \leq 0$ $(i = 0, 1, \ldots, n)$

(ii) $E_i(\hat{q}) = 0$ if $\hat{q}_i > 0$.

2.2   In the discussion below the following assumptions will also be made:

(c) $E_i(q)$ is homogeneous of degree 0.

(d)   The weak axiom of revealed preference holds in the sense that for any equilibrium price vector $\hat{q}$ and any other price vector q not proportional to $\hat{q}$ the inequality $\sum_{i=0}^{n} \hat{q}_i E_i(q) > 0$ prevails.

Assumption (d) immediately entails the uniqueness of the equilibrium price vector up to multiplication by positive scalars.

2.3   We take up one good, say the 0-th good, to play the role of *numéraire*. Let

$$p = (p_1, p_2, \ldots, p_n), \ p_i = q_i/q_0 \quad (i = 1, 2, \ldots, n)$$

$$F_i(p) = E_i(1, p_1, p_2, \ldots, p_n) \quad (i = 0, 1, 2, \ldots, n),$$

so that the letter p is used exclusively to designate *normalized* price vectors. Uzawa (1957, 1958, 1959–60) proposed the following iterative process corresponding to the Walrasian tâtonnement; that is,

$$p_i(t + 1) = \max[\rho F_i(p(t)) + p_i(t), 0], \quad (i = 1, 2, \ldots, n),$$

where ρ is a positive constant. This system is obtained from the classical formulation of price adjustment

$$p_i(t + 1) = \rho F_i(p(t)) + p_i(t), \quad (i = 1, 2, \ldots, n)$$

by taking into account the downward rigidity of prices below zero. He proved that given any small ε neighborhood of the equilibrium price vector $\hat{p}$ and any initial position $p(0) \geq 0$, the solution $p(t)$ of the above difference equation approaches and eventually reaches this prescribed neighborhood of $\hat{p}$ for small $\rho > 0$ depending on ε and $p(0)$, while the distance $p(t)$ from $\hat{p}$ monotonically decreases. The proof was done under assumptions (a), (b), and (d).

2.4 A differential equation analogous to the above equation is

$$\frac{dp_i}{dt} = \theta_i(p) - p_i, \quad (i = 1, 2, \ldots, n), \tag{1}$$

where

$$\theta_i(p) = \max[\rho F_i(p) + p_i, 0]. \tag{2}$$

In the process formulated by the difference equation stated above, the increments of prices are given by

$$\Delta p_i(t) = p_i(t + 1) - p_i(t)$$

$$= \max[\rho F_i(p(t)) + p_i(t), 0] - p_i(t), \quad (i = 1, 2, \ldots, n).$$

This suggests the replacement of Δp_i by dp_i/dt to get a differential equation version (1) of the process proposed by Uzawa. We are here concerned with the study of equation (1).

The main results of this note are summarized as follows:

PROPOSITION 1 (EXISTENCE) Under assumptions (a) and (c) equation (1) has one solution (tâtonnement path), starting from any given initial position $p(0) \geq 0$.

PROPOSITION 2 (STABILITY) If the price of each good is positive at equilibrium, i.e., $\hat{q}_i > 0$ $(i = 0, 1, \ldots, n)$, then under assumptions (a), (b), (c) and (d) any solution $p(t)$ of (1) converges to $\hat{p}$ for small $\rho > 0$. During the convergence of $p(t)$ to $\hat{p}$, the distance of $p(t)$ from $\hat{p}$ monotonically shrinks to zero.

2.5 Equation (1) avoids the various difficulties in the classical formulation of price adjustment in connection with the non-negativity of prices; it nevertheless retains the orthodox version of price flexibility in the sense that excess demand causes a rise in price, and excess supply entails a fall in price.[3] First, if $p_i = 0$, then $dp_i/dt = \theta_i(p) \geq 0$, so that prices are never negative. We next check on the pattern of price flexibility. In fact, whenever $\rho F_i(p) + p_i \geq 0$, the ith equation in (1) reduces to $dp_i/dt = \rho F_i(p)$. Furthermore, if $\rho F_i(p) + p_i < 0$, then $dp_i/dt = -p_i$, because $\theta_i(p) = 0$, and p_i decreases so long as $p_i > 0$, while satisfying $F_i(p) < -p_i/\rho \leq 0$.

The above consideration also makes it clear that if $\rho F_i(p) < -p_i$, the orthodox system $dp_i/dt = \rho F_i(p)$ is replaced by another one, namely, $dp_i/dt = -p_i$. Furthermore, the switch from one system to the other occurs not suddenly but always gradually and continuously. This built-in shock absorber prevents the changing price $p(t)$ from crashing against the bottom $p_i = 0$ and from penetrating into the negative domain $p_i < 0$. It slows down the price movement near the bottom and always insures a gentle sidewise crawling. This reminds us of a flap device which works when a jet airliner does a soft landing.

2.6 Introducing coefficients $k_i > 0$ of speed adjustment into (1) would cause no difficulties, and the method and results in this note equally apply to the equation

$$k_i \frac{dp_i}{dt} = \theta_i(p) - p_i \quad (i = 1, 2, \ldots, n),$$

either by reducing it to equation (1) through the change of units, or by using some suitably weighted distance function.

3   Proof of Proposition 1 (Existence)

3.1   We begin by proving three lemmas.

LEMMA 1.   Under assumptions (a) and (c) each $E_i(q)$ is bounded for $q \geq 0$, $\neq 0$; this in particular implies that $F_i(p)$ is bounded for $p \geq 0$.

Proof   Let $S_{n+1} = \{q \mid q_i \geq 0, \sum_{i=0}^{n} q_i = 1\}$. $E_i(q)$ is continuous on S_{n+1} which is compact. Hence $E_i(q)$ is bounded on S_{n+1}, that is, $|E_i(q)| \leq M_i$ on S_{n+1}. Then, by (c), $|E_i(q)| \leq M_i$ for all $q \geq 0$, $\neq 0$.

LEMMA 2   The functions $\theta_i(p) - p_i$ appearing in (1) are bounded for $p \geq 0$.

Proof   By Lemma 1, $|F_i(p)| \leq N \equiv \max(M_0, M_1, \ldots, M_n)$ for all $p \geq 0$. First, it is readily seen, in view of definition (2), that

$$|\theta_i(p) - p_i| \leq \max[\rho F_i(p), p_i],$$

because $\theta_i(p) - p_i$ equals either $\rho F_i(p)$ or $-p_i$.

Now, if $0 \leq p_i \leq \rho N$, the above inequality immediately implies that $|\theta_i(p) - p_i| \leq \rho N$. If, on the other hand, $\rho N < p_i$, then $\rho F_i(p) + p_i$ must be positive because $|\rho F_i(p)| \leq \rho N$. Hence, in this case, $\theta_i(p) - p_i$ actually equals $\rho F_i(p)$, so that $|\theta_i(p) - p_i| \leq \rho N$. Therefore, always

$$|\theta_i(p) - p_i| \leq \rho N.$$

LEMMA 3   Given any initial position $p(0) = p^0 \geq 0$, equation (1) has a solution in a small time interval $[0, \sigma]$, $\sigma > 0$, starting from p^0.

Proof   Let $|p| = (|p_1|, |p_2|, \ldots, |p_n|)$. The equation

$$\frac{dp_i}{dt} = \max[\rho F_i(|p|) + p_i, 0] - p_i \quad (i = 1, 2, \ldots, n) \tag{3}$$

has a solution in an interval $[0, \sigma]$, $\sigma > 0$, starting from p^0, by the Cauchy–Peano theorem,[4] since the right-hand side of (3) is continuous. If $p_i \leq 0$, then $\max[\rho F_i(|p|) + p_i, 0] - p_i \geq 0$ so that $p_i(t)$ never becomes negative. This can easily be rigorously proved, though it will not be given here. Therefore this solution $p(t)$ remains non-negative in $[0, \sigma]$ and satisfies equation (1).

3.2   *Proof of Proposition 1*   Let ω be the least upper bound of σ, such that the solution $p(t)$ of Lemma 3 can be continued to $[0, \sigma]$. Suppose that $\omega < +\infty$. It will be shown that this supposition leads to a contradiction. By definition, there is a solution $p(t)$ in $[0, \omega)$, and for any $0 \leq t_1 < t_2 < \omega$,

$$|p_i(t_2) - p_i(t_1)| \leq \int_{t_1}^{t_2} |\theta_i(p(s)) - p_i(s)| \, ds \leq \Gamma |t_1 - t_2|,$$

where Γ is a positive constant. Hence, $p_i(t_1) - p_i(t_2) \to 0$, as t_1 and t_2 tend to 0. This implies that

$$\lim_{t \to \omega} p_i(t) = p_i^\omega \quad (i = 1, 2, \ldots, n)$$

exist, and $p(t)$ can be continued to $[0, \omega]$ by setting $p(\omega) = p^\omega$. By Lemma 3, there is a solution $\bar{p}(t)$ of (1) starting from $p(\omega)$, in some $[0, \tau]$, $\tau > 0$; $p(t)$ can therefore be continued beyond ω to $[0, \omega + \tau]$, by defining $p(t) = \bar{p}(t - \omega)$ in $[\omega, \omega + \tau]$, which yields a contradiction. Accordingly, $\omega = +\infty$, and $p(t)$ can be continued to $[0, +\infty)$.

4   Proof of Proposition 2 (Stability)

Let us now take two sets X and Y; the symbol $X \setminus Y$ will stand for the difference set, i.e., $X \setminus Y = \{x \mid x \in X, x \notin Y\}$.

The proof will be carried out in the following four steps, (α) through (δ).

(α) By assumption, the unique normalized equilibrium price vector $\hat{p}$ is positive, i.e., $\hat{p}_i > 0$ $(i = 1, 2, \ldots, n)$, so that by condition (ii)

$$F_i(\hat{p}) = 0 \quad (i = 0, 1, 2, \ldots, n),$$

and hence $F_i(\hat{p}) + \hat{p}_i > 0$ $(i = 1, 2, \ldots, n)$. Since the $F_i(p)$'s are continuous for $p \geq 0$, given any constant ρ with $0 < \rho \leq 1$, there is a neighborhood[5,6] $U(\hat{p}, \varepsilon) \subset R_+^n$ such that

$$\rho F_i(p) + p_i > 0 \quad (i = 1, 2, \ldots, n) \quad \text{for } p \in U(\hat{p}, \varepsilon). \tag{4}$$

(β) By assumption (d), if $p \neq \hat{p}$,

$$f(p) \equiv F_0(p) + \sum_{i=1}^{n} \hat{p}_i F_i(p) > 0.$$

We next prove

LEMMA 4 $\inf_{p \notin U(\hat{p}, \varepsilon)} f(p) = M > 0.$

Proof   Clearly $M \geq 0$. Suppose that $M = 0$. Then it entails the existence of a sequence $\{p^\nu\}$ in $R_+^n \setminus U(\hat{p}, \varepsilon)$ such that $\lim_{\nu \to \infty} f(p^\nu) = M$.

Define the continuous mapping $\varphi \colon R_+^n \to S_{n+1}$ by the formulae

$$\varphi_0(p) = \frac{1}{1 + \sum_{i=1}^{n} p_i}, \quad \varphi_i(p) = \frac{p_i}{1 + \sum_{i=1}^{n} p_i} \quad (i = 1, 2, \ldots, n).$$

Because of the compactness of S_{n+1}, $\{\varphi(p^\nu)\}$ itself may be assumed[7] to converge to a q in S_{n+1}. By (c), we have

$$\varphi_0(\hat{p}) f(p) = \sum_{i=0}^{n} \varphi_i(\hat{p}) E_i(\varphi(p)),$$

so that, by continuity,

$$\sum_{i=0}^{n} \varphi_i(\hat{p}) E_i(q) = \lim_{\nu \to \infty} \varphi_0(\hat{p}) f(p^\nu) = \varphi_0(\hat{p}) M = 0.$$

Therefore, by (d), q is an equilibrium price vector, and q must equal $\varphi(\hat{p})$, since both of them lie in S_{n+1}. This, in particular, implies that $q_i > 0$ $(i = 0, 1, \ldots, n)$, especially $q_0 > 0$. Since

$$\lim_{v \to \infty} \varphi_0(p^v) = \lim_{v \to \infty} \frac{1}{1 + \sum p_i^v} = q_0 > 0,$$

$1 + \sum_{i=1}^n p_i^v$ converges to $1/q_0$, that is, $\{p^v\}$ is a bounded sequence in R_+^n, and therefore itself may be assumed[8] to converge to a p. But the closed set $\Delta = R_+^n \setminus U(\hat{p}, \varepsilon)$ contains p^v, and the limit p is contained in Δ. Then, by continuity,

$$f(p) = \lim_{v \to \infty} f(p^v) = M = 0,$$

from which it follows, by (d), $p = \hat{p}$. This implies a contradiction $\hat{p} \in \Delta$. Hence $M > 0$.

(γ) By Lemma 1, $F_i(p)$'s $(i = 1, 2, \ldots, n)$ are bounded for $p \geqq 0$. Therefore there is $L > 0$ such that

$$\sum_{i=1}^n F_i(p)^2 \leqq L.$$

(δ) We now prove that for any constant ρ fulfilling

$$0 < \rho < \min(2M/L, 1), \tag{5}$$

any solution $p(t)$ of (1) starting from any initial position $p(0) \geqq 0$ converges to $\hat{p}$. Step (δ) will be divided into the two portions (I) and (II).

(I)   If $p(t) \in U(\hat{p}, \varepsilon)$, then, by (4) and $\rho < 1$, system (1) reduces to the classical system

$$\frac{dp_i}{dt} = \rho F_i(p) \quad (i = 1, 2, \ldots, n).$$

Then, as is shown, e.g., in section 4.2 of the Arrow–Block–Hurwicz article (1959), if, following Liapounov, we define $2V = \sum_{i=1}^n (p_i - \hat{p}_i)^2$, we have

$$\frac{dV}{dt} = \rho \sum_{i=1}^n (p_i - \hat{p}_i) F_i(p)$$

$$= -\rho f(p) \quad \text{by } (b).$$

(II)   Now, by definition,

$\theta_i(p) = \rho F_i(p) + p_i \quad \text{if } \rho F_i(p) + p_i \geqq 0.$

and

$\theta_i(p) = 0 > \rho F_i(p) + p_i \quad \text{if } \rho F_i(p) + p_i < 0,$

from which it follows that $\theta_i(p)^2 \leqq |\rho F_i(p) + p_i|^2$. Thus, substituting $p_i + \dot{p}_i$ for $\theta_i(p)$ by (1), we have

$$(p_i + \dot{p}_i)^2 \leqq (\rho F_i(p) + p_i)^2 = \rho^2 F_i(p)^2 + 2\rho p_i F_i(p) + p_i^2.$$

Hence

$$\sum_{i=1}^{n} p_i^2 + 2 \sum_{i=1}^{n} p_i \dot{p}_i + \sum_{i=1}^{n} \dot{p}_i^2 \leqq \rho^2 \sum_{i=1}^{n} F_i(p)^2 + 2\rho \sum_{i=1}^{n} p_i F_i(p) + \sum_{i=1}^{n} p_i^2.$$

In view of the relation (b) $\sum_{i=1}^{n} p_i F_i(p) = -F_0(p)$, we have

$$\sum_{i=1}^{n} p_i \dot{p}_i \leqq \frac{1}{2} \left(\rho^2 \sum_{i=1}^{n} F_i(p)^2 - \sum_{i=1}^{n} \dot{p}_i^2 \right) - \rho F_0(p)$$

$$\leqq \frac{\rho^2}{2} \sum_{i=1}^{n} F_i(p)^2 - \rho F_0(p). \tag{6}$$

On the other hand, also by definition,

$\theta_i(p) \geqq \rho F_i(p) + p_i,$

which gives, in view of (1),

$\dot{p}_i = \theta_i(p) - p_i \geqq \rho F_i(p),$

and hence

$$\sum_{i=1}^{n} \hat{p}_i \dot{p}_i \geqq \rho \sum_{i=1}^{n} \hat{p}_i F_i(p). \tag{7}$$

Using (6) and (7),

$$\frac{dV}{dt} = \sum_{i=1}^{n} (p_i - \hat{p}_i)\dot{p}_i = \sum_{i=1}^{n} p_i \dot{p}_i - \sum_{i=1}^{n} \hat{p}_i \dot{p}_i$$

$$\leqq \frac{\rho^2}{2} \sum_{i=1}^{n} F_i(p)^2 - \rho \left[F_0(p) + \sum_{i=1}^{n} \hat{p}_i F_i(p) \right]$$

$$= \frac{\rho^2}{2} \sum_{i=1}^{n} F_i(p)^2 - \rho f(p).$$

If now $p(t) \notin U(\hat{p}, \varepsilon)$, by Lemma 4, ($\gamma$) and (5),

$$\frac{dV}{dt} \leq \frac{\rho^2}{2} \sum_{i=1}^{n} F_i(p)^2 - \rho f(p)$$

$$\leq \frac{\rho^2}{2} L - \rho M = \frac{\rho L}{2}(\rho - 2M/L) = -\delta,$$

where $\delta = (\rho L/2)(2M/L - \rho) > 0$.

On the basis of the above results (I) and (II), we always have

$$\frac{dV}{dt} \leq -\min[\delta, \rho f(p)], \tag{8}$$

from which it can be deduced that

$$\lim_{t \to \infty} V = 0 \quad \text{(monotonically)}.$$

In fact, since $f(p) \geq 0$ at all times, (8) implies that the non-negative function V of time is non-increasing. Accordingly, V monotonically converges to a non-negative limit η. If η were positive, $p(t) \notin U(\hat{p}, \eta/2)$ over time. In such a case, we can show, in exactly the same fashion as in the proof for Lemma 4, that $f(p) \geq \beta$ over time for a positive constant β. Therefore, in view of (8), dV/dt is majorized by a negative number, which yields a contradiction $\lim_{t \to \infty} V = -\infty$. This means that $\eta = 0$, and the proof is now complete.

5   Relations to the Arrow-Block-Hurwicz Result

5.1   Arrow, Block, and Hurwicz (1959) recently proved the global stability of the competitive market for a special case, namely, for the case in which all goods are gross substitutes. One important feature of their result is the broad generality of price adjustment; the rate of price change is not necessarily proportional to excess demand but is assumed to be only a sign-preserving function of excess demand. In this connection one may point out that the right-hand side of equation (1) is of the same sign as $F_i(p)$ for $p > 0$.[9] Accordingly, if one assumes gross substitutability, and if the initial position p^0 is positive, the stability proved in this note for equation (1) is implied by the Arrow–Block–Hurwicz result. However, generally speaking, the results of this note are different in several points from theirs, as will be elucidated below.

5.2 First, it is noted that we have proved the existence of a tâtonnement path, namely, a solution of the differential equation discussed in Section 3 without assuming any behavioral conditions on excess demand functions like gross substitutability or the weak axiom of revealed preference, while Arrow, Block, and Hurwicz assume a special condition[10] on the shape of excess demand functions to achieve the corresponding objective. Thus, our mathematical derivation of Proposition 1 differs in nature from theirs, in that the existence of a tâtonnement path is discussed under general conditions, separately from the stability problem. Second, attention should be called to the somewhat different role played by the weak axiom of revealed preference here in comparison with the Arrow–Block–Hurwicz article. They proved global stability for a narrower type of adjustment process in which the rates of price change are proportional to excess demands, by deriving the weak axiom of revealed preference from gross substitutability. When, however, general sign-preserving cases were discussed, they were based directly on gross substitutability, and did not rely upon the revealed preference axiom implied by substitutability. In this note, it has been shown that this axiom already suffices to establish global stability for a special, but sign-preserving, case. Finally, the initial position of the price tâtonnement in our case is assumed only to be non-negative and need not be strictly positive.

Notes

1. The authors are greatly indebted to Professor M. Morishima and the referee for invaluable criticisms and suggestions.

2. In what follows, for a vector q, the inequality $q \geqq 0$ means as usual that all the components of q are non-negative.

3. Here, the orthodox version of price flexibility is understood in such a broad sense that the rate of price change has the same sign as excess demend, but not necessarily depends on the amount of excess demand. See also the final section of this paper.

4. See, e.g., Coddington and Levinson 1955. The uniqueness of the solution is not insured here.

5. $U(\hat{p}, \varepsilon)$ is the set of vectors p whose distances to $\hat{p}$ are less than ε.

6. R^n_+ denotes the so-called non-negative orthant, namely the totality of all nonnegative vectors of the n-dimensional space R^n.

7. This can be done by passing to a suitable subsequence of $\{\varphi(p^{\nu})\}$.

8. This was done on a similar ground as remarked in footnote 7.

9. It should also be noted that the right-hand side of (1) may not be of the same sign as excess demand on the whole domain of all non-negative $p \geqq 0$. In fact, if $p_i = 0$, and $F_i(p) < 0$, then $\theta_i(p) - p_i = 0$, so that it does not have a sign-preserving nature in the exact sense.

10. See Lemma 6 in Arrow, Block and Hurwicz (1959).

References

Arrow, K. J. and G. Debreu (1954): Existence of an Equilibrium for a Competitive Economy, *Econometrica*, Vol. 22.

Arrow, K. J. and L. Hurwicz (1958): On the Stability of the Competitive Equilibrium, 1, *Econometrica*, Vol. 26.

Arrow, K. J., H. D. Block, and L. Hurwicz (1959): On the Stability of the Competitive Equilibrium, II, *Econometrica*, Vol. 27.

Coddington, E. A. and N. Levinson (1955): *Theory of Ordinary Differential Equations*, New York: McGraw-Hill.

Gale, D. (1955): The Law of Supply and Demand, *Mathematica Scandinavica*, Vol. 3.

Hahn, F. (1958): Gross Substitutes and the Dynamic Stability of General Equilibrium, *Econometrica*, Vol. 26.

McKenzie, W. L. (1954): On Equilibrium in Graham's Model of World Trade and Other Competitive Systems, *Econometrica*, Vol. 22.

—— (1958): A Contribution to the Theory of the Stability of Competitive Equilibrium, Report presented at *the Chicago Meeting of the Econometric Society*. December.

—— (1959): On the Existence of General Equilibrium for a Competitive Market, *Econometrica*, Vol. 27.

Negishi, T. (1958): A Note on the Stability of an Economy Where All Goods are Gross Substitutes, *Econometrica*, Vol. 26.

Nikaido, H. (1956): "On the Classical Multilateral Exchange Problem," *Metroeconomica*, Vol. VIII.

—— (1957): A Supplementary Note to Nikaido (1956), *Metroeconomica*, Vol. IX.

—— (1959): Stability of Equilibrium by the Brown–von Neumann Differential Equation, *Econometrica*, Vol. 27.

Uzawa, H. (1957): A Note on the Stability of Equilibrium, Technical Report No. 44, Dept. of Economics, Stanford University.

—— (1958): Iterative Methods for Concave Programming, in K. J. Arrow, L. Hurwicz, and H. Uzawa, *Studies in Linear and Nonlinear Programming*, Stanford: Stanford University Press.

—— (1959–60): Walras' Tâtonnement in the Theory of Exchange, *Review of Economic Studies*, Vol. 27.

Wald, A. (1936): Über die Produktionsgleichungen der Ökonomischen Wertlehre, *Ergebnisse eines mathematischen Kolloquiums*, Heft 7 (Vienna).

II Non-tâtonnement Price Dynamics

3 Economic Adjustments under Noncompetitive Pricing

1 Introduction

1.1 Summary of the Results

The market price mechanism is expected to implement an efficient re-source allocation through the parametric function of prices. This idealized mechanism worked well in the good old day's competitive economy where every agent was a price-taker. It achieved resource allocation by reconcil-ing individual ex ante price-taking behaviors of all agents, producers as well as consumers, and integrating them to mutually consistent feasible actions in the economy.

In the contemporary economy involving more or less monopolistic characteristics, however, the function is no longer perfect owing to the presence of price-making agents, especially, among producers. Nonethe-less, in order for the price mechanism to work, even though imperfectly, there must be price-taking agents. For otherwise all agents would intend to make prices, while nobody would take them as given parameters, and no transaction could result. Thus the economy whose working depends on a price mechanism includes price-takers. Their behaviors are functions of prices and therefore can more or less be controlled by agents making the prices. A demand or supply function with prices as arguments, available to a price-making agent, is an integration of behaviors of some price-taking agents behind it. He is thereby capable of controlling their behaviors by price adjustment.

Today, the price mechanism still works but imperfectly. Disequilibrium in the sense of imbalance of demand and supply does not necessarily result in a price adjustment that would reduce the excess demand or supply toward an equilibrium. Demand is brought in balance to supply through output adjustments rather than price adjustments. Prices function as price-makers' instruments to regulate the size and distribution of national income, that is, distribution between workers and capitalists on one hand and that among capitalists in various sectors on the other.

This view was developed somewhat extensively by the author in the two works (Nikaido 1974, 1975). In particular, it is shown in the second of them that sectoral levels of output can be uniquely and stably determined

From *Adaptive Economic Models* (New York: Academic Press, 1975). © 1975 Academic Press, Inc. Reprinted by permission.

at any possible price situation to meet the corresponding effective demand for goods. Thereby the capitalists can potentially regulate income distribution by way of controlling prices.

Some dynamics in output adjustments of this kind was also included. However, the exploration was not thoroughly done. The purpose of this paper is to supplement the dynamics in two typical adjustment processes, namely, adjustment under full cost pricing and that under perceived profit maximization. The case where the system Jacobian matrix possesses a uniformly column dominant negative diagonal, is then considered and stability is established using a result due to Karlin (1959, Chap. 9, Th. 9.5.1). The existence and uniqueness of a solution are also discussed for this case.

1.2   Basic Working of the Economy

The economy is depicted as a Leontief system of the standard type having an input coefficients matrix

$$A = (a_{ij}), \tag{1}$$

where a_{ij} denotes the amount of the ith good to produce one unit of the jth good in the jth sector with no joint production under constant returns to scale, $i, j = 1, 2, \ldots, n$. A is a nonnegative matrix and will be assumed to be indecomposable whenever required.

If labor is taken as a numeraire on the assumption of no money illusion, the price vector p is essentially determined by setting up a vector of sectoral profit per unit output π in the equation[1]

$$p' = p'A + l' + \pi', \tag{2}$$

where l is a given labor inputs vector, which is positive given the indispensability of labor. The solution $p = \sigma$ of equation (2) for $\pi = 0$ is the economy's labor value vector.

Let $F(p)$ be the demand vector of workers and $G(p, s_1, s_2, \ldots, s_j, \ldots, s_n)$ be the demand vector of capitalists' households, where s_j is the profit of the jth sector. Let further $L(p)$ be the supply of labor at p.

For a predetermined nonnegative profit per unit output vector π, which determines p in (2), the gross output vector $x = (x_i)$ is determined by:

J.B. Say's Case

$$x = Ax + F(p) + G(p, \pi_1 x_1, \pi_2 x_2, \ldots, \pi_n x_n). \tag{3}$$

Keynesian Case

$$x = Ax + F(p) + G(p, \pi_1 x_1, \pi_2 x_2, \ldots, \pi_n x_n) + \omega d \qquad (4)$$

both subject to full employment requirement

$$L(p) = l'x, \qquad (5)$$

where $d \geq 0^2$ is a given constant investment composition vector and ω is a nonnegative scalar indicating the level of investment.

In the work previously cited it was shown that the output levels, including ω, are uniquely determinate under appropriate conditions on F, G and L. The profit per unit output vector π therefore determines the output vector x and the scale of investment ω. They are thereby functions of π, $x = x(\pi)$ and $\omega = \omega(\pi)$, which are termed *objective demand functions*. Thus capitalists as producers are potentially capable of regulating the state of the economy by controlling π. Determination of π is ultimately dependent on monopolistic competition among sectors in one of its alternative forms, including, e.g., joint maximization of surplus value or aggregate profit, Cournot-Negishi noncooperative perceived profit maximization and so forth.

1.3 Dynamic Adjustments

In the economy whose basic working is characterized above, disequilibrium in the sense of excess demand for or supply of goods induces adjustments in output toward equilibrium, rather than changes in the prices of goods. Prices need not be sensitive to the imbalance of demand and supply. They are more apt to change through visible hands of producers. How the visible hands perform depends on the entrepreneurial behaviors of producers. A typical case of such a pricing is full cost pricing at fixed mark-up rates. It will be shown in Subsections 2.2 and 2.3 that the profit per unit output vector converges to an equilibrium state and that the sectorial output levels also converge to their equilibrium levels determined by equation (3) or (4) subject to (5), if output is adjusted in the direction of the excess of demand over supply while prices change on the full cost principle.

Another kind of the adjustment of the profit per unit output vector takes place in a dynamized process of the Cournot–Negishi noncooperative ex ante perceived profit maximization. Subsection 2.4 discusses convergence to a Cournot–Negishi solution along the objective demand schedules on the assumption that output adjustments to balance demand and supply are instantaneous.

1.4   Uniform Diagonal Dominance

In Nikaido 1975 fundamental workability of the economy, namely, existence and uniqueness of solution, is established by virtue of the Brouwer fixed point theorem and certain univalence theorems due to Gale and myself (1965). However, the Jacobian matrices of the relevant mappings have dominant diagonals for a set of weights constant throughout their domains. This fact simplifies the discussion for workability. It is remarkable that the existence and uniqueness of a solution can be proved simultaneously under this kind of uniform diagonal dominance. In Section 3 are presented a number of results in this line, inlcuding the one just mentioned.

2   Dynamic Processes

2.1   The Assumptions

The following conditions are assumed:

(P) A is productuve enough to meet positive amounts of final demand for goods. That is to say, the Hawkins–Simon conditions hold so that $I - A$ is invertible and $(I - A)^{-1}$ is nonnegative, where I is the identity matrix.

(W.1) $F(p) = (F_i(p))$ is a nonnegative, continuously differentiable vector-valued function of the positive price vector p.

(W.2)   The identity holds:

$$p'F(p) = L(p), \tag{6}$$

which implies, among other things, the nonnegativity and continuous differentiability of $L(p)$.

(W.3) $L(p)$ tends to zero when p_j ($j = 1, 2, \ldots, n$) tend to $+\infty$ simultaneously.

(W.4) $L(\sigma) > 0$.

(C.1) $G(p, s_1, s_2, \ldots, s_n) = (G_i(p, s_1, s_2, \ldots, s_n))$ is a nonnegative, continuous, vector-valued function of the positive p and nonnegative s_j's.

(C.2)   Each component function G_i has continuous partial derivatives, and those with respect to s_j satisfy

$$G_{ij} = \frac{\partial G_i}{\partial s_j} \geq 0 \quad (i,j = 1,2,\ldots,n), \tag{7}$$

that is, there are no inferior goods for capitalists' households.

(C.3)   For J. B. Say's case there holds the identity

$$p'G(p,s_1,s_2,\ldots,s_n) = \sum_{j=1}^{n} s_j. \tag{8}$$

(C.4)   For the Keynesian case the average propensity of capitalists' households to spend is uniformly less than unity, that is, there is a constant θ such that $1 > \theta > 0$ and

$$p'G(p,s_1,s_2,\ldots,s_n) \leq \theta \sum_{j=1}^{n} s_j. \tag{9}$$

(C.5)   For the Keynsian case the marginal propensities of capitalists' households to spend are not larger than unity, that is

$$\frac{\partial}{\partial s_j} p'G = \sum_{i=1}^{n} p_i \frac{\partial G_i}{\partial s_j} \leq 1 \quad (j = 1,2,\ldots,n). \tag{10}$$

There are immediate consequences from these assumptions. First of all, it is noted that in J. B. Say's case the full employment requirement (5) automatically follows from equation (3). For premultiplication of (3) by p' gives rise to (5) because of (2), (6) and (8).

Second, in view of the fact that ω is determined in equations (4) and (5) so that potential underemployment or labor-shortage equilibrium is avoided, the Keynesian case can be reudced to J. B. Say's case as long as the static workability of the economy is concerned. In fact this can be done by introducing an adjusted G function

$$G^*(p,s_1,s_2,\ldots,s_n) = G(p,s_1,s_2,\ldots,s_n)$$
$$+ \omega(p,s_1,s_2,\ldots,s_n)d \tag{11}$$

and formulating (3) for it, where

$$\omega(p,s_1,s_2,\ldots,s_n) = \left\{ \sum_{j=1}^{n} s_j - p'G(p,s_1,s_2,\ldots,s_n) \right\} \bigg/ p'd. \tag{12}$$

It is readily verified that G^* satisfies (C.3) by construction, and (C.2)

$$\frac{\partial G_i^*}{\partial s_j} = \frac{\partial G_i}{\partial s_j} + \left(1 - \frac{\partial}{\partial s_j} p'G\right)\Bigg/ p'd \geq 0$$

by (7) and (10).

2.2 Output Adjustments under Full Cost Pricing: J. B. Say's Case

Under full cost pricing the jth sector prices the jth good by adding a profit margin to the current direct material and labor cost by $100\, \delta_j$ per cent. Then, the prices change over time conforming to

$\dot{p}_j = \mu_j$ times the jth component of

$$R(p) = p'A(I + D) + l'(I + D) - p' \quad (j = 1, 2, \ldots, n), \tag{13}$$

where a dot means differentiation with respect to time, and μ_j are speeds of adjustment and

$$D = \begin{bmatrix} \delta_1 & & & 0 \\ & \delta_2 & & \\ & & \ddots & \\ 0 & & & \delta_n \end{bmatrix}. \tag{14}$$

Output is adjusted in the direction of excess of demand over supply, and the adjustment is represented by

$\dot{x}_i = \lambda_i$ times the ith component of

$$Q(x, p) = Ax + F(p) + G(p, \pi_1 x_1, \pi_2 x_2, \ldots, \pi_n x_n) - x \quad (i = 1, 2, \ldots, n) \tag{15}$$

where λ_i are speeds of adjustment and

$$\pi' = (p'A + l')D. \tag{16}$$

THEOREM 1   If the mark-up rates δ_i are small enough to permit $I - A(I + D)$ to have a nonnegative inverse, the movements of p and x determined by (13) and (15) are stable, and p and x converge to unique $\hat{p}$ and $\hat{x}$, respectively.

Proof (In this proof as well as in those following the basic assumptions will be used whenever required without explicit reference to them each time.) First of all, it is noted that the price movement is independent of and separated from the output movement, whereas the latter depends on the former. The convergence of the price vector to a unique equilibrium price vector $\hat{p}$ determined by

$$\dot{p}' = \dot{p}'A(I + D) + l'(I + D) \tag{17}$$

is well known. In fact, the invertibility of $I - A(I + D)$ with a nonnegative inverse implies the unique determination of $\hat{p}' = l'(I + D)\{I - A(I + D)\}^{-1}$ on the static side and the negative real parts of all eigenvalues of $A(I + D) - I$ on the dynamic side, and thereby ensures the convergence.

The moving price vector, which has started at a positive initial price vector, remains positive forever in the course of its convergence to $\hat{p}$. For $\dot{p}_j$ will be positive whenever p_j becomes too small by (13). This ensures, in particular, the positivity of the changing profit per unit output vector π' by (16). If the initial position of the output vector $x(0)$ is nonnegative, (15) generates an adjustment process forever. For $\dot{x}_i$ will be nonnegative by (15) and the positivity of π' whenever x_i reaches zero while x having remained nonnegative. Therefore it makes sense to see where the adjustment process will lead.

Equation (3) has a unique solution $x = \hat{x}$ for $p = \hat{p}$ and the corresponding $\pi = \hat{\pi}$, as established in my previously cited book or as will be shown alternatively in Section 3 below. It will be proved that the changing output vector converges to this $\hat{x}$.

To this end, first of all, let us examine the boundedness of x. The prices, which converge to the components of $\hat{p}$ while remaining positive, are bounded uniformly away from zero by common positive constants. Hence $L(p)$ is also bounded by continuity.

Let

$$\Lambda = \begin{pmatrix} \lambda_1 & & & 0 \\ & \lambda_2 & & \\ & & \ddots & \\ 0 & & & \lambda_n \end{pmatrix}$$

$$M = \begin{pmatrix} \mu_1 & & & 0 \\ & \mu_2 & & \\ & & \ddots & \\ 0 & & & \mu_n \end{pmatrix}.$$

Then, premultiplication of $\Lambda^{-1}\dot{x}$ by p' gives

$$\frac{d}{dt}(p'\Lambda^{-1}x) = \dot{p}'\Lambda^{-1}x + p'(A-I)x + p'F + p'G$$

$$= \dot{p}'\Lambda^{-1}x + (\dot{p}'M^{-1} - l' - \pi')x + L(p) + \pi'x$$

$$= L(p) - \{l' - \dot{p}'(\Lambda^{-1} + M^{-1})\}x \tag{18}$$

by (13), (15) and (16) together with (6) and (8). Since p and $\dot{p}$ tend to $\hat{p}$ and zero, respectively,

$$l' - \dot{p}'(\Lambda^{-1} + M^{-1}) \geqq \varepsilon p'\Lambda^{-1} \quad (\varepsilon = \text{a positive constant})$$

for large t. Hence (18) implies

$$\frac{d}{dt}(p'\Lambda^{-1}x) \leqq L(p) - \varepsilon p'\Lambda^{-1}x \tag{19}$$

when t becomes large, which ensures the boundedness of $p'\Lambda^{-1}x$ by that of $L(p)$. From this follows the boundedness of $\hat{p}'\Lambda^{-1}x$, whence that of x by its nonnegativity.

Next let us evaluate the Jacobian matrix of the compound system of (13) and (15), whose elements are bounded along the bounded trajectories of x and p. The Jacobian matrix is evaluated as

$$\begin{pmatrix} \Lambda & 0 \\ 0 & M \end{pmatrix} \begin{bmatrix} A + \left(\dfrac{\partial G_i}{\partial s_j}\right)\Pi - I & N \\ 0 & (I+D)A' - I \end{bmatrix} \tag{20}$$

where

$$\Pi = \begin{bmatrix} \pi_1 & & & 0 \\ & \pi_2 & & \\ & & \ddots & \\ 0 & & & \pi_n \end{bmatrix}$$

and $N = (n_{ij})$ is a square matrix of order n and n_{ij} is the partial derivative of the right-hand side of the ith equation in (15) with respect to p_j.

Now, partially differentiating (3) with respect to s_j, we have

$$p'\left(\frac{\partial G_i}{\partial s_j}\right) = (1, 1, \ldots, 1). \tag{21}$$

Then, (13) and (21) imply

$$p' \left\{ A + \left(\frac{\partial G_i}{\partial s_j} \right) \Pi - I \right\} = \hat{p}' M^{-1} - l',$$

so that

$$\hat{p}' \left\{ A + \left(\frac{\partial G_i}{\partial s_j} \right) \Pi - I \right\} \leqq -\frac{l'}{2} < 0' \tag{22}$$

along the trajectory for large t.

Additionally, $\hat{p}'(|n_{ij}|)$ is bounded along the trajectory, and hence

$$m' \{ (I + D)A' - I \} + \hat{p}'(|n_{ij}|) \leqq -c' < 0' \tag{23}$$

for constant positive vectors m and c by the invertibility of $I - A(I + D)$ with a nonnegative inverse.

Note that

$$A + \left(\frac{\partial G_i}{\partial s_j} \right) \Pi \quad \text{and} \quad (I + D)A'$$

are nonnegative matrices under (7). Then (22) and (23) imply that the Jacobian matrix has a negative dominant diagonal with respect to column sum with the weight vector

$$(\hat{p}'\Lambda^{-1}, m'M^{-1})$$

along the trajectory for large t. Therefore, following the idea of Karlin (1959, Chap. 9, Th. 9.5.1.) and defining the Liapounov function

$$V(x, p) = \sum_{i=1}^{n} (\hat{p}_i/\lambda_i)|\lambda_i Q_i(x, p)| + \sum_{j=1}^{n} (m_j/\mu_j)|\mu_j R_j(p)|$$

we can show that

$$\frac{d^+ V}{dt} \leqq - \sum_{j=1}^{n} (l_j/2)|\lambda_j Q_j(x, p)| - \sum_{i=1}^{n} c_i|\mu_i R_i(p)|$$

along the trajectory for large t, where d^+/dt denotes one-sided differentiation. Hence the convergence of x to $\hat{x}$ follows. This completes the proof of Theorem 1.

2.3   Output Adjustments under Full Cost Pricing: The Keynesian Case

The adjustment process applies to J. B. Say's case transformed from the Keynesian case through (11) as well. In such a situation, however, ω is adjustment instantaneously following the adjustments of x and p. This is somewhat unsymmetrical.

In order to adjust ω in a manner similar to x let us assume that ω changes in the direction of excess of total profit over the sum of spending from profit and investment demand. Then

$$\dot{\omega} = \lambda_0 [\pi' x - p'\{G(p, \pi_1 x_1, \pi_2 x_2, \ldots, \pi_n x_n) + \omega d\}]$$

$\dot{x}_i = \lambda_i$ times the ith component of

$$Q(\omega, x, p) = Ax + F(p) + G(p, \pi_1 x_1, \pi_2 x_2, \ldots, \pi_n \pi_n) + \omega d - x$$

$$(i = 1, 2, \ldots, n) \tag{24}$$

while the behavior of p is regulated by (13) as before.

THEOREM 2   Under the same conditions on δ_j as in Theorem 1, the movements of ω, x and p determined by (13) and (24) are stable, and there will be convergence of ω, x and p to unique $\hat{\omega}$, $\hat{x}$ and $\hat{p}$ determined by equations (4), (5) and (17).

Proof   A sketch of an analogous proof will be given. p tends to $\hat{p}$ while remaining positive, as in Theorem 1. x_i and ω will never become negative, and can be generated without limit. The nonnegativity of ω follows from $\dot{\omega} \geq 0$ whenever ω reaches zero while x, ω having remained nonnegative, since $\pi' x - p'G \geq (1 - \theta)\pi' x \geq 0$ by (9). The nonnegativity of x is ensured for similar reasons.

It can readily be verified in the light of (6) that equation (5) is equivalent to

$$\pi' x = p'(G + \omega d)$$

under equation (4). Hence the critical point of the compound system of (13) and (24) is uniquely determined as $\hat{\omega}$, $\hat{x}$ and $\hat{p}$ by (4), (5) and (17), to which the convergence of the solution is asserted.

The boundedness of the solution can be seen as follows. The boundedness of ω will immediately follow by the first equation in (24) regulating $\dot{\omega}$ once x proves bounded. Next the boundedness of x can be seen by considering the following inequality, similar to (19),

$$\frac{d}{dt} p'\Lambda^{-1}x + \lambda_0^{-1}\dot{\omega} \leq L(p) - \varepsilon p'\Lambda^{-1}x,$$

which holds for large t and a positive constant ε, and the fact that the first equation in (24) implies $(1 - \theta)\pi'x < \omega p'd$ in case $\dot{\omega} < 0$.

The Jacobian matrix of the compound system of (13) and (24) is evaluated as

$$\begin{bmatrix} \lambda_0 & 0 & 0 \\ 0 & \Lambda & 0 \\ 0 & 0 & M \end{bmatrix} \begin{bmatrix} -p'd & \pi' - p'\left(\dfrac{\partial G_i}{\partial s_j}\right)\Pi & N \\ d & A + \left(\dfrac{\partial G_i}{\partial s_j}\right)\Pi - I & \\ 0 & 0 & (I + D)A' - I \end{bmatrix} \qquad (25)$$

where $N = (n_{ij})$ is an $(n + 1) \times n$ matrix. It is noted that

$$\pi' - p'\left(\frac{\partial G_i}{\partial s_j}\right)\Pi \geq 0'$$

by (10). Clearly

$$p'd > 0, \quad d \geq 0$$

$$A + \left(\frac{\partial G_i}{\partial s_j}\right)\Pi \geq 0, \quad (I + D)A' \geq 0.$$

Finally, the Jacobian matrix has a negative dominant diagonal with respect to column sum with the positive weight vector

$$(\rho, \hat{p}', m') \begin{bmatrix} \lambda_0^{-1} & 0 & 0 \\ 0 & \Lambda^{-1} & 0 \\ 0 & 0 & M^{-1} \end{bmatrix}$$

along the trajectory for large t, provided a scalar $\rho > 1$ and a positive vector m are suitably chosen, similarly as in Theorem 1. Thereby Karlin's method can be applied. This completes the proof.

2.4 Adjustments toward the Cournot–Negishi Solution

It is now assumed that output is adjusted instantaneously in response to the predetermined profit per unit output vector toward the level determined by the objective demand function $x(\pi)$. Nonetheless producers need not know the true shapes of the objective demand schedules. They

perceive subjective demand schedules and try to price their product so as
to maximize the expected profit along the schedules. But the economy
must find itself on the objective demand function, so long as all the markets are actually cleared. Thus, the Cournot–Negishi solution is defined to
be such a point on the objective demand function that all producers are
simultaneously maximizing their expected profits there. For a detailed
discussion see Nikaido 1975.

Let

$$q_j = p_j - \eta_j(p, x)(y_j - x_j) \quad (j = 1, 2, \ldots, n) \tag{26}$$

be an inverse demand function perceived by the jth sector when supply
x is currently cleared at the prices p. q_j is the expected price when the
planned output y_j is supplied. The perceived demand functions are down-
ward-sloping, so that $\eta_j(p, x) > 0$.

The jth sector maximizes the expected profit

$$\left\{(1 - a_{jj})q_j - \sum_{i \neq j} a_{ij}p_i - l_j\right\}y_j.$$

The maximization is worked out subject to the nonnegativity constraint
$y_j \geq 0$. Nonetheless it always results in marginal conditions with vanishing
derivatives, yielding

$$(1 - a_{jj}) - \sum_{i \neq j} a_{ij}p_i - l_j = (1 - a_{jj})\eta_j y_j \quad (j = 1, 2, \ldots, n). \tag{27}$$

The right-hand side in the jth equation of (27) is the profit per unit output
expected by the jth sector which is evaluated as

$$\pi_j(p, x) = \frac{1}{2}\{(1 - a_{jj})\eta_j(p, x)x_j + \pi_j\} \quad (j = 1, 2, \ldots, n) \tag{28}$$

The Cournot–Negishi solution is a situation such that

$$\pi_j = \pi_j(p, x(\pi)) \quad (j = 1, 2, \ldots, n) \tag{29}$$

and is obtained as a fixed point under the mapping $\pi \rightarrow (\pi_j(p, x(\pi))$.

Now, assume producers price goods in the direction of their expectation
(28) while the economy is moving on the objective demand function. Then,
the actual profit per unit output changes conforming to

$$\dot{\pi}_j = \alpha_j(\pi_j(p, x(\pi)) - \pi_j) \quad (j = 1, 2, \ldots, n). \tag{30}$$

If $\eta_j(p, x)$ are continuous for positive p and nonnegative x, system (30) is well-behaved, since $\dot{\pi}_j \geq 0$ when π_j reaches zero while π having started at a nonnegative initial position and remained nonnegative.

Now, suppose for simplicity that η_j are positive constants. Then, (30) is explicitly given as

$$\dot{\pi}_j = \alpha_j((1 - a_{jj})\eta_j x_j(\pi) - \pi_j) \quad (j = 1, 2, \ldots, n), \tag{31}$$

where the speeds of adjustment α_j are rearranged so as to include $1/2$.

THEOREM 3   The solution π of equation (31) converges to a Cournot–Negishi solution, provided the η_j are sufficiently small.

Proof   It has already been noted that π remains nonnegative. $p \geq \sigma > 0$ for the labor value vector σ when $\pi \geq 0$. Therefore $x(\pi)$ is bounded for $\pi \geq 0$ by continuity, (5) and (W.3). Therefore the solution π of equation (30) is bounded. $x(\pi)$ has continuous partial derivatives, which are therefore bounded along the trajectory. Hence the Jacobian matrix of (31) has a negative dominant diagonal with respect to column sum with constant positive weights along the trajectory provided the η_j are sufficiently small. The convergence to a critical point can thereby be proved by Karlin's method.   Q.E.D.

3   Systems Having Uniformly Dominant Diagonals

3.1   Uniformly Dominant Diagonals

As is well known, a square matrix $T = (t_{ij})$ has a dominant diagonal, if there are positive weights α_i such that

$$\alpha_j |t_{jj}| > \sum_{i \neq j} \alpha_i |t_{ij}| \quad (j = 1, 2, \ldots, n). \tag{32}$$

Alternatively, T has a dominant diagonal, if there are positive weights α_j such that

$$\alpha_i |t_{ii}| > \sum_{i \neq j} \alpha_j |t_{ij}| \quad (i = 1, 2, \ldots, n). \tag{33}$$

The two definitions are equivalent, since both are equivalent to the fulfillment of the Hawkins–Simon conditions by the matrix (t_{ij}^*) whose elements are given by

$$t_{ij}^* = \begin{cases} |t_{ii}| & \text{if } i = j \\ -|t_{ij}| & \text{otherwise.} \end{cases}$$

For general information about dominant diagonals we may consult McKenzie (1960).

If T, whose elements are functions defined on a set, has a dominant diagonal throughout the set, the weights α_i in (32) are generally different from palace to place in the set. Thus in the case of a matrix whose elements are functions we may strengthen diagonal dominance to

DEFINITION 1 T has a uniformly dominant diagonal with respect to column sum (abbr. c-u.d.d.), if there are constant positive weights α_i such that (32) holds uniformly.

DEFINITION 2 T has a uniformly dominant diagonal with respect to row sum (abbr.r-u.d.d.), if there are constant positive weights α_j such that (33) holds uniformly.

It goes without saying that both versions of uniform diagonal dominance need not be equivalent. Uniform diagonal dominance remarkably simplifies discussion not only of stability but also of static workability (uniqueness and/or existence of a solution).

3.2   Uniqueness by Uniform Diagonal Dominance

Consider a system of equations

$$f_i(x) = 0 \quad (i = 1, 2, \ldots, n) \tag{34}$$

where the functions on the left-hand side are continuously differentiable in a convex domain X of the n-dimensional Euclidean space.

THEOREM 4   If the Jacobian matrix of (34) has a c-u.d.d. in X, then its solution is unique.

Proof   Let

$$f_{ij}(x) = \frac{\partial f_i}{\partial x_j} \quad (i, j = 1, 2, \ldots, n).$$

The diagonal elements f_{jj} never vanish but are of a definite sign. Therefore, it may be assumed by replacing f_j by $-f_j$ if necessary that the Jacobian matrix has a positive c-u.d.d.

Suppose that there are two solutions $a = (a_j)$ and $b = (b_j)$ of (34). If $a_j < b_j$ for some components j, we can perform linear transformations $x_j \to -x_j$, $f_j \to -f_j$ simultaneously for all such j. The Jacobian matrix of the transformed system still has a positive c-u.d.d. on the new transformed convex domain. Therefore we may assume, without loss of generality, that $a \geq b$.

Define

$$\phi(t) = ta + (1 - t)b \quad (1 \geq t \geq 0).$$

Then, in view of the positive c-u.d.d.,

$$\frac{d}{dt} \sum_{i=1}^{n} \alpha_i f_i(\phi(t)) = \sum_{j=1}^{n} \sum_{i=1}^{n} \alpha_i f_{ij}(\phi(t))(a_j - b_j)$$

$$\geq \sum_{j=1}^{n} \left(\alpha_j f_{jj} - \sum_{i \neq j} \alpha_i |f_{ij}| \right)(a_j - b_j) > 0,$$

which contradicts

$$\sum_{i=1}^{n} \alpha_i f_i(a) = \sum_{i=1}^{n} \alpha_i f_i(b) = 0.$$

Q.E.D.

THEOREM 5   If the Jacobian matrix of (34) has a r-u.d.d. in X, then its solution is unique.

Proof   It suffices to consider such two solutions a and b of (34) having a positive r-u.d.d. that $a \geq b$, as in Theorem 4. Let

$$\theta = \max_{j} \frac{a_j - b_j}{\alpha_j} = \frac{a_k - b_k}{\alpha_k} > 0.$$

Then, in view of the positive r-u.d.d.,

$$\frac{d}{dt} f_k(\phi(t)) = \sum_{j=1}^{n} f_{kj}(\phi(t))(a_j - b_j)$$

$$\geq f_{kk}(a_k - b_k) - \sum_{j \neq k} |f_{kj}|(a_j - b_j)$$

$$\geq \theta \left(f_{kk} \alpha_k - \sum_{j \neq k} |f_{kj}| \alpha_j \right) > 0,$$

which contradicts

$$f_k(a) = f_k(b) = 0.$$

Q.E.D.

3.3   Existence and Uniqueness by Uniform Diagonal Dominance

Further strengthening of uniform diagonal dominance enables us to establish existence and uniqueness simultaneously in a simple way along with the idea in Nikaido 1972.

In this subsection the functions in equation (34) are assumed to satisfy the following conditions. (A) Their common domain is the nonnegative orthant, namely, the set of all nonnegative x. (B) The off-diagonal elements of the Jacobian matrix are nonpositive

$$f_{ij}(x) \leq 0 \quad (i \neq j) \tag{35}$$

and (C)

$$f_i(x) \leq 0 \tag{36}$$

whenever the ith component of x is zero.

Now we have

THEOREM 6   If the Jacobian matrix has a psoitive c-u.d.d. in the further stringent sense that

$$(\alpha_1, \alpha_2, \ldots, \alpha_n)(f_{ij}(x)) \geq (\beta_1, \beta_2, \ldots, \beta_n) \tag{37}$$

uniformly for positive constants α_i, β_i, then equation (34) has a unique solution.

Proof   The proof will be worked out by induction on n simultaneously for existence and uniqueness. If $n = 1$, system (34) consists of a single equation of a scalar variable

$$f_1(x) = 0 \tag{38}$$

(37) in this case is specified to $\alpha_1 f_{11}(x) \geq \beta_1$, whence $f_{11}(x) \geq \beta_1/\alpha_1 > 0$ uniformly. Hence $f_1(x)$ monotonically increases without limit, as x increases from zero toward infinity. Thus a solution exists by continuity, since $f_1(0) \leq 0$ by (C), and the solution must be unique by monotonicity.

Suppose now the truth of the assertion for $n - 1$. For convenience of discussion let us rewrite (34) as

$$f_i(x_1, x_2, \ldots, x_{n-1}, x_n) = 0 \quad (i = 1, 2, \ldots, n-1) \tag{39}$$

$$f_n(x_1, x_2, \ldots, x_{n-1}, x_n) = 0 \tag{40}$$

and consider the system of equations in the $n-1$ variables $x_1, x_2, \ldots, x_{n-1}$, (39), for each fixed nonnegative value of x_n.

This system satisfies all the assumptions of the theorem. In fact, (A), (B) and (C) are automatically met. Its Jacobian matrix is the principal submatrix J_n of order $n-1$ in the upper left corner of that of the original system. Since (37) holds and $f_{nj}(x) \leq 0$ ($j < n$) by (35), we have

$$(\alpha_1, \alpha_2, \ldots, \alpha_{n-1})J_n \geq (\beta_1, \beta_2, \ldots, \beta_{n-1}). \tag{41}$$

Therefore, (39) has a unique solution $(x_1, x_2, \ldots, x_{n-1})$ for each fixed nonnegative value of x_n by the induction hypothesis for $n-1$, whence these x_j ($j = 1, 2, \ldots, n-1$) are functions of x_n

$$x_j = g_j(x_n) \quad (j = 1, 2, \ldots, n-1) \tag{42}$$

which satisfy by construction

$$f_i(g_1(x_n), g_2(x_n), \ldots, g_{n-1}(x_n), x_n) = 0 \quad (i = 1, 2, \ldots, n-1) \tag{43}$$

identically for $x_n \geq 0$.

Let

$$g(x_n) = f_n(g_1(x_n), g_2(x_n), \ldots, g_{n-1}(x_n), x_n). \tag{44}$$

Then equation (34) has a unique solution if and only if

$$g(x_n) = 0 \tag{45}$$

is uniquely solvable in the nonnegative unknown x_n.

The rest of the proof is to see that equation (45) satisfies all the assumptions of the theorem for $n = 1$. In fact, (A) is clearly met, while (B) is meaningless, (C) is also met, since

$$g(0) = f_n(g_1(0), g_2(0), \ldots, g_{n-1}(0), 0) \leq 0$$

by (C) for the original system. Equations (35) and (37) imply that $(f_{ij}(x))$ is invertible with a nonnegative inverse, whence

$$(\alpha_1, \alpha_2, \ldots, \alpha_n) \geq (\beta_1, \beta_2, \ldots, \beta_n)(f_{ij}(x))^{-1}. \tag{46}$$

Let the elements of the nth column of $(f_{ij}(x))^{-1}$ be $h_{in}(x)$ ($i = 1, 2, \ldots, n$), which are nonnegative. Then, from (46) follows in particular

$$\alpha_n \geq \sum_{i=1}^{n} \beta_i h_{in}(x) \geq \beta_n h_{nn}(x),$$

which reduces to

$$\alpha_n \geq \beta_n \frac{\det J_n}{\det(f_{ij}(x))}. \tag{47}$$

Clearly $\det(f_{ij}(x)) > 0$ and $\det J_n > 0$ by the Hawkins–Simon conditions. Hence (47) can be written as

$$\alpha_n \frac{\det(f_{ij}(x))}{\det J_n} \geq \beta_n. \tag{48}$$

Now, the $n - 1$ functions (42) are continuously differentiable by the implicit function theorem, and, upon differentiation, we have

$$\frac{dg}{dx_n} = \frac{\det(f_{ij}(x))}{\det J_n}$$

evaluated for the functions (42). Hence

$$\alpha_n \frac{dg}{dx_n} \geq \beta_n$$

by (48). Thus all the assumptions are satisfied and equation (45) is uniquely solvable by virtue of the assertion for $n = 1$ already proved.   Q.E.D.

THEOREM 7   If the Jacobian matrix has a positive r-u.d.d. in the further stringent sense that

$$(f_{ij}(x)) \begin{bmatrix} \alpha_1 \\ \alpha_2 \\ \vdots \\ \alpha_n \end{bmatrix} \geq \begin{bmatrix} \beta_1 \\ \beta_2 \\ \vdots \\ \beta_n \end{bmatrix} \tag{49}$$

uniformly for positive constants α_j, β_j then equation (34) has a unique solution.

Proof   The proof can be worked out in essentially the same way as in Theorem 6 and is left to the reader.

It is finally remarked that the static workability of the basic economy is within the reach of Theorem 6. In fact, if the ith component of the excess of the left-hand side over the right-hand side in (3) is denoted by $f_i(x)$, equation (3) is rewritten as equation (34), with the corresponding Jacobian matrix

$$(f_{ij}(x)) = I - \left(A + \left(\frac{\partial G_i}{\partial s_j}\right)\Pi\right).$$

Assumptions (A), (B) and (C) are clearly met. Moreover

$$p'(f_{ij}(x)) = l'$$

holds as a special case of (37). Therefore Theorem 6 can be applied. The Keynesian case (4), (5) can be transformed to J. B. Say's case, as was already noted.

Notes

This work was supported by the Japan Economic Research Foundation.

1. Here, as well as in the sequel, a prime denotes transposition.

2. Here, as well as in what follows, the following semi-order for vectors $x = (x_i)$, $y = (y_i)$ will be used:

$x \geqq y$ if $x_i \geqq y_i$ $(i = 1, 2, \ldots, n)$

$x \geq y$ if $x \geqq y$, and $x \neq y$

$x > y$ if $x_i > y_i$ $(i = 1, 2, \ldots, n)$.

References

Gale, D. and H. Nikaido (1965): The Jacobian Matrix and Global Univalence of Mappings, *Mathematische Annalen*, 159.

Karlin, S. (1959): *Mathematical Methods and Theory in Games, Programming and Economics*, Vol. I, Reading Mass.: Addison-Wesley.

McKenzie, L. W. (1960): Matrices with Dominant Diagonals and Economic Theory, *Mathematical Methods in Social Sciences 1959*, Stanford: Stanford University Press.

Nikaido, H. (1972): Relative Shares and Factor Price Equalization, *Journal of International Economics*, Vol. 2.

———— (1974): What is an Objective Demand Function?, *Zeitschrift für Nationalökonomie*, 34.

———— (1975): *Monopolistic Competition and Effective Demand*, Princeton: Princeton University Press.

4 Dynamics of Wage-Price Spirals and Stagflation in the Leontief–Sraffa System

with
Susumu
Kobayashi   0210
0230
1342

DSO
EII
E31

1 Introduction

Generally, inflation is a compound process of cost-push and demand-pull.[1] Nonetheless, insofar as supply of goods is sufficiently elastic, quantity adjustment is faster than price adjustment in the present day market mechanism. Supply is rapidly or instantaneously balanced to demand both on their effective, rather than notional, levels, as disequilibrium dynamics theorists presume, while price change is governed not any longer by the classical law of demand and supply but by an alternative force, most crucially generated by mark-ups.

Thus, aside from their monetary and other complex aspects, the current inflationary processes chronically prevailing in advanced capitalist economies may be characterized as cost-pushed wage-price spirals. The purpose of this paper is to formulate and analyze these spiral processes in the many good world in such a simplistic dynamic setting that they are driven by price mark-ups and wage bargaining.

The spirals have income distribution aspects, so that they are formulated and analyzed with special regard to the aspects, and the dynamics of the spirals is ultimately dictated by what takes place over time in the income distribution side of the system. As was pertinently elucidated by Sraffa in his seminal work (1960) the trade-off relation between profits and wages, which otherwise would seem complex in appearance, becomes so transparent, when expressed in terms of the standard commodity, that in real terms they always sum up to the same pie, i.e., certain constant units of the standard commodity per unit labor input. We will therefore formulate and examine the spirals within the framework of Sraffa.

Sraffa rightly emphasizes that his theory assumes nothing about the degree of returns to scale and factor proportions. Nonetheless this generality is possible only if the system stands still. In general the very concept of a standard commodity crucially depends on the output levels on which the system is frozen. A standard commodity which remains invariant and retains the same labor value over time seems to be very difficult to conceive, unless constant returns to scale and fixed factor proportions prevail. For this reason and because both price changes and output changes

With Susumu Kobayashi. From *International Economic Review* 19, no. 1 (February 1978): 83–102. Reprinted by permission.

altogether come to the picture simultaneously, the Sraffa world will be dynamized in the standard Leontief system.

Competitive equilibrium is incompatible with positive profits under constant returns to scale, as is the case with the situation in question. It is therefore presumed that such amounts of goods as meet effective demand are supplied so that commodity markets are always cleared. Thus prices of goods are not determined by the notional demand-supply situation but marked up at a desired positive rate of profit.

On the other hand, wages chase price changes in the bargaining between capital as a whole and labor as a whole at a pace varying from time to time under the influence of their bargaining powers, which reflect several factors, among others, the disequilibrium situation of labor market. Indeed, unemployment strengthens the bargaining power of capital and weakens that of labor, but under circumstances they can still countervail so as to generate a price rise under unemployment, an important aspect of the so-called stagflation. This pattern of wage change somewhat parallels with the Phillips curve constructions, though there is some difference between them in what among disequilibrium features of labor market is presumed to influence most crucially wage change.

The wage-price spirals are generated and driven by these price markups and wage bargaining, and it will be shown that eventually the spirals either converge to the static situation of Sraffa corresponding to a desired uniform rate of profit, or else approach a persistent state of stagflation, according to the relative magnitudes of the relevant parameters. The final section expounds the results of the analysis both in the basic version and in the presence of technical progress.

2   Background Facts in the Leontief–Sraffa System

Suppose that the economy is depicted by a standard Leontief system consisting of n sectors, each of which produces a distinct single good under constant returns to scale by using material inputs and one common indispensable primary factor of production, labor.[2] Let a_{ij} and l_j be the constant inputs of the i-th goods and labor per unit output of the j-th good, where $a_{ij} \geqq 0$ and $l_j > 0$ $(i, j = 1, 2, \ldots, n)$. The square matrix of the n-th order $A = (a_{ij})$ is a nonnegative matrix, which is assumed to be indecomposable and productive enough to satisfy the Hawkins–Simon conditions,[3] i.e., $I - A$ has a nonnegative inverse, where I is the identity matrix.

Let further p_i $(i = 1, 2, \ldots, n)$ and w be the prices of the i-th goods and the rate of money wage. Then, for a given positive rate of money wage w there is a unique set of positive prices p_i $(i = 1, 2, \ldots, n)$ such that

$$p_j = (1 + r) \sum_{i=1}^{n} a_{ij} p_i + w l_j \quad j = 1, 2, \ldots, n \tag{1}$$

provided the rate of profit r is admissible in the sense that the matrix $I - (1 + r)A$ has a nonnegative inverse, or, what amounts to the same thing, $1/\lambda - 1 > r \geq 0$, where $\lambda = \lambda(A)$, the dominant Frobenius eigenvalue of A.

Sraffa's standard commodity is a basket of n goods $(c_1, \ldots, c_j, \ldots, c_n)$ whose composition gives rise to a positive column eigenvector of A associated with λ, unique up to multiplication by a scalar. Hence

$$\sum_{j=1}^{n} a_{ij} c_j = \lambda c_i \quad i = 1, 2, \ldots, n. \tag{2}$$

For convenience a unit of the standard commodity is chosen so as to fulfill

$$\sum_{j=1}^{n} c_j l_j = 1 - \lambda. \tag{3}$$

The rate of real wage ω is given in terms of the unit standard commodity by

$$\omega = \frac{w}{p}, \tag{4}$$

where the price level p is defined as

$$p = \sum_{j=1}^{n} c_j p_j. \tag{5}$$

Thus an admissible rate of profit r and the rate of real wage ω associated with it satisfy the linear equation

$$r/R + \omega = 1, \tag{6}$$

a representation of Sraffa's trade-off relation, where $R = 1/\lambda - 1$.

Suppose that more generally than in (1), at the current prices p_i $(i = 1, 2, \ldots, n)$ and the current rate of money wage w the rates of profit of sectors are r_j, so that

$$p_j = (1 + r_j) \sum_{i=1}^{n} a_{ij} p_i + w l_j \quad j = 1, 2, \ldots, n. \tag{7}$$

The rates of profits are not necessarily uniform among sectors in (7). Nevertheless, (7), when summed up with c_j as weight for the j-th equation and divided through by $(1 - \lambda)p$, is aggregated to

$$g/R + \omega = 1, \tag{8}$$

the trade-off relation between the rate of real wage (4) and the average rate of profit g, where

$$\frac{g}{R} = \frac{\sum_{j=1}^{n} r_j \sum_{i=1}^{n} a_{ij} p_i c_j}{(1 - \lambda)p}. \tag{9}$$

g/R represents the aggregate real profits per unit net output in terms of the standard commodity. Regardless of whether the rates of profit are uniform, the current income distribution is of such a nature that the shares of capital and labor in one unit of the standard commodity are g/R units and ω units of the commodity, respectively.

Needless to say, the composition of goods in the standard commodity need not coincide with that of the actual net outputs of goods. We can still conceive a virtual state of balanced growth in which goods are produced in the composition of the standard commodity. If $\gamma(t)c_i$ $(i = 1, 2, \ldots, n)$, where $\gamma(t)$ is the amount of employment at t, are the net outputs at a moment of time t, then, assuming instantaneous adjustment of supply to effective demand, we have

$$x_i = \sum_{j=1}^{n} a_{ij} x_j + \gamma(t)c_i \quad i = 1, 2, \ldots, n \tag{10}$$

with the corresponding gross outputs being

$$x_j = \frac{\gamma(t)c_j}{1 - \lambda} \quad j = 1, 2, \ldots, n \tag{11}$$

and the existing circulating capital stock of the i-th good being

$$\sum_{j=1}^{n} a_{ij} x_j = \frac{\gamma(t)\lambda c_i}{1 - \lambda} \quad i = 1, 2, \ldots, n. \tag{12}$$

Assume that capitalists save but do not consume while workers consume but do not save, as is often done. If the rate of real wage is ω at t, workers consume $\gamma(t)\omega$ units, and capitalists save and invest $\gamma(t)g/R$ units of the standard commodity. Thus the capital stock increases subject to

$$\frac{d}{dt}\frac{\gamma(t)\lambda c_i}{1-\lambda} = \frac{\gamma(t)gc_i}{R} \quad i = 1, 2, \ldots, n, \tag{13}$$

from which follows in the light of $R = 1/\lambda - 1$

$$\frac{1}{\gamma}\frac{d\gamma}{dt} = g. \tag{14}$$

Therefore g is the rate of balanced growth at t, and (8) is also the trade-off relation between the rate of real wage and the rate of growth.

3 The Wage-Price Spiral Process

With all the facts summarized above about the world of Sraffa in mind, let us consider the following dynamic process. Suppose that capitalists always stick to an admissible fixed rate of profit r, which will be referred to as a normal rate of profit, and that they mark up prices at this rate of profit. Hence the prices are adjusted subject to

$$\frac{dp_j}{dt} = (1+r)\sum_{i=1}^{n} a_{ij}p_i + wl_j - p_j \quad j = 1, 2, \ldots, n. \tag{15}$$

(15) represents a full cost pricing by capital as a whole, but not by individual capitalists, so that the coefficients of adjustment speed, which (15) has on the right-hand side, are uniform among sectors, and assumed to be unity without loss of generality. (15) is a counterpart in continuous time formulation of a markup process

$$p_j(t+1) = (1+r)\sum_{i=1}^{n} a_{ij}p_i(t) + w(t+1)l_j \quad j = 1, 2, \ldots, n.$$

We adopt the continuous time formulation for the sake of a simpler and more transparent mathematical analysis, which reveals better the essential dynamics of the process, though the analysis could be worked out in the discrete time formulation at the cost of more mathematical intricateness.

Here the formulation (15) of a process of price changes solely as markups underlies the presumption of so instantaneous adjustment of supply, under constant returns to scale, to effective demand in commodity markets that there is no inducement to price changes from discrepancies between demand and supply. This is a situation where quantities are faster adjusted than prices, whose changes are governed by factors other than competitive market mechanism.

On the other hand the rate of money wage is adjusted in such a way that its rate of change is proportional to that of the price level, with downward rigidity, that is,

$$\frac{1}{w}\frac{dw}{dt} = \max\left[\theta\frac{1}{p}\frac{dp}{dt}, 0\right] \tag{16}$$

where θ is a scalar index which reflects the bargaining powers of capital and labor, and varies from time to time, as will be explained.

Admittedly the formulation of wage rate adjustment in (16) concentrates on one of the most important factors governing wage rate adjustment and neglects the others, so that its formulation is somewhat ad hoc. Still θ can be thought of as an aggregative indicator of multiple factors influencing the labor market, among others, the bargaining powers of capital and labor in the wage determination.

The bargaining powers of both parties need not be exogenous but may be influenced by the other aspects of the system. As one of the most important aspects we pay exclusive attention to the relation between supply of labor and employment. We recall the virtual state of balanced growth at the current growth rate g determined by the current real wage rate ω, as discussed in the previous section. Since net output of one unit of the standard commodity is produced with one unit of labor input, employment grows at the rate g. Assume that labor force grows at an exogenous fixed rate η. Therefore it may be presumed that a rise of g influences the bargaining power of capital adversely and that of labor favorably and vice versa, and we assume

$$\theta = \alpha + \beta\frac{g}{\eta}. \tag{17}$$

α, β are parameters, which are nonnegative constants, positive in the most interesting case.[4]

This formulation does not exactly accommodate but parallels the findings of Phillips (1958) that the rate of change of money wage rate is a function of the rate of unemployment. In our formulation the rate of change of wage rate is related to the discrepancy between the growth rate of employment g and that of labor supply η, in other words, to the rate of change of the rate of unemployment or employment, rather than to the rate of unemployment or employment.

However, since we are mainly concerned with the long-run eventual state of the system and since the convergence of g to a constant level will make the discrepancy eventually persistent, we may construct our Phillips curve on this good simple proxy variable, a persistent magnitude of which leads to an eventual definite demand-supply situation of labor market.

Now g is determined by the current real wage rate ω in (8), so that θ is given by

$$\theta = \alpha + \beta \frac{R(1 - \omega)}{\eta}. \tag{18}$$

We have a complete system of differential equations (15), (16) with (4), (5), (18) in the variables w and p_i ($i = 1, 2, \ldots, n$), which depicts the wage-price spiral process in question.

The process, starting at an arbitrary initial position $p_j(0) \geqq 0$ ($j = 1, 2, \ldots, n$), $w(0) > 0$, continues without limit over time. In particular, $w(t)$ remains positive, so that $p_j(t)$ remains nonnegative because $dp_j/dt > 0$ whenever p_j approaches 0 in (15). It will be shown in the following parts that the eventual state of the process depends crucially on the magnitudes of the parameters α, β, r, η and their relationships.

A few additional remarks will be made about the formulation of the spiral process before we proceed to the analysis of its dynamic performance in the sequel.

The current prices and rate of money wage satisfy (7) with the corresponding rates of profit. Thus subtraction of (7) from (15) gives rise to

$$\frac{dp_j}{dt} = (r - r_j) \sum_{i=1}^{n} a_{ij} p_i \quad j = 1, 2, \ldots, n. \tag{19}$$

The substantial meaning of the full cost pricing in (15) is that prices are adjusted in the direction toward the discrepancies between the intended uniform rate of profit and the current rates of profit.

An actual deflator relevant to the tastes of workers may be based on a basket of goods whose composition may differ from that of the standard commodity. Nonetheless the movement of the rate of money wage generated subject to some laws based on the actual deflator reveals its essential nature when it is measured in terms of the very deflator based on the standard commodity. This nature is what most vitally governs the spiral. (16) directly formulates this fact. In interpretation (16) should be thought of as the essential movement of the rate of money wage, rather than its actual one in appearance.

4 The Underlying Macrodynamics of the Aggregative Variables

The wage-price spiral generates movements of the prices of goods and the rate of money wage over time, and we are concerned with the eventual state toward which the system tends. Specifically, our great concern is whether they converge to the equilibrium levels associated with the normal rate of profit r and whereto an undamped spiral will bring the system.

In the spiral process an increase in the rate of money wage directly gives rise to changes in prices. On the other hand there will be damping force powerful enough to let the spiral eventually die out if $\theta < 1$, that is, the money wage increase is behind the price increase, otherwise if $\theta > 1$. The dynamic destiny of the spiral ultimately hinges on the behavior of the rate of money wage. However, the dynamics of the spiral is of such a character that the behavior of the rate of money wage is determined exclusively by the dynamics among the relevant aggregative variables, including it, namely, the price level p, the rate of money wage w and the rate of real wage ω, independently of the behaviors of the individual prices of goods. Thus, to begin with, in this section we will deal with the dynamics of the aggregative variables.

To this end, first of all, let us examine the dynamics of the rate of real wage. In fact, multiplying the j-th equation in (15) by c_j and summing up over all $j = 1, 2, \ldots, n$, in view of (2), (3), (4), (5), we have

$$\frac{1}{p}\frac{dp}{dt} = (1 - \lambda)(r/R + \omega - 1). \tag{20}$$

On the other hand, from (4), (16) follows

$$\frac{1}{\omega}\frac{d\omega}{dt} = \frac{1}{w}\frac{dw}{dt} - \frac{1}{p}\frac{dp}{dt} = \max\left[(\theta - 1)\frac{1}{p}\frac{dp}{dt}, -\frac{1}{p}\frac{dp}{dt}\right]. \tag{21}$$

Hence (18), (20) and (21), combined together, give rise to

$$\frac{1}{\omega}\frac{d\omega}{dt} = (1 - \lambda)\max\left[\left(\alpha + \beta\frac{R(1 - \omega)}{\eta} - 1\right)\left(\frac{r}{R} + \omega - 1\right),\right.$$

$$\left. -\left(\frac{r}{R} + \omega - 1\right)\right], \tag{22}$$

the differential equation governing the change of ω.

We examine the dynamic behavior of ω and the corresponding ones of p and w on the assumption of the positivity of β, as the most relevant premise. We recall that r is fixed at an admissible level in the sense explained in Section 2, and is called a normal rate of profit. It is a target rate of profit intended by capital as a whole within the admissibility range. Let ω_N be the unique rate of real wage satisfying Eq. (6) and call it the normal rate of real wage. On the other hand, let ω_S be the unique rate of real wage satisfying the equation

$$\theta = 1, \tag{23}$$

that is,

$$\alpha + \beta\frac{R(1 - \omega)}{\eta} = 1. \tag{24}$$

Call ω_S the stagflation rate of real wage. The reason for this nomenclature will become self-explanatory in the sequel.

By admissibility ω_N fulfills

$$1 \geqq \omega_N > 0, \tag{25}$$

whereas ω_S can be any value, either positive, even greater than one, or nonpositive, depending on the parameters α, β, r, η.

The dynamics vitally hinges on the relation between ω_N and ω_S, and the resulting situations are classified to three cases.

Case 1

$$\omega_S > \omega_N, \tag{26}$$

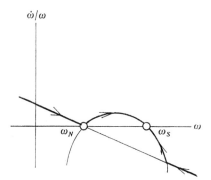

Figure 4.1

or the parameters satisfy

$$\alpha + \beta \frac{r}{\eta} > 1, \tag{27}$$

that is, the catch-up ratio θ is greater at the growth rate r than one. The continuous function of ω on the right-hand side of (22) has two vanishing values, ω_N and ω_S, and its graph is given, with arrows indicating the movement of the point $(\omega, \dot{\omega}/\omega)$ on it, in Fig. 4.1.

(22) has two stationary solutions $\omega = \omega_N$ and $\omega = \omega_S$. The former is stable so long as disturbances happen to lower ω below ω_N. However, ω approaches ω_S, a stable state, once ω ever reaches any value beyond ω_N. w remains constant and p decreases toward a positive level in the movement of ω toward ω_N from below. On the other hand $dp/p\,dt$ is positive and increasing when $\omega > \omega_N$. Moreover, since θ converges to unity, we eventually have

$$\frac{1}{w}\frac{dw}{dt} = \theta \frac{1}{p}\frac{dp}{dt} \tag{28}$$

$$\theta \geqq \text{positive constant less than one.} \tag{29}$$

Therefore both p and w increase to infinity.

The growth rate at ω_S is $g_S = R(1 - \omega_S)$, which is lower than the normal rate of profit $r = R(1 - \omega_N)$. Furthermore, if labor is aggressive enough to have $\alpha + \beta > 1$, the rate g_S is also lower than the growth rate of labor force η, because of $\alpha + \beta g_S/\eta = 1$. Hence in the vicinity of ω_S as well as at

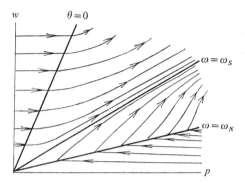

Figure 4.2

ω_S capital demands the rate of profit r and labor demands the rate of real wage proximate to ω_S, so that the price level and the rate of money wage increase without limit, while unemployment and growth at a lower rate than r eventually persist. This is a state of coexisting inflation and unemployment. Fig. 4.2 gives the trajectories of the point (p, w) with arrows indicating the directions of movement.

Case 2

$$\omega_N > \omega_S, \tag{30}$$

or, the parameters satisfy

$$\alpha + \beta \frac{r}{\eta} < 1, \tag{31}$$

that is, the catch up ratio θ is less at the growth rate r than one. This time the function on the right-hand side of (22) has just one vanishing value ω_N, and the corresponding stationary solution $\omega = \omega_N$ is globally stable, as is clear from the graph of the function given in Fig. 4.3.

w remains constant and p decreases to a positive level, when ω approaches ω_N from below. When ω approaches ω_N from above, w remains constant for very low levels of p, but we eventually have (28) and

$$\theta \leqq \sigma, \tag{32}$$

where σ is a positive constant less than one, because θ tends to its value at ω_N which is positive and less than one. Hence, by the positivity of $dp/p \, dt$,

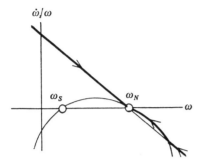

Figure 4.3

(28), (32) imply

$$\frac{1}{w}\frac{dw}{dt} \leqq \sigma \frac{1}{p}\frac{dp}{dt},$$

and, integrating we have

$$w \leqq Mp^{\sigma}, \quad M = \text{constant.} \tag{33}$$

If p tends to infinity, ω would tend to zero with the right-hand side of the rearranged form of (33)

$$\omega = \frac{w}{p} \leqq Mp^{\sigma-1},$$

a contradiction. Therefore the increasing p is bounded and convergent. Then, the increasing w is also bounded and convergent by (33). Thus all the aggregative variables converge. Fig. 4.4 gives the trajectories of the point (p, w) with arrows indicating the directions of movement. It will be shown in the next section that the individual prices of goods are also convergent, so that the spiral dies out to the equilibrium state.

Case 3

$$\omega_N = \omega_S \tag{34}$$

or, the parameters satisfy

$$\alpha + \beta\frac{r}{\eta} = 1, \tag{35}$$

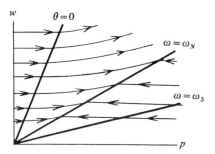

Figure 4.4

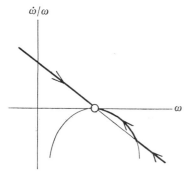

Figure 4.5

that is, the catch-up ratio θ is just one at the growth rate r. The corresponding illustrations are given in Figs. 4.5 and 4.6.

The unique stationary state $\omega = \omega_N = \omega_S$ is globally stable. Nonetheless, the behaviors of p and w are pathological while ω always approaches $\omega_N = \omega_S$. This is due to the dual characters of the level $\omega_N = \omega_S$ which originate with the coincidence of ω_N and ω_S.

Clearly, w remains constant and p decreases to a positive value when ω approaches $\omega_N = \omega_S$ from below. p and w are unchanged just at the stationary state $\omega = \omega_N = \omega_S$. However, peculiarity occurs and both p and w increase without limit to infinity, when ω approaches $\omega_N = \omega_S$ from above. To see this peculiarity we have to know the relation between ω and p more explicitly than in the two preceding cases.

In fact, when ω approaches $\omega_N = \omega_S$ from above, we eventually have[5]

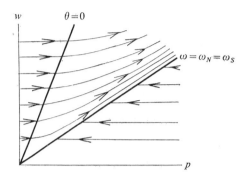

Figure 4.6

$$\frac{1}{\omega}\frac{d\omega}{dt} = \left(\alpha + \beta\frac{R(1-\omega)}{\eta} - 1\right)\frac{1}{p}\frac{dp}{dt}, \tag{36}$$

in (22), so that the differentials $d\omega$ and dp fulfill

$$\frac{d\omega}{\omega\left(\alpha + \beta\dfrac{R(1-\omega)}{\eta} - 1\right)} = \frac{dp}{p}. \tag{37}$$

Integrating (37) we have

$$\frac{\omega}{1 - \left(\alpha + \beta\dfrac{R(1-\omega)}{\eta}\right)} = \varepsilon p^{\alpha + \beta(R/\eta)-1}, \tag{38}$$

where ε is a constant of integration.

Assumption(35) and $R > r$ imply $\alpha + \beta(R/\eta) > 1$, so that the exponent of p is positive on the right-hand side of (38). The left-hand side tends to infinity, as the nominator and denominator tend to $\omega_N = \omega_S$ and zero, respectively. Therefore p tends to infinity. Convergence of p to infinity is monotone, because $dp/p\,dt$ is positive for $\omega > \omega_N = \omega_S$ in (20). When (36) holds, we simultaneously have (28), with θ approaching one. Hence w is increasing, and tends to infinity, as p and ω tend to infinity and $\omega_N = \omega_S > 0$, respectively, in the expression $w = \omega p$. Thus inflation persists in the region $\omega > \omega_N = \omega_S$. Fig. 4.6, which would result with the shrinkage of the fan-like region between the two rays $\omega = \omega_N$ and $\omega = \omega_S$ in Fig. 4.2 to the ray $\omega = \omega_N = \omega_S$, illustrates this situation.

On the alternative premise $\beta = 0$ three similar situations arise, which can be regarded as variants of the three cases above, respectively. This time (22) simplifies to

$$\frac{1}{\omega}\frac{d\omega}{dt} = (1 - \lambda)\max\left[(\alpha - 1)\left(\frac{r}{R} + \omega - 1\right), -\left(\frac{r}{R} + \omega - 1\right)\right], \qquad (39)$$

whose right-hand side is kinked just at ω_N but nowhere else. The three situations are case i: $\alpha > 1$, case ii: $\alpha < 1$ and case iii: $\alpha = 1$, which are (27), (31) and (35) for $\beta = 0$, respectively. However, there is no counterpart of ω_S in cases i and ii, whereas any value of ω can be regarded as an ω_S in case iii. Nonetheless, substantially cases i, ii and iii are variants of cases 1, 2 and 3, respectively. In all cases w remains constant and p decreases to a positive value, while ω approaches ω_N, starting at a level less than ω_N.

When ω starts at a level higher than ω_N, the results are as follows. In case i, ω, p, and w increase to infinity. In case ii, ω approaches ω_N, and p and w are convergent. In case iii, p and w increase to infinity, while keeping ω unchanged from an initial value other than ω_N. Derivation of these results is similar to, but easier than that under the premise $\beta > 0$, and is left to the reader.

5 Convergence of Individual Prices

So far only the convergence of p, w has been seen and it remains to prove that of the current prices to certain limits in case 2 and case ii. This result could be proved by relying on the standard representation of the solution of (15) in terms of the basic matrix solution of the associated system of linear homogeneous equations.[6] But alternatively we will prove it, along with the line in a method of proof due to Karlin (1959, Ch. 9, Theorem 9.5.1) by showing that the very presence of the standard commodity ensures a negative dominant diagonal for the system Jacobian matrix.

As has been shown, ω monotonically converges to ω_N, either increasingly from below or decreasingly from above. w remains unchanged and p decreases to a positive level in the state of the increasing ω. In this state w and p are related by a single-valued differentiable function

$$w = f(p), \tag{40}$$

whose derivative fulfills

$$f'(p) = 0. \tag{41}$$

On the other hand we eventually have (28) with the increasing p and w in the state of the decreasing ω. Hence w is a single-valued differentiable function (40) of p. This time the derivative of (40) fulfills

$$f'(p) = 0\frac{f(p)}{p} \tag{42}$$

on the trajectory.[7] For we have (40) and

$$\frac{dw}{dt} = f'(p)\frac{dp}{dt} > 0 \tag{43}$$

in (28). It is noted that the function (40) depends on, but is determined by the initial conditions.

In the light of the above remark the current prices can be regarded as a solution of

$$\frac{dp_j}{dt} = H_j(p_1, p_2, \ldots, p_n) \tag{44}$$

$$H_j(p_1, p_2, \ldots, p_n) = (1 + r)\sum_{i=1}^{n} a_{ij}p_i + f(p)l_j - p_j \quad j = 1, 2, \ldots, n, \tag{45}$$

where $f(p)$ is given by the initial conditions in (40).

Then, the elements of the Jacobian matrix J are evaluated as

$$\frac{\partial H_j}{\partial p_i} = (1 + r)a_{ij} + f'(p)c_i l_j - \delta_{ij} \quad i, j = 1, 2, \ldots, n$$

$$\geq 0 \quad (\text{if } i \neq j), \tag{46}$$

where δ_{ij} are Kronecker's deltas. By multiplying the j-th equation in (46) by c_j and summing up over all j for each i, we have, in view of the definition of the unit standard commodity (2), (3),

$$\sum_{j=1}^{n} c_j \frac{\partial H_j}{\partial p_i} = c_i(1 - \lambda)(r/R + f'(p) - 1) \quad i = 1, 2, \ldots, n. \tag{47}$$

Next define

$$\Phi(p_1, p_2, \ldots, p_n) = \sum_{j=1}^{n} c_j |H_j(p_1, p_2, \ldots, p_n)| \tag{48}$$

as a function of p_1, p_2, ..., p_n. This function, when evaluated on the trajectory, is not differentiable but still has a right-hand side derivative $d^+\Phi/dt$, which can be evaluated by performing ordinary differentiation for terms with nonvanishing H_j and right-hand side differentiation for terms with vanishing H_j in (48), and which therefore satisfies, in the light of (41), (42) and (47),

$$\frac{d^+\Phi}{dt} \leq \sum_{i=1}^{n} \left(\sum_{j=1}^{n} c_j \frac{\partial H_j}{\partial p_i} \right) |H_i|$$

$$= \begin{cases} (1 - \lambda)(r/R - 1)\Phi, & \text{if } \omega < \omega_N \tag{49} \\ (1 - \lambda)(r/R + \theta\omega - 1)\Phi, & \text{if } \omega > \omega_N. \tag{50} \end{cases}$$

$r/R - 1 < 0$ in (49). On the other hand ω converges to ω_N from above and θ converges to a positive value less than one in (50). Therefore there is such a positive ε that

$$(1 - \lambda)(r/R + \theta\omega - 1) \leq -\varepsilon$$

$$< (1 - \lambda)(r/R + \omega_N - 1)$$

$$= 0$$

eventually holds in (50).

Hence, in both (49) and (50),

$$\frac{d^+\Phi}{dt} \leq -\varepsilon\Phi \tag{51}$$

for a positive ε, respectively, and (51) implies

$$\lim_{t \to \infty} \Phi = 0.$$

Whence the left-hand side and w approach 0 and w^*, respectively, in (15) as t tends to infinity. Rearranging (15) by means of the nonnegative elements b_{ij} of the inverse of $I - (1 + r)A$, we have

$$p_j = \sum_{i=1}^{n} b_{ij}(wl_i - dp_i/dt) \quad j = 1, 2, \ldots, n \tag{52}$$

(52) converges to

$$p_j = \sum_{i=1}^{n} b_{ij} w^* l_i,$$

the unique solution of (1) for $w = w^*$, as $t \to +\infty$.

We have thereby shown that in case 2 and its variant case ii the spiral dies out to the state where the rate of profit and the rate of real wage are r and ω_N. We may also note that convergence of prices based on (49) applies to the phase of the spiral with the unchanging rate of money wage occurring in any of the cases in question.

6   Relative Prices in the Stagflation

It has been shown that p and w tend to infinity in case 1 while ω approaches ω_S in the region $\omega > \omega_N$. Therefore the individual prices also tend to infinity. Nonetheless it may be of some interest to see what the relative prices p_j/p $(j = 1, 2, \ldots, n)$ will be in the limit. They remain nonnegative likewise as p_j $(j = 1, 2, \ldots, n)$ and add up with weights c_j to unity

$$\sum_{j=1}^{n} c_j(p_j/p) = 1, \tag{53}$$

so that they are bounded. Moreover the relative prices $q_j = p_j/p$ $(j = 1, 2, \ldots, n)$ converge to certain limits, as will be seen by considering the system of differential equations that governs their behaviors.

In fact, upon differentiation we have

$$\frac{dq_j}{dt} = \frac{1}{p}\frac{dp_j}{dt} - \frac{q_j}{p}\frac{dp}{dt},$$

which, combined with (15), (20) leads to

$$\frac{dq_j}{dt} = (1 + r) \sum_{i=1}^{n} a_{ij} q_i + \omega l_j - \{\lambda + (1 - \lambda)(r/R + \omega)\} q_j \quad j = 1, 2, \ldots, n. \tag{54}$$

In the present case we have

$$\lim_{t \to \infty} \frac{d\omega}{dt} = 0 \tag{55}$$

in general, and especially

$$\frac{d\omega}{dt} = 0 \tag{56}$$

over time just at the state $\omega = \omega_s$.

Let the right-hand side of (54) be denoted by

$$G_j(q_1, q_2, \ldots, q_n, \omega) \quad j = 1, 2, \ldots, n. \tag{57}$$

Then, their partial derivatives are evaluated as

$$\frac{\partial G_j}{\partial q_i} = (1 + r)a_{ij} - \{\lambda + (1 - \lambda)(r/R + \omega)\}\delta_{ij}$$

$$\tag{58}$$

$$\frac{\partial G_j}{\partial \omega} = l_j - (1 - \lambda)q_j \quad i, j = 1, 2, \ldots, n,$$

where δ_{ij} are Kronecker's deltas. Similarly as in Section 5 we have

$$\sum_{j=1}^{n} c_j \frac{\partial G_j}{\partial q_i} = -(1 - \lambda)\omega c_i \quad i = 1, 2, \ldots, n, \tag{59}$$

$$\frac{\partial G_j}{\partial q_i} \geqq 0 \quad (\text{if } i \neq j), \tag{60}$$

$$\sum_{j=1}^{n} c_j \left| \frac{\partial G_j}{\partial \omega} \right| \text{ is bounded on the trajectory.} \tag{61}$$

Next define

$$\psi(q_1, q_2, \ldots, q_n, \omega) = \sum_{j=1}^{n} c_j |G_j(q_1, q_2, \ldots, q_n, \omega)| \tag{62}$$

as a function of $q_1, q_2, \ldots, q_n, \omega$. This function, when evaluated on the trajectory, is continuous with respect to t and has a right-hand side derivative $d^+\psi/dt$, which can be evaluated in the light of (59) and (60), similarly as in Section 5, obtaining

$$\frac{d^+\psi}{dt} \leqq \sum_{i=1}^{n} \left(\sum_{j=1}^{n} c_j \frac{\partial G_j}{\partial q_i} \right) |G_i| + \sum_{j=1}^{n} c_j \left| \frac{\partial G_j}{\partial \omega} \right| \left| \frac{d\omega}{dt} \right|$$

$$= -(1 - \lambda)\omega\psi + \sum_{j=1}^{n} c_j \left| \frac{\partial G_j}{\partial \omega} \right| \left| \frac{d\omega}{dt} \right| \tag{63}$$

There is a positive ε such that we eventually have

$$(1 - \lambda)\omega \geqq \varepsilon, \tag{64}$$

since $(1 - \lambda)\omega$ approaches $(1 - \lambda)\omega_S$, which is larger than $(1 - \lambda)\omega_N > 0$. Because of (55) and (61) the second summation term in (63) converges to zero. Hence for any positive δ there is a moment of time t_0 from which on we have

$$\sum_{j=1}^{n} c_j \left| \frac{\partial G_j}{\partial \omega} \right| \left| \frac{d\omega}{dt} \right| \leqq \varepsilon\delta \quad t \geqq t_0. \tag{65}$$

Thus, (63) implies

$$\frac{d^+ \psi}{dt} \leqq -\varepsilon\psi + \varepsilon\delta \quad t \geqq t_0. \tag{66}$$

We denote by $\psi(t)$ the value of ψ evaluated on the trajectory. Let τ be the least upper bound of ξ, not less than t_0, such that the inequality

$$\psi(t) \leqq m(t) \tag{67}$$

holds on the interval $[t_0, \xi]$, where

$$m(t) = (\psi(t_0) - 2\delta)e^{\varepsilon(t_0 - t)} + 2\delta.$$

The definition of τ makes sense because $\psi(t_0) = m(t_0)$. Suppose that τ is finite. Then

$$\psi(\tau) = m(\tau) \tag{68}$$

by continuity, and there is a decreasing sequence $\{t_v\}$ tending to τ from above such that

$$\psi(t_v) > m(t_v).$$

Hence

$$\frac{\psi(t_v) - \psi(\tau)}{t_v - \tau} > \frac{m(t_v) - m(\tau)}{t_v - \tau},$$

which becomes in the limit

$$\frac{d^+}{dt}\psi(\tau) \geqq \varepsilon\{2\delta - m(\tau)\}. \tag{69}$$

Now, (66) at $t = \tau$, (68) and (69) altogether lead to a contradiction $0 \geqq \varepsilon\delta$. Hence $\tau = +\infty$ and (67) holds for $t \geqq t_0$. The first term in the expression of $m(t)$ converges to zero, as t tends to infinity. Hence from a further larger value t_1 on we have $\psi(t) \leqq 3\delta$ $(t \geqq t_1)$. This implies

$$\lim_{t \to \infty} \psi(t) = 0. \tag{70}$$

Accordingly, the relative prices converge to those determined by the system of equations

$$\{\lambda + (1 - \lambda)(r/R + \omega_S)\}q_j = (1 + r) \sum_{i=1}^{n} a_{ij}q_i + \omega_S l_j \quad j = 1, 2, \ldots, n. \tag{71}$$

But they are not even the relative prices that ensure a uniform rate of profit among all the sectors for the rate of real wage ω_S. For suppose that a uniform rate of profit r_S prevails at them for ω_S. Then

$$q_j = (1 + r_S) \sum_{i=1}^{n} a_{ij}q_i + \omega_S l_j \quad j = 1, 2, \ldots, n. \tag{72}$$

Subtracting the j-th equation in (72) from that in (71), we obtain

$$\rho q_j = (r - r_S) \sum_{i=1}^{n} a_{ij}q_i \quad j = 1, 2, \ldots, n, \tag{73}$$

where

$$\rho = (1 - \lambda)(r/R + \omega_S - 1) > 0. \tag{74}$$

Summation of the equations in (73) with weights c_j gives

$$\rho = (r - r_S)\lambda$$

because of (53). Whence $\rho/(r - r_S) = \lambda$ and (73) imply that $(q_1, q_2, \ldots, q_n)$ is a row eigenvector of the input coefficients matrix associated with its dominant Frobenius eigenvalue λ. Then (71) immediately reduces to $q_j = l_j/(1 - \lambda)$, which is possible only in the special case of equal organic compositions[8] and very unlikely to occur in general. Thus, even if the nominal prices are marked up at the normal rate of profit in the spiral process, the system approaches a state where nonuniform rates of profit prevail.

7   Allegory of the Results

The present analysis does not intend to formulate a wage-price spiral on a microeconomic foundation. Its principal purpose is to elucidate the dynamics of wage-price spirals in special regard to their income distribution aspects, both as their driving force and as their resulting political economy implications, within the framework of Sraffa's theory on distribution of income to capital and labor. The spiral formulated here is not a direct depiction of what is proceeding in appearance, but the essence of its dynamics driven by the combined effects of bargaining powers of capital as a whole and labor as a whole.

Thus the analysis is focused exclusively on the aspects relevant to Sraffa's theory, but abstracts attention from other complex factors such as monetary ones. Moreover the formulation of the process involves various ad hoc features, among others, an ad hoc setup of wage rate adjustment (16). Nevertheless its results provide us with lessons of interest insofar as they elucidate the parts played by capital and labor in determining the state whereto the spiral will lead.

Generally, what most crucially governs the dynamic character of the spiral is the magnitude θ indicating how the rate of money wage follows up the change of price level. It reflects many factors influencing wage determination, among others, the bargaining powers of capital and labor, and depends on the parameters α, β, η and the endogenous variable g. α, β can be regarded as indicators of the bargaining power of labor. η is the growth rate of labor force. g is the current growth rate of output as well as the current average rate of profit.

The ultimate destiny of the spiral hinges on the relative magnitudes of the parameters α, β, η, and the intended rate of profit r, as was classified in (27), (31) and (35). $\alpha + \beta r/\eta$ is just the value of the catch-up ratio θ at the growth rate r, and its relation to unity dictates the destiny. Under the given η the larger α, β and r become, the more stagflation-oriented the system gets.

Suppose that $\alpha + \beta r/\eta > 1$ and stagflation is unavoidable. Still it might be damped, if either capital becomes modest enough to lower r or labor becomes modest enough to lower α, β or both, so as to lower $\alpha + \beta r/\eta$ below one.

Nonetheless even too modest capital can not lower $\alpha + \beta r/\eta$ below one, if labor is too aggressive to lower α, β. For even too modest capital is not expected to accept a negative rate of profit. Thus the situation of stag-flation, $\alpha + \beta r/\eta > 1$ seems to be typical of the present day advanced capitalist economies.

The case of a converging spiral is characterized by the condition $\alpha + \beta r/\eta < 1$, as was shown. This condition can hold for small α, β, even if $r > \eta$. But the growth rate of output, which eventually becomes r, can hardly be higher in persistent growth than the growth rate of labor force η. Thus r is tacitly presumed not to exceed η.

Finally, it is noted that the results presented above can readily be adapted to the wage-price spiral process under Harrod neutral technical change. In fact, with μ the rate of labor-augmenting technical change, the process is formulated by a modified form of (15), which is obtained from (15) by replacing l_j by $e^{-\mu t}l_j$, and an alternative equation governing the change of money wage rate

$$\frac{1}{w}\frac{dw}{dt} = \max\left[\theta\frac{1}{p}\frac{dp}{dt}, 0\right] + \mu. \tag{75}$$

where we redefine

$$\theta = \alpha + \beta\frac{g - \mu}{\eta} \tag{76}$$

instead of (17). Labor-augmenting technical change reduces the amount of labor input per unit output at the rate μ, so that employment grows at the rate $g - \mu$ while output grows at the rate g. This fact necessitates replace-ment of (17) by (76).

Now, if one performs the transformation $w_\mu = e^{-\mu t}w$, then $(p_1(t), p_2(t), \ldots, p_n(t), w_\mu(t))$ is nothing but a solution of (15), (16), with $\alpha - \beta\mu/\eta$ as a new value of α, so that all the results above can be carried over to the process under this type of technical change.

It is noted that at each moment of time the trade-off relation between the current growth rate g, the average rate of profit at the same time, and the rate of real wage ω is

$$g/R + \omega e^{-\mu t} = 1 \tag{77}$$

instead of (8). This is no wonder, because $e^{-\mu t}$ units of labor input is used to produce one unit of the standard commodity at t. Alternatively (77) can be put in the form

$$g/R + \omega_\mu = 1 \tag{78}$$

in terms of

$$\omega_\mu = \omega e^{-\mu t} = w/pe^{\mu t}. \tag{79}$$

ω_μ is labor's share in the distribution of one unit of the standard commodity, and can also be interpreted as the rate of real wage measured in terms of $e^{\mu t}$ units of the standard commodity producible at t with one unit of labor input.

What is remarkable is that technical change has an effect of lowering α to $\alpha - \beta\mu/\eta$ to make the system less stagflation-oriented. The system can possibly achieve growth at the rate r without inflation so long as $\alpha + \beta(r - \mu)/\eta < 1$, while stagflation would be unavoidable without technical change $\alpha + \beta r/\eta > 1$. Therefore technical change raises potential rate of growth without inflation. However, if such a high rate of profit is demanded that $\alpha + \beta(r - \mu)/\eta > 1$, stagflation will be unavoidable, in which the actual growth rate g is higher by μ than that without technical change, but the growth rate of employment $g - \mu$ is unchanged from $(1 - \alpha)\eta/\beta$, that without technical change.

Notes

1. The authors acknowledge with many thanks the valuable criticism received in many opportunities, especially the referee's, but, needless to say, assume responsibility for any remaining errors. The first author is supported by Japan Economic Research Foundation.

2. Throughout this paper formulations and their analysis will be made in the Leontief–Sraffa circulating capital model simply because of our strong emphasis on special regard to Sraffa's work in its original version. It should be noted, however, that all the results summarized in this section and obtained in the subsequent sections can readily be reformulated and adapted without essential modifications to the case with fixed capital. In fact this can be done by defining a unit standard commodity as a positive column eigenvector c associated to the dominant Frobenius eigenvalue of the matrix $B(I - A)^{-1}$ and normalized so as to have unit labor value, where B is a given fixed capital coefficients matrix. We acknowledge with many thanks the valuable suggestion of the referee in this regard.

3. In what follows certain by now familiar rudimentary results on nonnegative matrices, such as the Hawkins–Simon conditions and Frobenius theorem, will be used freely and without references to the source material. . Debreu and Herstein 1953 is a general reference to the results. Also Nikaido 1970 might be named as one of the materials that compile them in a book form.

4. θ can be a more general type of function of g and η without essential modification of the analysis such that $\partial\theta/\partial g > 0$, $\partial\theta/\partial\eta < 0$.

5. The differential equation (37) or its explicit integration (38) can be used in cases 1 and 2, although one could dispense with them there.

6. For example, see Ch. 1, Theorem 4, p. 14 in Bellman (1953).

7. We can obtain an explicit form of $f(p)$, but (42) suffices to prove the result.

8. See Ara 1975.

References

Ara, K. (1975): Parable and Realism in the Theory of Capital: A Generalization of Prof. Samuelson's Theory of Surrogate Production Function, in Japanese, *The Economic Studies Quarterly* XXVI.

Bellman, R. (1953): *Stability Theory of Differential Equations*, New York: McGraw-Hill.

Debreu, G. and I. N. Herstein (1953): Nonnegative Square Matrices, *Econometrica* XXI.

Karlin S. (1959): *Mathematical Methods and Theory in Games, Programming and Economics*, Vol. I, Reading: Addison-Wesley.

Nikaido, H. (1970): *Introduction to Sets and Mappings in Modern Economics*, Amsterdam: North-Holland.

Phillips, A. W. (1958): The Relation between Unemployment and the Rate of Change of Money Wage Rates in the United Kingdom, 1861–1957, *Economica* XXV.

Sraffa, P. (1960): *Production of Commodities by means of Commodities*, Cambridge: Cambridge University Press.

5 Wage-Price Spirals under Monopoly: "What Is an Objective Demand Function?" Set in Motion

1 What Will Happen in Disequilibrium?

The aggregate demand function derived within the traditional IS-LM framework is independent of the level of money wage rate. Thus a downward shift of the supply curve caused by a money wage cut would send its intersecting point with the demand curve rightward, thereby increasing the equilibrium level of output and hence employment except in an extremely Keynesian situation of liquidity trap or interest rate inelastic investment.

This is due to the ignorance of the class composition of the aggregate demand, especially, different propensities to save of wageearners and profit income earners. Kaldor's model of income distribution (1956) takes a good deal of advantage of the difference in thriftiness so as to elucidate income distribution in a full employment situation. But it tells nothing about underemployment situations just because of the ignorance of price variables, or the fix-price presumption.

In the standard IS-LM model the crucial dependence of aggregate demand on the price level originates in the money market except in a few exceptional variants, which let the IS curve, too, depend on the price level.

Nevertheless, even if monetary factors are set aside, an aggregative demand function relevant to income distribution is derivable by simply including the price level and the money wage rate in Kaldor's model. This was done, and the derived function was termed an *objective* demand function in distinction from a monopolist's *perceived* one and used to work out monopolistic and oligopolistic equilibria in a previous work (Nikaido 1974).

The function represents an aggregation of all price-taking household behaviors of employed workers and profit income earners under a given level of demand pertaining to investment.

A giant monopolist therefore can always sell all his supply of output, so long as he lies on this demand curve, and he can potentially regulate economy-wide income distribution by so doing. But this need not mean that he can *actually* do so. Imperfect information makes him more or less incapable of correctly perceiving the true shape of the demand curve.

From *Zeitschrift für Nationalökonomie* 39 (1979): 299–313. © 1979 Springer-Verlag. Reprinted by permission.

He may imagine a perceived demand curve, downward sloped with a finite elasticity, but more or less different from the true demand curve, and seek for a maximum profit on the former, rather than on the latter. Or, alternatively, he may price output just by simply marking up the cost at a desired rate.

Each of these two alternative typical modes of the monopolist's behavior, namely, profit maximization on a perceived demand curve, perceived profit maximization in short, and full cost pricing gives rise to a supply curve. The corresponding specific monopolistic equilibrium position is characterized as the intersection of the true demand curve with a supply curve of the monopolist under a given rate of money wage.

This view was expounded and worked out in the two illustrative situations, full cost pricing and perceived profit maximization in the work. But scope was so limited that only static equilibrium positions were considered without any attention paid to what would happen in disequilibrium. The purpose of this paper is to consider certain dynamic situations depicting wage-price spirals, which emerge when the work is set in motion.

In the dynamized situations considered here there are two main driving forces caused by disequilibria in certain parts of the economy.

Output is supplied by a monopolist, or all firms as a whole presumed to behave as a single monopolist, who always finds himself on his specific supply curve by *actually* employing a certain amount of labor to produce and supply the corresponding level of output at the price level determined by the supply function. Generally the aggregate demand does not equal the supply, so that there is disequilibrium. If there is excess demand, this is met by a decrease in inventory. On the other hand excess supply results in an unintended increase of inventory. Thus transactions are always actually made at his supply price, while disequilibrium is converted to unintended inventory investment. However disequilibrium makes the monopolist unhappy and lets him crawl on the supply curve, which is one of the driving forces.

At the same time disequilibrium in the labor market causes a change in money wage rate, somewhat accelerated by anticipated inflation, a Phillips curve phenomenon, and thereby shifts both the demand and supply curves, which is the other driving force.

These two driving forces set the economy in motion. After all, its dynamic destiny depends on the supply function. It will be examined in the two most typical cases, namely, full cost pricing and perceived profit maximization, as in Nikaido 1974.

2 The Dynamic Process

In the macromodel of a national economy considered here, exactly as in Nikaido (1974), one single homogeneous aggregative good is produced at a constant unit labor input l (and implicitly with capital), consumed and invested.

There are two income earning classes, *employed* workers and profit earners, whose propensities to save, assumed to be constant, are s_π, s_ω satisfying $s_\pi > s_\omega \geqq 0$, respectively. Given a level of investment d in real terms, also assumed to be constant, then the level of output y in real terms, the price level p and the money wage rate w satisfy in equilibrium

$$(1 - s_\omega)wly + (1 - s_\pi)(py - wly) + pd = py$$

by the principle of effective demand. From the equation above follows

$$p = \phi(y, w) = \frac{(1 - s_\omega/s_\pi)wly}{y - d/s_\pi} \tag{1}$$

a representation of the objective demand function, which embodies all possible market clearing situations resulting from price-taking behaviors of all agents save the *ex ante* behavior of a monopolist who monopolizes the production and supply of output. The incomes of profit earners originate in the monopoly profit.

The monopolist can *potentially* charge any price level beyond $(1 - s_\omega/s_\pi)$ wl through (1) while keeping market clearing. But this need not mean that he can *actually* do so. Because of imperfect information he can not necessarily be capable of correctly perceiving the true shape of the objective demand function. Here, the imperfection of his perception should not be considered implausible just on the ground that (1) is a hyperbola very simplistic in shape.

This imperfect information leads him to a *supply* function

$$p = \psi(y, w), \tag{2}$$

such that he charges the price (2) for the supply level of output y at a given money wage rate w in a specific way depending on the mode of his behavior as a monoplistic price-setter.

A monopolistic equilibrium is characterized and located on the objective demand curve (1) as the point at which the supply curve (2) crosses (1), as was formulated in Nikaido 1974.

Let us formulate what takes place when the economy is off the monopolistic equilibrium position. Generally there are disequilibria prevailing in both commodity and labor markets. The presumption relevant to the contemporary economy is that prices, namely p and w, are so inflexible at each moment of time that the disequilibria cannot be instantaneously resolved. Price inflexibility in the short-run may be accounted for on several grounds. Here it will be attributed to certain monopoly factors.

It is presumed that in the commodity market the monopolist always sticks to his supply price (2). He supplies y at the price (2), so that there is generally disequilibrium, which is resolved by an unintended accumulation or decumulation Δv of inventories. It is noted that he always actually employs ly units of labor, carries out production and supplies the level of output y at the price (2). There is just a unique level of the unintended level of inventory investment Δv such that the price level given by the objective demand function (1) is equated to the predetermined supply price (2) by replacing d by $d + \Delta v$. Specifically, Δv is determined by

$$\Delta v = s_\pi y - d - \frac{(s_\pi - s_\omega)wly}{\psi(y, w)} \tag{3}$$

Excess demand ($\Delta v < 0$) stimulates him to increase supply, and excess supply ($\Delta v > 0$) to decrease it. Thus, the level of output y is presumed to vary subject to

$$\frac{dy}{dt} = \alpha \left[d - s_\pi y + \frac{(s_\pi - s_\omega)wly}{\psi(y, w)} \right], \tag{4}$$

where α is a positive constant. For simplicity the inventory level v will not explicitly be taken into account.

On the other hand, in the labor market the rate of change of the money wage rate is in a trade-off relation to the rate of unemployment by a price expectations-adjusted Phillips curve. Explicitly

$$\frac{1}{w}\frac{dw}{dt} = Q(1 - ly/L) + \beta e, \tag{5}$$

where

$Q(u)$ = a strictly decreasing differentiable function of the rate of unemployment u, representing a Phillips curve,

L = a constant level of labor supply,

e = the expected rate of price change,

β = a positive constant.

The expected rate of price change e evolves conforming to adaptive expectation, so that

$$\frac{de}{dt} = \gamma\left(\frac{1}{p}\frac{dp}{dt} - e\right), \tag{6}$$

where γ = a positive constant,

$$\frac{1}{p}\frac{dp}{dt} = \frac{1}{\psi(y,w)}\left(\frac{\partial\psi}{\partial y}\frac{dy}{dt} + \frac{\partial\psi}{\partial w}\frac{dw}{dt}\right) \tag{7}$$

= the rate of change of the *actual* price level (2), which is a function of y, w, e by (4), (5).

Thus, (4), (5), (6) form a system of three differential equations in the three variables y, w, e, which, with appropriate mathematical backgrounds, formulates a wage-price spiral process.

The dynamic destiny of the process crucially hinges on the supply function and will be examined in the two typical specific cases, full cost pricing and perceived profit maximization, in the following sections.

In the two cases the supply functions are very simplistic functions of y, w, differentiable in both variables. Thus the right-hand sides of (4), (5), (6) are functions differentiable in y, w, e.

In addition to the aforementioned ones the Phillips curve is presumed to have the following properties: $Q(u)$ is defined between 0 and 1, and becomes negative in the neighborhood of 1 and tends to plus infinity as u approaches 0. Therefore there is a unique level u^* by continuity and strict monotonicity such that $Q(u^*) = 0$.

3 Full Cost Pricing

In full cost pricing the monopolist charges the price for the level of output y by marking up the current cost of production, either simply the labor cost or together with a fixed overhead cost at a desired rate. If production causes him to incur a fixed overhead cost a, an amount of output in real terms, and his mark-up rate is θ, the supply price level p is determined so as to satisfy

$$py = (1 + \theta)(pa + wly),$$

from which follows the corresponding supply function

$$p = \psi(y, w) = \frac{(1 + \theta)wly}{y - (1 + \theta)a}. \tag{8}$$

(8) reduces to the case of simple mark-up of the labor cost, when $a = 0$, e.g. fixed overhead cost is absent or ignored by him. When a is positive, (8) gives a positive supply price for the level of output $y > (1 + \theta)a$, and it decreases with the increase of level of supply due to decreasing cost.

Both objective demand curve (1) and supply curve (8) are hyperbolas and intersect just once to determine the corresponding monoplistic equilibrium position, provided

$$\frac{d}{s_\pi} > (1 + \theta)a. \tag{9}$$

The fixed overhead cost a is presumed to originate in the depreciation of capital (only implicitly taken into consideration). (9) is met, if θ is low in the plausible situation of nonnegative net investment $d \geqq a$.

Substituting (8) into (4), we have

$$\frac{dy}{dt} = \alpha \left[d - (s_\pi - s_\omega)a - \frac{(s_\omega + s_\pi\theta)y}{1 + \theta} \right] \tag{4.F}$$

and (4.F), (5), (6) formulate the wage-price spiral process under full cost pricing.

The dynamics of the process is very simple. The right-hand side of (4.F) is a downward sloping linear function of y and independent of the other variables w, e. Starting at an arbitrary level, y approaches the equilibrium level

$$y_F = \frac{(1 + \theta)[d - (s_\pi - s_\omega)a]}{s_\omega + s_\pi \theta} \tag{10}$$

which is positive by (9).

Now, from (8) follows

$$\frac{1}{p}\frac{dp}{dt} = \frac{1}{w}\frac{dw}{dt} + \frac{1}{y}\frac{dy}{dt} - \frac{1}{y - (1 + \theta)a}\frac{dy}{dt}. \tag{11}$$

Hence, in the light of (5), (11), we can put (6) in the form

$$\frac{de}{dt} = \gamma\left[Q(1 - ly/L) - \frac{(1 + \theta)a}{y(y - (1 + \theta)a)}\frac{dy}{dt} + (\beta - 1)e\right]. \tag{12}$$

(12) can be regarded as a linear differential equation in e with

$$\gamma\left[Q(1 - ly/L) - \frac{(1 + \theta)a}{y(y - (1 + \theta)a)}\frac{dy}{dt}\right] \tag{13}$$

regarded as a forcing term.

Let us now examine two possible cases I_F, II_F separately.

Case I_F

$L > ly_F$. Because of the convergence of y and dy/dt to y_F and 0, the forcing term converges to

$\gamma Q(u_F)$, $u_F = 1 - ly_F/L$

a finite number.

Then, in Solow's situation of money illusion, $1 > \beta$, (Solow 1969),

$$\lim_{t \to \infty} e = \frac{Q(u_F)}{1 - \beta} \tag{14}$$

and also, from (5), (11)

$$\lim_{t \to \infty}\frac{1}{w}\frac{dw}{dt} = \lim_{t \to \infty}\frac{1}{p}\frac{dp}{dt} = \frac{Q(u_F)}{1 - \beta} \tag{15}$$

Thus the economy approaches the state in which the level of output is y_F, and the money wage rate and the actual and expected price levels change at the constant rate $Q(u_F)/(1 - \beta)$.

In Friedman's situation of no money illusion, $\beta = 1$, (Friedman 1968), Eq. (12) is integrated to

$$e = e_0 + \int_0^t \gamma Q(1 - ly/L)\,dt + \gamma\left[\log\frac{y}{y - (1 + \theta)a}\right]_0^t \tag{16}$$

where e_0 is the initial value of e.

Therefore, the eventual behaviors of e and the rates of change of the money wage rate and price level are affected by the initial values of the variables y, w, e, rather than merely by the point of a long-run Phillips curve corresponding to the level of output y_F.

Case II_F

$L \leqq ly_F$. If $L = ly_F$, then

$$\lim_{t \to \infty} Q(1 - ly/L) = +\infty$$

while y tending to y_F. If $L < ly_F$ the monotonically changing rate of unemployment reaches zero at a finite moment of time t_1, so that

$$\lim_{t \to t_1} Q(1 - ly/L) = +\infty.$$

Thus, regardless of money illusion, the rates of change of all the price variables tend to infinity as t tends to infinity or t_1.

Under full cost pricing the dynamic destiny and associated income distribution between both workers and profit earners are crucially affected by the mark-up rate θ. The monopolistic equilibrium level of output (10) is strictly decreasing from

$$y_M = \frac{d - (s_\pi - s_\omega)a}{s_\omega}$$

to

$$y_m = \frac{d}{s_\pi}$$

as θ ranges from 0 to $d/(s_\pi a) - 1$. The corresponding rate of unemployment u_F is strictly increasing from

$$u_M = 1 - \frac{l[d - (s_\pi - s_\omega)a]}{s_\omega L}$$

to

$$u_m = 1 - \frac{ld}{Ls_\pi}.$$

The intervals (y_m, y_M), (u_M, u_m) depend on the technology l, a, the thriftiness s_π, s_ω, the supply of labor L and the level of gross investment d, and shift with them. Nonetheless the mark-up rate θ uniquely determines the equilibrium level of output y_F and the corresponding rate of unemployment u_F in these intervals. Thus under the same parametrical conditions the lower the mark-up rate, the more inflationary the economy becomes within the intervals.

Suppose now that the parametrical conditions give rise to a situation $u_M < u^* < u_m$. Then, there is a uniquely determinate mark-up rate θ^* at which $u_F = u^*$. In the presence of money illusion the economy approaches the state in which the level of output is y_F, and the rate of money wage and price level remain to be unchanged, while the expected rate of price change is zero. In the absence of money illusion, however, (5), (11), (16) imply the rates of change of the price level and money wage rate and the expected rate of price change are equal to e_0, an arbitrary initial value. Therefore any rate of inflation can be compatible with the rate of unemployment, so that only a vertical Phillips curve persists.

4 Perceived Profit Maximization

The monopolist is now presumed to imagine a downward sloping perceived demand curve

$$p = p_0 - \eta(y - y_0) \tag{17}$$

passing through the observed point (y_0, p_0), where η is a positive constant.

(17) gives rise to a family of perceived demand curves

$$p = \varepsilon - \eta y \tag{18}$$

indexed by $\varepsilon = p_0 + \eta y_0$.

On each of curves (18) corresponding to a value of the parameter ε, the monopolist chooses a unique level of output to maximize the expected profit

$$(p - wl)y = (\varepsilon - \eta y - wl)y. \tag{19}$$

Then the pair of the profit maximizing level of y and the corresponding price level p generates a locus, his supply curve, as ε ranges over all nonnegative values.

For $\varepsilon \geq wl$ the pair consists of

$$y = \frac{\varepsilon - wl}{2\eta}, p = \frac{\varepsilon + wl}{2}, \tag{20}$$

and generates a supply curve

$$p = \psi(y, w) = \eta y + wl, \tag{21}$$

which is obtained by eliminating ε from (20).

For $\varepsilon < wl$, the pair would be $(0, \varepsilon)$, which can be replaced by $(0, wl)$, the pair given by (21) for $y = 0$ and securing the same level of profit.

Thus, substituting (21) into (4), we have

$$\frac{dy}{dt} = \alpha \left[d - s_\pi y + \frac{(s_\pi - s_\omega)wly}{\eta y + wl} \right], \tag{4.P}$$

and (4.P), (5), (6), together with (7) for (21), formulate the wage-price spiral process under perceived profit maximization.

For a given level of money wage rate the supply curve (21) intersects the objective demand curve (1) just once to determine a monopolist equilibrium position under perceived profit maximization. The equilibrium position depends on and varies with the rate of money wage rate. It ranges from d/s_π to d/s_ω as the rate of money wage rate varies from zero to infinity.

Although manifold possibilities are conceivable as to the position of the range of the equilibrium level of output relative to the domain of the Phillips curve, we will consider the most important situation in which

$$\frac{d}{s_\pi} < \frac{(1 - u^*)L}{l} < \frac{d}{s_\omega} \tag{22}$$

or

$$1 - \frac{ld}{Ls_\omega} < u^* < 1 - \frac{ld}{Ls_\pi}. \tag{23}$$

where u^* is the rate of unemployment to ensure no change in the rate of money wage, $Q(u^*) = 0$.

Let

$$y_P = \frac{(1 - u^*)L}{l} \tag{24}$$

and let w_P be the unique level of money wage rate at which y_P is the monopolistic equilibrium level of output. Also let $e_P = 0$. Then the point (y_P, w_P, e_P) is a critical point of the system (4.P), (5), (6).

Let $f(y, w, e)$, $h(y, w, e)$ be the functions on the right-hand side of (4.P), (6), respectively and $g(y, w, e)$ the function multiplied by w on the right-hand side of (5). Then

$$f(y, w, e) = \alpha\left[d - s_\pi y + \frac{(s_\pi - s_\omega)wly}{\eta y + wl}\right]$$

$$g(y, w, e) = w[Q(1 - ly/L) + \beta e] \tag{25}$$

$$h(y, w, e) = \gamma\left[\frac{\eta f(y, w, e) + lg(y, w, e)}{\eta y + wl} - e\right].$$

Denoting the partial derivatives of f, g, h by appropriate subscripts, we can evaluate

$$f_w(y, w, e) > 0 > f_y(y, w, e) \quad (y, w > 0) \tag{26}$$

$$g_y(y, w, e) > 0 \quad (L/l > y \geq 0, w > 0) \tag{27}$$

$$g_w(y_P, w_P, e_P) = 0. \tag{28}$$

Then at the critical point the Jacobian matrix J of the system has

$$\text{trace of } J = f_y(y_P, w_P, e_P) + \gamma\left(\frac{\beta w_P l}{\eta y_P + w_P l} - 1\right) < 0 \quad (1 \geq \beta \geq 0) \tag{29}$$

$$\text{norm of } J = \gamma f_w(y_P, w_P, e_P)g_y(y_P, w_P, e_P) > 0 \quad \text{(independent of } \beta\text{).} \tag{30}$$

In a three-variable system, (29), (30) imply that one eigenvalue is real positive and the other two (possibly, one of double multiplicity) are either real negative or conjugate complex with negative real parts. Therefore in both situations with $(1 > \beta \geq 0)$ and without $(\beta = 1)$ money illusion the critical point is locally a saddle point. It is either a stable node or vortex within the surface generated by all trajectories converging to it, while trajectories off the surface diverge towards the direction of the eigenvector associated with the positive eigenvalue.

The direction of the eigenvector is also readily tractable to detect. To this end we note that the characteristic polynomial can be put in the form

$$\left[\lambda + \gamma\left(1 - \frac{\beta w_P l}{\eta y_P + w_P l}\right)\right] \left|\begin{array}{cc} \lambda - f_y - f_w & -g_y \\ -g_y & \lambda \end{array}\right| - \frac{\beta \gamma w_P f_w(\eta \lambda + l g_y)}{\eta y_P + w_P l} \tag{31}$$

and that the determinant in (31) must be positive when (31) equals zero at the positive eigenvalue λ for β such as $1 \geqq \beta > 0$. Therefore, all the principal minors of the determinant, whose off-diagonal elements are negative, are positive, so that the Hawkins–Simon conditions hold. The components σ, τ, v of an eigenvector associated with the positive eigenvalue λ satisfy

$$(\lambda - f_y)\sigma - f_w\tau = 0$$
$$-g_y\sigma + \lambda\tau = \beta w_P v. \tag{32}$$

Thus, if we take a positive v, then the other σ, τ determined by (32) must also be positive because of the Hawkins–Simon conditions.

When $\beta = 0$, the determinant vanishes at the positive eigenvector, and σ, τ are determined as positive number uniquely up to scalar multiplication. The third component v determined by the third equation in

$$(\lambda I - J)\begin{pmatrix} \sigma \\ \tau \\ v \end{pmatrix} = 0$$

must be nonnegative because of the continuous dependence of the positive eigenvalue λ and proportions of the associated eigenvector on β.

Thus, in the neighborhood of the critical point the level of output y, the rate of money wage w and the expected rate of price change e have tendency either to rise together (inflationary) or to fall together (deflationary) except on the bordering surface where they are converging towards y_P, w_P, e_P respectively.

Their global behaviors are, however, less tractable. Nevertheless there is a certain region in the (y, w, e) space where inflationary processes persist and their eventual destinies are tractable, as will be shown.

Let us consider the region Δ formed by all such points in the positive orthant of the (y, w, e)-space as satisfy the inequalities

$$f(y, w, e) > 0 \tag{33}$$

$$Q(1 - ly/L) > 0. \tag{34}$$

As is readily verified, under (26), (27) the vector (f, g, h) points inward on the boundary of Δ except at the critical point (y_P, w_P, e_P) at which the eigenvector (σ, τ, v) points inward. Hence no trajectory leaves Δ, so that a trajectory passing through a point in Δ remains to stay forever in Δ.

Clearly we have

$$f(y, w, e) < \alpha(d - s_\omega y) \leq 0 \quad (y \geq d/s_\omega, w > 0). \tag{35}$$

It is also easy to see, in view of (26), (27), that any point (y, w, e) in Δ satisfies

$$y > y_P, \ w > w_P. \tag{36}$$

Let us now examine two possible cases I_P, II_P separately.

Case I_P

$d/s_\omega < L/l$. In the light of (34), (35), y is bounded in Δ. A trajectory passing through a point in Δ continues to stay forever in Δ, as was shown. Along it therefore y is increasing and bounded, so that y must converge to a finite limit y_∞. On the other hand w increases to infinity in Δ by (5) in which $e > 0$, and $Q(1 - ly/L)$ is increasing with y. Then $f(y, w, e)$, while remaining positive, converges to

$$\alpha(d - s_\omega y_\infty),$$

which must be zero. Hence $y_\infty = d/s_\omega$.

With these results in mind, first let us see what will happen under money illusion $1 > \beta \geq 0$. $h(y, w, e)$ can be majorized from above by

$$\gamma[\eta f(y, w, e)/wl + Q(1 - ly/L)] + \gamma(\beta - 1)e,$$

in which the expression in the brackets is bounded along the trajectory. Thus e would be sent back whenever it is ready to become too large. Hence e is bounded along the trajectory.

Then, rearranging terms, we can put (6) with (7) for (21) in the form

$$\frac{de}{dt} = \gamma \frac{\eta[f(y, w, e) - \beta ye]/wl + Q(1 - ly/L)}{\eta y/wl + 1} + \gamma(\beta - 1)e. \tag{37}$$

(37) can be thought of as a linear differential equation in e with the first term regarded as a forcing term, which is known to converge to $\gamma Q(1 - ld/Ls_\omega)$ along the trajectory. Hence

$$\lim_{t \to \infty} e = \frac{Q(1 - ld/Ls_\omega)}{1 - \beta}. \tag{38}$$

Thus (5) becomes in the limit

$$\lim_{t \to \infty} \frac{1}{w} \frac{dw}{dt} = \frac{Q(1 - ld/Ls_\omega)}{1 - \beta}, \tag{39}$$

and also

$$\lim_{t \to \infty} \frac{1}{p} \frac{dp}{dt} = \frac{Q(1 - ld/Ls_\omega)}{1 - \beta}. \tag{40}$$

As a static equilibrium situation the level of output $y = d/s_\omega$ is realizable only in the case where the objective demand curve (1) intersects a special *competitive* supply curve (21) with $\eta = 0$, at the market clearing price p equal to the unit wage cost wl, and hence there is no profit. Under a monopolist maximizing the profit along a linear perceived demand curve the wage-price spiral eliminates the profit more and more to bring the economy toward this situation. The rate of inflation is given by the long-run Phillips curve in (38)–(40).

Let us examine the case of no money illusion $\beta = 1$, w tends to infinity, as was already noted. Hence, given an arbitrary large positive number M, we have

$$\frac{\eta f(y, w, e)/wl + Q(1 - ly/L)}{\eta y/wl + 1} > Q(1 - ld/Ls_\omega)/2$$

$$\frac{\eta y/wl}{\eta y/wl + 1} < \frac{Q(1 - ld/Ls_\omega)}{4M}$$

from a moment of time t_0 on in (37) for $\beta = 1$. Thus (37) for $\beta = 1$ gives rise to

$$\frac{de}{dt} > (\gamma/2)Q(1 - ld/Ls_\omega)\left(1 - \frac{e}{2M}\right) \tag{41}$$

for $t \geqq t_0$. (41) implies that e must eventually saitsfy $e > M$. Therefore

$$\lim_{t \to \infty} e = +\infty. \tag{42}$$

Hence (5) for $\beta = 1$ becomes in the limit

$$\lim_{t \to \infty} \frac{1}{w} \frac{dw}{dt} = +\infty \tag{43}$$

and also

$$\lim_{t \to \infty} \frac{1}{P} \frac{dp}{dt} = +\infty.$$

Case II_P

$d/s_\omega \geqq L/l$. If $d/s_\omega = L/l$, we have

$$\lim_{t \to \infty} Q(1 - ly/L) = +\infty,$$

and it can readily be seen, as in the situation $\beta = 1$ of Case I_P, that regardless of money illusion $dw/w\,dt$, $dp/p\,dt$, e tend to infinity.

If $d/s_\omega > L/l$, the rising output level y approaches L/l, and $Q(1 - ly/L)$ tends to infinity as t tends to a moment of time, from which on the system is unworkable.

5 Summary and Concluding Remarks

In both inflationary wage-price spiral processes the wage increase, which is caused by the current state of the economy in real terms, i.e., the level of output y, through a Phillips curve, and the prevailing expectation for the rate of price change, gives rise to a feed-back effect on the commodity market to induce a change in the level of output and thereby a change in the actual price level. At the same time the expected rate of price change evolves by chasing its actual rate so as to entail a feed-back effect on the labor market.

On the price-variable side of the processes, the less money illusion, the more accelerated will be inflation. Nonetheless the degree of money illusion does not dictate the ultimate state in real terms toward which the economy tends. On the real-variable side the economy approaches a specific state in real terms in each of both processes, whether money illusion is present or absent. Indeed, the ultimate rate of inflation is given by a non-vertical long-run Phillips curve at the point corresponding to the state under money illusion, while it is a point on a vertical long-run Phillips curve corresponding to the state in the absence of the illusion. But the illusion only decelerates the processes and does not dictate the ultimate destiny of the economy in real terms, which is determined by the pattern of monopolistic price making, that is, the shape of the corresponding supply function.

The dynamic modelling here is built on the direct footing of the previous paper (Nikaido 1974), whose purpose was to illustrate monopolistic equilibria in as the simplest setting as possible. It sets aside all other factors such as monetary factors, capital accumulation, productivity increase and so forth. It concentrates on the examination of what happens in situations where both demand and supply curves simultaneously shift with the changing money wage rate, so that a complex of demand-pull and cost-push is operative. This is an important aspect of inflation, which is vital even to more general situations.

Note

This research was carried out during my visit at the Department of Economics, University of Southern California, to which many thanks are due for its support of my visit.

References

Friedman, M. (1968): The Role of Monetary Policy, *American Economic Review* 58.

Kaldor, N. (1956): Alternative Theories of Distribution, *Review of Economic Studies* 23.

Nikaido, H. (1974): What is an Objective Demand Function?, *Zeitschrift für Nationalökonomie* 34.

Solow, R. M. (1969): *Price Expectations and the Behaviour of the Price Level*, Manchester: Manchester University Press.

6 Prices and Income Distribution in a Leontief Economy

1 Introduction

The neoclassical line of thought presumes the parametric function of prices
to regulate the amounts of goods demanded and supplied and thereby to
bring markets into equilibrium. Contrastingly, in the Keynesian tradition,
commodity markets, though not necessarily the labor market, are cleared
by virtue of the adjustment of output levels rather than prices, which are
assumed to be rigid. Within this framework the state of the economy,
including income levels, output, and employment, can be determined by
virtue of the principle of effective demand. Does this mean that prices do
not matter? On the contrary they do. Nonetheless various questions about
the role of prices in an output-adjusting economy have received little
attention in the traditional economic literature.

One question that has been discussed is how to account for price rigidity as such, or, in other words, how to establish microeconomic foundations for macro theory. One view attributes the rigidity to monopolistic
behavior. A second view explains the phenomenon as a behavioral adjustment arising from transactions that must take place according to quantity
constraints ensuing from a notional disequilibrium situation. This second
view, a currently fashionable one, is associated with the works of Barro
and Grossman (1971, 1976), Leijonhufvud (1968), Negishi (1974), and was
originally advocated by Clower (1965) and Patinkin (1965). Close inspection, however, reveals that this latter approach is equivalent to the former.
This is because the quantity conscious behavior depicted in the effective
demand approach is essentially that of a monopolist facing an imperfectly
elastic demand schedule. Consequently, kinky demand functions arise in
a manner essentially equivalent to the Sweezy theory of price rigidities
(1939).

The further question, as to how the state of the economy is determined,
given the price rigidities, wherever they originate, is yet to receive ade-
quate theoretical treatment. Such states cannot be independent of, but
must be affected by, the very levels at which prices are fixed. Therefore the
state of the economy must in substance, if not in appearance, be regulated

From *Journal of Economic Behavior and Organization* 1 (1980): 61–79. © North-Holland 1980. Reprinted with kind permission from Elsavier Science B. V., Amsterdam, The
Netherlands.

by pricing. This provides the market price mechanism with a latent socio-economic function.

Certain aspects of this socioeconomic function were considered in the simple framework of the Leontief system in a previous work by the author (1975) on the basis of the concept of objective demand functions. Although that work assumed full employment mainly for the purpose of having an economy-wide picture of monopolistic competition, the analysis can readily be adapted to a Keynesian situation in which insufficient effective demand may give rise to unemployment. In a related work (Nikaido 1974) the potential controllability of the economy by pricing was elucidated. These, however, precluded specific results about the extent to which pricing can regulate the state of the economy, one of whose most important features is income distribution.

The purpose of this paper is to analyze the link between prices and income distribution given a specific form of the propensities to consume. Specifically a one-to-one link is shown to exist between all possible unit profits (hence, price systems) and all possible states of income distributions. Comparative static results are then attained which show how a change in a given sector's unit profit affects the income level in that sector more than in any other, and conversely, i.e., a change in a given sector's income level affects the unit profit in that sector more than any other.

Finally, dynamic adjustments based on excess intersectoral demand are considered in which some sectoral unit profits and some sectoral income levels are adjustable, while the complementary parameters are fixed. These adjustments are shown to converge to a unique Keynesian equilibrium. Of special interest to readers of this chapter is the case in which all adjustments occur through unit profits with income levels fixed. Such a system is the analog of a cost mark-up process, and suggests an interesting possible relationship in an imperfectly competitive economy between a common pricing rule of thumb and the ability of particular managerial groups to maintain income levels.

Of course it must be remembered that the results of this paper are limited for the very special Leontief technology and need not be expected to hold generally. Nonetheless, our results indicate the possibility of obtaining rigorous relationships between economic states and the underlying parameters of technology and behavior when price rigidities and other non-neoclassical behavioral irregularities prevail.

2   Background Preliminaries

2.1   The Basic Leontief System

The basic framework of the economy's production is the standard Leontief system consisting of n sectors $j = 1, 2, .., n$ with material inputs coefficients $a_{ij} \geq 0$ $(i, j = 1, 2, \ldots, n)$ and labor input coefficients $l_j > 0$ $(j = 1, 2, \ldots, n)$.

The system is assumed to be productive enough to satisfy Hawkins–Simon's conditions, so that both the output determining equation

$$x_i = \sum_{j=1}^{n} a_{ij} x_j + c_i, \quad i = 1, 2, \ldots, n, \tag{1}$$

and the price determining equation

$$p_j = \sum_{i=1}^{n} a_{ij} p_i + w l_j + \pi_j, \quad j = 1, 2, \ldots, n, \tag{2}$$

are solvable in the non-negative unknowns of output levels x_j $(j = 1, 2, \ldots, n)$ and prices p_i $(i = 1, 2, \ldots, n)$, respectively, for arbitrarily given non-negative amounts of final demand c_i $(i = 1, 2, \ldots, n)$ and non-negative levels of wage rate w and sectoral profits per unit output π_j $(j = 1, 2, \ldots, n)$.

If b_{ij} $(i, j = 1, 2, \ldots, n)$ are elements of the non-negative inverse $(I - A)^{-1}$ of $I - A$, where I is the identity matrix and $A = (a_{ij})$ is the material input coefficients matrix, both solutions of (1) and (2) are given as

$$x_i = \sum_{j=1}^{n} b_{ij} c_j, \quad i = 1, 2, \ldots, n, \tag{3}$$

$$p_j = w\sigma_j + \sum_{i=1}^{n} b_{ij} \pi_i, \quad j = 1, 2, \ldots, n, \tag{4}$$

where

$$\sigma_j = \sum_{i=1}^{n} b_{ij} l_i, \quad j = 1, 2, \ldots, n,$$

is the labor value of the jth good. The labor values of goods are positive. Moreover A is assumed to be indecomposable, so that b_{ij} are all positive.

2.2   Determination of Incomes

Let y_j $(j = 0, 1, \ldots, n)$ represent the levels of the wage bill and sectoral profit incomes, which will henceforth be referred to simply as sectoral incomes, with the households of employed workers as the zeroth sector. Then

$$y_0 = w \sum_{j=1}^{n} l_j x_j,$$

$$y_j = \pi_j x_j, \quad j = 1, 2, \ldots, n.$$

(5)

Let further the jth sector's average propensities to spend on the ith good be denoted by γ_{ij} $(i = 1, 2, \ldots, n; j = 0, 1, \ldots, n)$. They are non-negative constants and satisfy

$$\gamma_j = \sum_{i=1}^{n} \gamma_{ij} < 1, \quad j = 0, 1, \ldots, n.$$

(6)

Now suppose that d_i $(i = 1, 2, \ldots, n)$ non-negative amounts of all items of final demand, other than households' consumption, taken together and simply called investment, are exogenously given. Then, as is well-known, sectoral income levels y_j $(j = 1, 2, \ldots, n)$ can be uniquely determined as solutions of the system of linear equations

$$y_0 = w \sum_{j=1}^{n} \sigma_j \left(\frac{1}{p_j} \sum_{k=0}^{n} \gamma_{jk} y_k + d_j \right),$$

$$y_i = \pi_i \sum_{j=1}^{n} b_{ij} \left(\frac{1}{p_j} \sum_{k=0}^{n} \gamma_{jk} y_k + d_j \right), \quad i = 1, 2, \ldots, n,$$

(7)

provided w, π_i $(i = 1, 2, \ldots, n)$ are arbitrarily fixed without being zero simultaneously. The determinacy comes from the fact that the kth column sum of non-negative coefficients on the right-hand side in (7) is less than one by (4) and (6), and hence the coefficients matrix of (7) satisfies Hawkins–Simon's conditions.

The above facts are the very well-known side of the coin. They are summarized here briefly just to prepare for the exploration of its other hidden side, which is our main objective in this paper.

3   Summary of the Results

Sectoral income levels y_j $(j = 0, 1, \ldots, n)$ determinate in the system of linear equations (7) are given by multiplying a given investment scheme vector (d_i) by the corresponding matrix multiplier. If the input coefficients

a_{ij} and propensities to spend γ_{ij} are stable, the multiplier depends solely on the wage rate w and profits per unit output π_i $(i = 1, 2, \ldots, n)$. Thus, the multiplier and hence sectoral income levels are subjected to and regulated by sectoral profits per unit output as parameters. How and to what extent the former can potentially be regulated by the latter? Our purpose here is to unveil the way the latter regulate the former behind the very well-known side of the coin, income determination by multipliers.

First, our examination reveals the extent to which the regulation can achieve income distribution. Our finding is that any income distribution can be achieved by this parametric regulation. That is, an arbitrarily given set of sectoral income levels y_j $(j = 0, 1, \ldots, n)$ is achievable in the income determination process (7) under a suitable set of the wage rate w and sectoral profits per unit output π_i $(i = 1, 2, \ldots, n)$. This fact will be elucidated in Theorem 1, section 4.1, which gives a more general finding that if either an income level y_i or a profit level per unit output π_i is arbitrarily claimed in each of $n + 1$ sectors, including the workers' households as a sector, the level of the remaining variable, either the profit per unit output or income, exists in each of $n + 1$ sectors so as to satisfy eq. (7).

Second, as to the number of ways in which the parametric regulation achieves the aim, our finding is the unique determination of levels of the relevant parameters. Theorem 2, section 4.2, asserts that the determination of levels of the remaining variables is unique for claimed variable levels in Theorem 1, section 4.1. This result tells in a special case that the levels of wage rate and sectoral profits per unit output which bring about a claimed income distribution are unique.

These two findings reveal the basic relationship, latent in the well-known income determination by multipliers in (7), the global one-to-one correspondence between all possible schemes of income distribution (relative shares and absolute levels of sectoral incomes) and all possible price situations [levels of wage rate and sectoral profits per unit output underlying prices w, p_i $(i = 1, 2, \ldots, n)$ via eq. (2)]. The relationship, termed the relevant link, is capable of functioning as a socioeconomic framework in which claims to a specific scheme.of income distribution are materialized in the appearance of market clearing by equality of demand and supply at the corresponding specific prices.

Our further examination brings to light certain comparative statics and dynamic properties with which the relevant link is provided. Through the relevant link a change in the profit per unit output in a sector affects income levels in all sectors, but more in this sector than in any others. Likewise, a change in the income level in a sector affects profits per unit output in all sectors, but more in this sector than in any others. These comparative statics results are elucidated in Theorems 3 and 4, section 5.2.

The levels of incomes and profits per unit output corresponding in the relevant link to claimed levels of the complementary parameters are such levels as fully adjusted to the claims. A certain property of the relevant link enables a stable dynamic process to work out in which these levels adjust themselves gradually under the persistent claimed levels of the complementary parameters toward the fully adjusted state.

In appearance the process goes as a multiplier process in which output levels change in the direction of excess demand. But in substance the process functions in the following way. In each of the sectors whose income level is fixed to claimed ones the profit per unit output π_i is adjusted so as for the current level of income to follow up the claimed one. In each of sectors whose profit levels per unit output are fixed to claimed ones the income level y_i changes in the direction of excess demand. The process functions essentially as price mark-ups in sectors with fixed income levels and as multiplier processes in those with fixed profit levels per unit output. Theorem 5, section 6, ensures the stability of this dynamic process.

4   Unique Determinacy of Prices by Income Distribution

4.1   From Income Distribution to Prices

The question now is to see to what extent a given scheme of income distribution y_i $(i = 0, 1, \ldots, n)$ is attainable through output adjustment at a system of fixed prices. The Leontief system can produce any bill of final demand. But its limited overall technological substitutability allows the corresponding output levels x_i $(i = 1, 2, \ldots, n)$ to lie only within a certain range, rather than in any proportions. Specifically, the vector of output levels $x = (x_i)$ is always a weighted sum of the n positive column vectors of the matrix $(I - A)^{-1}$, so that no output levels can be attainable outside of this range for any bill of final demand.

Naturally this fact also applies to the present case where incomes are spent at a system of prices subject to stable propensities to spend. Nonetheless the situation is different for income distribution. Actually any scheme of income distribution is attainable at a suitable unique system of prices through the corresponding output adjustment for a given scheme of investment, as will be formulated and proved below.

Moreover, this is not the whole story about the linkage which connects the price system with income distribution via (7). The linkage is provided with more general capability of unique determination in the range of possible systems of prices and scheme of income distribution.

For notational simplicity let

$$\pi_0 = w,\tag{8}$$

$$b_{0j} = \sigma_j, \quad j = 1, 2, \ldots, n,\tag{9}$$

and henceforth π_0, too, will be referred to as the zeroth sector's profit per unit output. Then (4) and (7) are

$$p_j = \sum_{i=0}^{n} b_{ij}\pi_i, \quad j = 1, 2, \ldots, n,\tag{10}$$

$$y_i = \pi_i \sum_{j=1}^{n} (b_{ij}/p_j) \sum_{k=0}^{n} \gamma_{jk} y_k + \pi_i m_i, \quad i = 0, 1, \ldots, n,\tag{11}$$

where

$$m_i = \sum_{j=1}^{n} b_{ij} d_j, \quad i = 0, 1, \ldots, n\tag{12}$$

are derived positive constants.

In the value side of the system profits per unit output π_i ($i = 0, 1, \ldots, n$) are more fundamental and more essential than prices p_j ($j = 1, \ldots, n$), which are linear functions of π_i in (10). The linkage connects the system of profits per unit output $(\pi_0, \pi_1, \ldots, \pi_n)$ with the scheme of income distribution $(y_0, y_1, \ldots, y_n)$ by way of (10), (11). The capability of unique determination which the linkage is provided with will be formulated and proved in the following theorems:

THEOREM 1 (existence)   Let L and M be disjoint subsets of the set of all $n + 1$ sectors $N = \{0, 1, \ldots, n\}$ with $L \cup M = N$. Given arbitrarily prescribed levels of sectoral incomes y_i^* ($i \in L$) and levels of profits per unit output π_i^* ($i \in M$), all non-negative but not all zero, a given non-negative investment scheme d_j ($j = 1, 2, \ldots, n$) not all items zero, there are levels of profits per unit output $\hat{\pi}_i$ ($i \in L$) and levels of sectoral incomes $\hat{y}_i$ ($i \in M$), all non-negative, which altogether satisfy (10), (11).

Proof As is well-known and also recalled in the foregoing sections, an arbitrary semipositive vector $\pi = (\pi_i)$, with the ith sector's profit per unit output π_i as its ith component uniquely determines positive prices by (10) and non-negative sectoral incomes by (10) and (11), so that they are functions $p_j(\pi)$ $(j = 1, 2, \ldots, n)$, $y_i(\pi)$ $(i = 0, 1, \ldots, n)$ of π. From (10), (11) it is also obvious that they are continuous and homogeneous of the first degree. Needless to say, they satisfy (10), (11) identically. Then the assertion to be proved can be stated in terms of these functions as the existence of a solution vector π of the system of $n + 1$ equations

$$y_i(\pi) = y_i^*, \quad i \in L,$$
$$\pi = \pi_i^*, \quad i \in M. \tag{13}$$

To prove the assertion define $n + 1$ continuous non-negative-valued functions

$$\phi_i(\pi) = y_i^* \Big/ \left(\sum_{j=1}^{n} (b_{ij}/p_j(\pi)) \sum_{k=0}^{n} \gamma_{jk} y_k(\pi) + m_i \right), \quad i \in L,$$

$$= \pi_i^*, \quad i \in M, \tag{14}$$

on the set of all semipositive vectors π. Then construct the continuous mapping

$$\pi \to \psi(\pi) = (\psi_i(\pi)), \tag{15}$$

$$\psi_i(\pi) = \phi_i(\pi) \Big/ \sum_{t=0}^{n} \phi_t(\pi), \tag{16}$$

from the simplex formed by all semipositive vectors π with unit component sum into itself, on the basis of the positivity of the denominator in (16) ensured by that of some of $y_i^* \in L$, $\pi_i^* \in M$. Hence there is a fixed point $\bar{\pi} = (\bar{\pi}_i)$ in the simplex by the Brouwer fixed point theorem.

At this point we have

$$\lambda\bar{\pi}_i = \phi_i(\bar{\pi}), \quad i = 0, 1, \ldots, n, \tag{17}$$

where

$$\lambda = \sum_{t=0}^{n} \phi_t(\bar{\pi}). \tag{18}$$

The functions $\phi_i(\pi)$ are homogeneous of degree zero, so that (17) implies

$$\hat{\pi}_i = \phi_i(\hat{\pi}), \quad i = 0, 1, \ldots, n \qquad (19)$$

for $\hat{\pi} = (\hat{\pi}_i) = (\lambda \bar{\pi}_i)$. Then, (19) means

$$y_i(\hat{\pi}) = \hat{\pi}_i \left(\sum_{j=1}^{n} (b_{ij}/p_j(\hat{\pi})) \sum_{k=0}^{n} \gamma_{jk} y_k(\hat{\pi}) + m_i \right)$$

$$= y_i^*, \quad i \in L,$$

$$\hat{\pi}_i = \pi_i^*, \quad i \in M,$$

by the definitions of the functions $\phi_i(\pi)$, $y_i(\pi)$ $(i = 0, 1, \ldots, n)$, and therefore $\hat{\pi}$ is a solution of (13). Finally $\hat{\pi}_i$ $(i \in L)$, $\hat{y}_i = y_i(\hat{\pi})$ $(i \in M)$ form a solution whose existence is asserted.

4.2 Unique Determinacy

Now that any prescribed set of an income distribution scheme in a group of sectors L and profits per unit output in the complementary group of sectors M can be attained through output adjustment for a suitable set of profits per unit output in L and an income distribution scheme in M, the next question is to see how many solutions exist under the prescription. This question is answered by

THEOREM 2 (uniqueness)   There is at most one solution for a prescription y_i^* $(i \in L)$, π_i^* $(i \in M)$ in Theorem 1 under the same assumptions.

Proof   Define $n + 1$ functions

$$f_i(\pi_0, \pi_1, \ldots, \pi_n, y_0, y_1, \ldots, y_n) = \pi_i \sum_{j=1}^{n} (b_{ij}/p_j) \sum_{k=0}^{n} \gamma_{jk} y_k + \pi_i m_i - y_i,$$

$$i = 0, 1, \ldots, n, \quad (20)$$

as the excess of the right-hand side over the left-hand side in (11), where p_j, m_i are given by (10), (12).

These functions, when the $n + 1$ assigned arguments set equal to the prescribed values $y_i = y_i^*$ $(i \in L)$, $\pi_i = \pi_i^*$ $(i \in M)$, are functions of the remaining $n + 1$ arguments π_s $(s \in L)$, y_s $(s \in M)$. Under these circumstances the system of equations, the existence of whose solution is established in Theorem 1 and for which the uniqueness of solution is to be proved, is

$$f_i(\pi_0, \pi_1, \ldots, \pi_n, y_0, y_1, \ldots, y_n) = 0, \quad i = 0, 1, \ldots, n, \qquad (21)$$

in the unknowns π_s ($s \in L$), y_s ($s \in M$) under the prescription $y_i = y_i^*$ ($i \in L$), $\pi_i = \pi_i^*$ ($i \in M$).

First, assume that the prescription satisfies

$$y_i^* > 0, \quad i \in L, \quad \pi_i^* > 0, \quad i \in M. \tag{22}$$

Then it is clear from (20) that any solution must also satisfy

$$\pi_s > 0, \quad s \in L, \quad y_s > 0, \quad s \in M. \tag{23}$$

Hence we have only to prove the uniqueness of solution in the domain characterized by (23). We perform simple linear transformations

$$y_s = -z_s, \quad s = 0, 1, \ldots, n, \tag{24}$$

and examine the uniqueness in the open rectangular region Γ characterized by

$$\pi_s > 0, \quad s \in L, \quad z_s < 0, \quad s \in M. \tag{25}$$

To this end let us evaluate the system Jacobian matrix $J = (\partial f_i / \partial \pi_s, \partial f_i / \partial z_s)$ of (21) as transformed by (24) under the prescription (22) in Γ, obtaining

$$\frac{\partial f_i}{\partial \pi_s} = -\delta_{is} \left\{ \sum_{j=1}^{n} (b_{ij}/p_j) \sum_{k=0}^{n} \gamma_{jk} z_k - m_i \right\}$$

$$+ \pi_i \sum_{j=1}^{n} (b_{ij} b_{sj}/p_j^2) \sum_{k=0}^{n} \gamma_{jk} z_k, \quad s \in L, \tag{26}$$

$$\frac{\partial f}{\partial z_s} = \delta_{is} - \pi_i \sum_{j=1}^{n} (b_{ij}/p_j)\gamma_{js}, \quad s \in M. \tag{27}$$

where δ_{is} are Kronecker's deltas. J has all its offdiagonal elements nonpositive

$$\frac{\partial f_i}{\partial \pi_s} \leqq 0, \quad i = 0, 1, \ldots, n, i \neq s, \quad s \in L, \tag{28}$$

$$\frac{\partial f_i}{\partial z_s} \leqq 0, \quad i = 0, 1, \ldots, n, i \neq s, \quad s \in M, \tag{29}$$

as is clear from (26), (27). J also has all its column sums positive

$$\sum_{i=0}^{n} \frac{\partial f_i}{\partial \pi_s} = m_s > 0, \quad s \in L, \tag{30}$$

$$\sum_{i=0}^{n} \frac{\partial f_i}{\partial z_s} = 1 - \gamma_s > 0, \quad s \in M. \tag{31}$$

Hence Hawkins–Simon's conditions hold, and J has all its principal minors positive. Thus the solution in question is unique by virtue of a theorem due to Gale and myself (1965, 1968, ch. 7) on mappings having a p-Jacobian matrix.

Second, essentially the same method of proof can be worked out even in the absence of condition (22). In fact, some, though not all, of the prescribed values are still positive by assumption. Therefore, if there are positive π_i^* among M, the prices p_j are always positive in (10) for all $\pi_s \geq 0$ ($s \in L$). Hence the functions (20) are continuously differentiable and have a Jacobian matrix satisfying (26)–(31) in the closed rectangular region characterized by

$$\pi_s \geq 0, \quad s \in L, \quad z_s \leq 0, \quad s \in M.$$

If all π_i^* vanish for $i \in M$, there are positive y_i^* among L. Let L^+ be the set of i's among L for which y_i^* is positive. The solution must satisfy $\pi_s > 0$ ($s \in L^+$), so that we have the same situation in the rectangular region characterized by

$$\pi_s > 0, \quad s \in L^+, \quad \pi_s \geq 0, \quad s \in L \backslash L^+, \quad z_s \leq 0, \quad s \in M$$

In both general cases which lack (22) the theorem due to Gale and myself can be applied to ensure uniqueness. It is noted that the unique determinate value of a variable π_s is zero if and only if the corresponding prescribed value y_s^* vanishes, and the same is true for y_s and π_s^*. The proof is thereby complete.

4.3 The Relevant Link

The foregoing results have established the relevant link between the set of all sectorial profits per unit output and the state of all schemes of income distribution. The link is given by the system of eqs. (21). An arbitrary prescription of non-negative values, at least one positive, for an arbitrary set of $n + 1$ arguments among the $2(n + 1)$ arguments $\pi_0, \pi_1, \ldots, \pi_n, y_0, y_1, \ldots, y_n$ such as has all its members differently numbered can uniquely determine the non-negative values of the remaining $n + 1$ arguments so as to let (21) hold. In other words, any such $n + 1$ arguments are globally defined implicit functions of the $n + 1$ remaining arguments.

The well-known classical result that the sectoral income levels can be uniquely determined by (10), (11), at arbitrarily fixed $\pi_0, \pi_1, \ldots, \pi_n$, that is, by a matrix multiplier, is one partial aspect of the link hitherto revealed to us. The corresponding determined sectoral income levels are functions of $\pi_0, \pi_1, \ldots, \pi_n$,

$$y_s = \Psi_s(\pi_0, \pi_1, \ldots, \pi_n), \quad s = 0, 1, \ldots, n, \tag{32}$$

a particular instance of the implicit functions.

Conversely, for each set of non-negative sectoral incomes $y_0, y_1, \ldots, y_n$ not all of them zero, there is a unique set of non-negative sectoral profits per unit output, not all of them zero. These profits are functions of $y_0, y_1, \ldots, y_n$, that is, the inverse of (32)

$$\pi_t = \Psi_t^{-1}(y_0, y_1, \ldots, y_n), \quad t = 0, 1, \ldots, n. \tag{33}$$

another particular instance of the implicit functions.

In the neoclassical world everything can be determinate by market clearing through parametric function of prices. Here the system of equations always represents commodity market clearing as equality of effective demand with effective supply through output adjustments accompanied by price adjustments under circumstances, still leaving the $n + 1$ degrees of freedom of indeterminacy.

There may be an objection that suggests a possibility of treating the investment scheme $d_1, d_2, \ldots, d_n$ as functions of the arguments. But this would not bring any additional equations to (21) but merely such complication as threatens the existence and/or uniqueness of solution without reducing the degree of freedom. The present simplified situation where the investment scheme is exogenously given is a special case in which $d_1, d_2, \ldots, d_n$ are constant-valued functions of the arguments. Introduction of another variable affecting the investment scheme, e.g., the rate of interest, would also bring another equation, while leaving the indeterminacy unaffected.[1]

Another line of objection would take the labor market into account. Nonetheless the indeterminacy still remains whenever involuntary unemployment is universal, in other words, it is inevitable at any price–income state not below its minimum subsistence state, which may limit the range of $(\pi_0, p_1, p_2, \ldots, p_n)$ from below, and hence that of $(\pi_0, \pi_1, \ldots, \pi_n)$. The degree of freedom would decrease only by one at best in a lucky coincidental situation of full employment.

In order for prices to be determined so as to clear markets, the income levels must be predetermined or prescribed in essence but latently some way round. In the light of this fact the socioeconomic implication of price rigidity is the persistence of more or less specific schemes of income distribution. Notwithstanding these essential aspects prices clear markets and thereby determine income distribution in appearance.

5   Comparative Statics Laws

5.1   Properties of the Relevant Link

The set of all semipositive vectors $y = (y_i)$ of incomes is completely in one-to-one correspondence by the relevant link with the set of all semipositive vectors $\pi = (\pi_i)$ of profits per unit output. The correspondence has several important properties, as will be noted.

(α)   The correspondence is continuous in both directions, as is clear from the continuity of the functions in (20).

(β)   The correspondence is homogeneous of the first order, for the functions in (20) are homogeneous of the first order in $\pi_0, \pi_1, \ldots, \pi_n, y_0, y_1, \ldots, y_n$. Therefore doubling all profits unit output gives rise to doubled incomes and vice versa.

(γ) $y_s\ (s = 0, 1, \ldots, n)$ as functions of $\pi_0, \pi_1, \ldots, \pi_n$ in (32) identically fulfill

$$\sum_{s=0}^{n} (1 - \gamma_s) y_s = \sum_{j=1}^{n} p_j d_j = \sum_{t=0}^{n} m_t \pi_t, \tag{34}$$

and $\pi_t\ (t = 0, 1, \ldots, n)$ as functions of $y_0, y_1, \ldots, y_n$ in (33) identically fulfill (34), too. This can be verified by summing up the equations in (11) and taking account of (10), (12).

(δ)   In the correspondence $\pi_i = 0$ for an i if and only if $y_i = 0$.

(ε)   Despite the first order homogeneity the correspondence is non-linear.

5.2 Comparative Statics Laws

Since there are $2(n + 1)$ variables π_i, y_j $(i, j = 0, 1, \ldots, n)$ among which $n + 1$ functional relations (21) hold, any $n + 1$ variables chosen from among them, regarded as parameters whose values are exogenously determined, say, institutionally or politically in a latent way, uniquely determine the values of the other $n + 1$ variables. Then, a parametrical change, that is, a change in the underlying latent socioeconomic situation, induces changes in the $n + 1$ variables.

Specifically, (32) gives the values of $n + 1$ sectoral incomes under prescribed values of $n + 1$ profits per unit output regarded as parameters. A change in the value of one of the parameters induces changes in the levels of sectoral incomes. How much and in what directions? The same questions can be asked about the effects of a change in the level of income in a sector on the levels of profits per unit output through (33). The following two theorems answer these questions to a certain extent.

THEOREM 3 (comparative statics 1)   Let Δy_s $(s = 0, 1, \ldots, n)$ be the increments of the sectoral incomes y_s $(s = 0, 1, \ldots, n)$ as functions of profits per unit output π_t $(t = 0, 1, \ldots, n)$ in (32) when π_k is increased from a positive level by $\Delta\pi_k$ in the kth sector while π_t $(t \neq k)$ remaining unchanged in the other sectors. Then

(i) $\Delta y_k > 0,$

(ii) $\dfrac{\Delta y_k}{y_k} > \dfrac{\Delta y_s}{y_s},\quad s \neq k,$

provided all π_t are positive.

Proof   For the sake of analytical convenience perform linear transformations

$$y_s = -z_s \geqq 0, \quad s = 0, 1, \ldots, n, \tag{35}$$

as in (24). Then (21) is converted to

$$f_i(\pi_0, \pi_1, \ldots, \pi_n, -z_0, -z_1, \ldots, -z_n) = 0, \quad i = 0, 1, \ldots, n. \tag{36}$$

By partially differentiating (32) with (35) and (36) with respect to π_k, we have

$$\sum_{s=0}^{n} \frac{\partial f_i}{\partial z_s} \frac{\partial z_s}{\partial \pi_k} + \frac{\partial f_i}{\partial \pi_k} = 0, \quad i = 0, 1, \ldots, n. \tag{37}$$

Suppose that

$$\frac{\partial z_k}{\partial \pi_k} \geq 0. \tag{38}$$

Then, from (37) follow n equations

$$\sum_{s \neq k} \frac{\partial f_i}{\partial z_s} \frac{\partial z_s}{\partial \pi_k} = -\frac{\partial f_i}{\partial z_k} \frac{\partial z_k}{\partial \pi_k} - \frac{\partial f_i}{\partial \pi_k}, \quad i \neq k. \tag{39}$$

In the light of the evaluations of the partial derivatives in (26), (27), we see

$$\frac{\partial f_i}{\partial z_k} \leq 0, \quad \frac{\partial f_i}{\partial \pi_k} \leq 0, \quad i \neq k,$$

so that the n equations in (39) have the right-hand side non-negative by (38). Moreover, also in the light of the reasoning in the proof of Theorem 2, the matrix of (39) as a system of equations in the unknowns $\partial z_s / \partial \pi_k$ ($s \neq k$), has Hawkins–Simon's conditions. Hence the principal minor matrix obtained by deleting the kth row and column in the matrix, which is the coefficient matrix of (39) as a system of equations in the unknowns $\partial z_s / \partial \pi_k$ ($s \neq k$), has the same properties. These results altogether imply

$$\frac{\partial z_s}{\partial \pi_k} \geq 0, \quad s \neq k. \tag{40}$$

But (38), (40) contradict

$$\sum_{s=0}^{n} (1 - \gamma_s) z_s + \sum_{t=0}^{n} m_t \pi_t = 0, \tag{41}$$

which results from (34) by the transformations (35).

Thus (38) is ruled out, so that

$$\frac{\partial z_k}{\partial \pi_k} < 0, \tag{42}$$

and therefore

$$\frac{\partial y_k}{\partial \pi_k} > 0, \tag{43}$$

and hence the proposition (i).

To prove (ii), in addition to (37) we note

$$\sum_{s=0}^{n} \frac{\partial f_i}{\partial z_s} z_s + \pi_i m_i = 0, \quad i = 0, 1, \dots, n, \tag{44}$$

which follow from (36) because of the homogeneity of degree one of $f_i - \pi_i m_i$ in the z variables.

On the basis of the negativity of $z_k = -y_k < 0$ ensured by the positivity of π_k as remarked in (δ), section 5.1, let

$$\theta = \frac{1}{z_k} \frac{\partial z_k}{\partial \pi_k}. \tag{45}$$

Then θ is positive by (42). (45) also implies

$$\frac{\partial z_k}{\partial \pi_k} - \theta z_k = 0. \tag{46}$$

In view of (46), subtracting θ times the ith equation in (44) from the ith one in (37), we have

$$\sum_{s \neq k} \frac{\partial f_i}{\partial z_s} \left(\frac{\partial z_s}{\partial \pi_k} - \theta z_s \right) = \theta m_i \pi_i - \frac{\partial f_i}{\partial \pi_k}, \quad i \neq k. \tag{47}$$

Again, in the light of the evaluations (26), (27), all the equations in (47) are positive on the right-hand side, and the coefficient matrix $(\partial f_i / \partial z_s)$ of order n on the left-hand side, having non-positive offdiagonal elements, satisfies Hawkins–Simon's conditions, as was remarked above. Hence

$$\frac{\partial z_s}{\partial \pi_k} - \theta z_s > 0, \quad s \neq k. \tag{48}$$

Now (48) implies, because of the negativity of z_s,

$$\frac{1}{y_s} \frac{\partial y_s}{\partial \pi_k} = \frac{1}{z_s} \frac{\partial z_s}{\partial \pi_k} < \theta = \frac{1}{z_k} \frac{\partial z_k}{\partial \pi_k} = \frac{1}{y_k} \frac{\partial y_k}{\partial \pi_k}, \tag{49}$$

which proves (ii) in an infinitesimal increment form.

(49) implies that each of $y_s/y_k (s \neq k)$ as a function of π_k is strictly decreasing. Therefore $y_s/y_k > (y_s + \Delta y_s)/(y_k + \Delta y_k)$ for the increments Δy_s, Δy_k corresponding to $\Delta \pi_k > 0$, whence follows (ii).

Corresponding to (33) we have likewise:

THEOREM 4 (comparative statics 2)   Let $\Delta \pi_t$ $(t = 0, 1, \ldots, n)$ be the increments of the profits per unit output π_t $(t = 0, 1, \ldots, n)$ as functions of sectional incomes y_s $(s = 0, 1, \ldots, n)$ in (33) when y_k is increased from a positive level by Δy_k in the kth sector while y_s $(s \neq k)$ remaining unchanged in the other sectors. Then

(i) $\Delta \pi_k > 0$

(ii) $\dfrac{\Delta \pi_k}{\pi_k} > \dfrac{\Delta \pi_t}{\pi_t}, \quad t \neq k,$

provided all y_s are positive.

The proof of Theorem 4 essentially duplicates that of Theorem 3.

Both Theorems 3 and 4 are typical comparative statics laws inherent in the relevant link as revealed in the specific directions of determination (32) and (33). Comparative statics laws such as proposition (i) in both Theorems are inherent in other directions of determinations as well. In fact, for a decomposition $\{L, M\}$ of the $n + 1$ sectors as in Theorems 1 and 2 profits per unit output π_t $(t \in L)$ and sectoral incomes y_s $(s \in M)$ are functions of sectoral incomes y_i $(i \in L)$ and profits per unit output π_j $(j \in M)$. Then, a partial positive increment $\Delta \pi_k$ in a sector k in M gives rise to $\Delta y_k > 0$, and a partial positive increment Δy_k in a sector k in L gives rise to $\Delta \pi_k > 0$. These laws can be proved in the same ways as in both Theorems. Nevertheless propositions of type (ii) seem to fail to hold, unless one of L, M is empty.

6   Dynamic Adjustments

Let $\{L, M\}$ be a decomposition of all the sectors. Then an adjustment process, in which sectoral income levels in L and profits per unit output in M remain to be unchanged because of some latent socioeconomic rigidities, is formulated as

$$\frac{d\pi_i}{dt} = -\lambda_i f_i(\pi_0, \pi_1, \ldots, \pi_n, y_0, y_1, \ldots, y_n), \quad i \in L,$$

$$\qquad\qquad = 0, \qquad\qquad\qquad\qquad\qquad i \in M, \qquad\qquad (50)$$

$$\frac{dy_i}{dt} = 0, \qquad\qquad\qquad\qquad\qquad i \in L,$$

$$\qquad\qquad = \mu_i f_i(\pi_0, \pi_1, \ldots, \pi_n, y_0, y_1, \ldots, y_n) \qquad i \in M, \qquad (51)$$

where λ_i, μ_i are positive constants, and f_i are the functions in (20).

Output levels x_i and income levels y_i are related by

$$\pi_i x_i = y_i, \quad i = 0, 1, \ldots, n.$$

If y_i^* are constant income levels in L, and π_i^* are constant profits per unit output in M, then

$$\pi_i x_i = y_i^*, \quad i \in L, \qquad\qquad\qquad\qquad\qquad (52)$$

$$\pi_i^* x_i = y_i, \quad i \in M. \qquad\qquad\qquad\qquad\qquad (53)$$

Hence by (20), (50), (52) we have

$$\frac{1}{x_i}\frac{dx_i}{dt} = -\frac{1}{\pi_i}\frac{d\pi_i}{dt} = \lambda_i \times \text{excess demand for the } i\text{th good}, \quad i \in L. \qquad (54)$$

By (20), (51), (53) we also have

$$\frac{dx_i}{dt} = \mu_i \times \text{excess demand for the } i\text{th good}, \quad i \in M. \qquad\qquad (55)$$

Thus in the surface appearance the process works itself out as a multiplier process.

One special case where L is empty and M includes all the sectors is the well-known standard mutliplier process under fixed prices. Another extreme case where L includes all the sectors and M is empty works itself out as a multiplier in appearance, but is a price mark-up process

$$\frac{d\pi_i}{dt} = \lambda_i$$

(ith sector's income $- \pi_i \times$ demand for the ith good), $\quad i = 0, 1, \ldots, n,$

in essence, in which fixed levels of income persist.

As to the dynamic performances we have:

THEOREM 5 (stability)   Any solution of the system (50), (51), starting at any positive initial position, converges to the profit per unit output–income scheme $(\pi_0^\infty, \pi_1^\infty, \ldots, \pi_n^\infty, y_0^\infty, y_1^\infty, \ldots, y_n^\infty)$, which is a unique solution of the system of eqs. (20), $y_i = y_i^*$ $(i \in L)$, $\pi_i = \pi_i^*$ $(i \in M)$, where y_i^* $(i \in L)$, π_i^* $(i \in M)$ are prescribed constant levels, assumed to be positive.

Proof   Having started at a positive initial position and remained to be positive up to this moment of time, the trajectory will never leave the positive orthant, since

$$\frac{d\pi_i}{dt} > 0 \text{ whenever } \pi_i = 0, \quad i \in L,$$

and

$$\frac{dy_i}{dt} > 0 \quad \text{whenever } y_i = 0, \quad i \in M.$$

Next, by performing the linear transformations (35), we can put the system in the form

$$\frac{d\pi_i}{dt} = -\lambda_i f_i(\pi_0, \pi_1, \ldots, \pi_n, -z_0, -z_1, \ldots, -z_n), \quad i \in L, \tag{56}$$

$$\frac{dz_i}{dt} = -\mu_i f_i(\pi_0, \pi_1, \ldots, \pi_n, -z_0, -z_1, \ldots, -z_n), \quad i \in M, \tag{57}$$

with

$$\begin{aligned} y_i &= y_i^*, \quad i \in L, \\ \pi_i &= \pi_i^*, \quad i \in M. \end{aligned} \tag{58}$$

In the light of the evaluations (26), (27) and the reasoning thereafter, and because of the positivity of π_i's and the negativity of z_i's, the system Jacobian matrix has positive offdiagonal elements and a dominant negative diagonal in regard to column sum with positive constant weights $1/\lambda_i$ for $i \in L$ and $1/\mu_i$ for $i \in M$. Therefore, the system is globally stable by virtue of a theorem due to Karlin (1959, ch. 9, thm. 9.5.1).

Notes

Research carried out during the author's visit at University of Southern Calirornia, to which many thanks are due for its support of the visit. He owes much to the anonymous referees for invaluable comments, but any remaining error is his sole responsibility.

1. Suppose d_i $(i = 1, 2, \ldots, n)$ are functions of interest rate r. Then, adding to the system of eqs. (21) one more equation equating a demand function for real money balances of r and sectoral income levels y_i $(i = 1, 2, \ldots, n)$ deflated by p, a weighted sum of prices, to an exogeneously given level of nominal money supply also deflated by p, one gets a multi-sector IS-LM model. y_i $(i = 1, 2, \ldots, n)$, π_i $(i = 1, 2, \ldots, n)$ and r have $n + 1$ degrees of freedom.

References

Barro, R. J. and H. I. Grossman (1971): A general disequilibrium model of income and employment, *American Economic Review*, 61.

Barro, R. J. and H. I. Grossman (1976): *Money, employment and inflation*, Cambridge: Cambridge University Press.

Clower, R. W. (1965): The Keynesian counterrevolution: A theoretical appraisal, in F. Hahn and F. Brechling, eds., *The theory of interest rates*, London: Macmillan.

Gale, D. and H. Nikaido (1965): The Jacobian matrix and global univalence of mappings, *Mathematische Annalen*, 159.

Karlin, S. (1959): *Mathematical methods and theory in games, programming and economics*, Vol. 1, Reading: Addison-Wesley.

Leijonhufvud, A. (1968): *On Keynesian economics and the economics of Keynes*, New York: Oxford University Press.

Negishi, T. (1974): Involuntary unemployment and market imperfection, *Economic Studies Quarterly*, 25.

Nikaido, H. (1968): *Convex structures and economic theory*, New York: Academic Press.

——— (1974): What is an objective demand function?, *Zeitschrift für Nationalökonomie*, 34.

——— (1975): *Monopolistic competition and effective demand*, Princeton: Princeton University Press.

Patinkin, D. (1965): *Money, interest, and prices*, 2nd ed., New York: Harper and Row.

Sweezy, P. M. (1939): Demand under conditions of oligopoly, *Journal of Political Economy*, 47.

III GROWTH AND CYCLES

7 Persistence of Continual Growth Near the von Neumann Ray: A Strong Version of the Radner Turnpike Theorem [1964]

It seems that nothing has been more challenging to mathematical economists during the last two or three years than the "turnpike" problem.[1] It is concerned with a question of whether or not optimal paths of economic growth trace out catenary motions near the balanced growth path, the so-called turnpike, as the span of programming periods gets longer.[2] It will continue to bewitch many people, since only some very special cases of turnpike phenomena have definitely been brought to light by a few authors[3] such as Hicks (1961), Morishima (1961), and Radner (1961) whose results jointly embellish the February, 1961 issue of *The Review of Economic Studies*. Among these results, Radner's seems to be the most suggestive for further studies in the formulation of the problem as well as in the method of proof. Radner proved, in an elegant way, that, for any thin neighbouring cone of the balanced growth ray, any optimal paths starting at a common initial position stay within the cone except for a finite common number of periods. In spite of this splendid result, however, Radner's theorem has been criticized because of one dubious point left untouched. The criticism points out that there is no assurance that the system will not run off the neighbouring cone around the half-way point of the entire programming period. An optimal path may several times enter and leave the neighbouring cone at intermediate periods which are far from both the initial and the terminal periods. In other words, no evidence has yet been given for the belief that these running-off periods are concentrated around the initial and terminal periods. On this ground, Radner's results are often referred to as a "weak" turnpike theorem,[4] or, more jokingly, as a "hop-skip-jumping" turnpike theorem.

The purpose of this paper is to show that this phenomenon of half-way turning off does not really occur in the Radner case, provided some additional, but plausible, assumptions are explicitly imposed upon technological possibilities and the society's preferences about the terminal states of paths of economic growth. In non-mathematical terms, the additional assumption about technology implies that goods can be combined as inputs *in any proportion* to produce some outputs which may, or may not, be zero. This suggests, but need not imply, the presence of some costless disposal processes. On the other hand, another assumption requires that society prefers one state to another if the former provides a larger amount of each good than the latter.

From *Econometrica* 32, nos. 1–2 (January–April 1964): 151–162. Reprinted by permission.

It is also assumed that the von Neumann ray is generated by a positive vector.

These assumptions are sufficiently general to be satisfied by almost all economically meaningful cases. The discussion in the following sections is intended to justify the writer's belief that the Radner theorem should be classified as a "strong," rather than a "weak," turnpike theorem, as one assuring true catenary movements near the turnpike. To be more precise, it will be shown in this paper that under these additional assumptions, the Radner turnpike theorem can be put in the following form:

For any thin neighbouring cone of the balanced growth ray there is a number k such that any optimal path $x(t)$ starting at a common initial state continually stays within the cone except for the k initial periods and the k terminal periods, that is, during most periods t of the program given by $k \leq t \leq N - k$, regardless of the whole span N of programming periods.

The writer believes that this result suggests the powerfulness of the Radner theorem.

For simplicity's sake, the proof will proceed in two steps. The first step will give a proof for the case where free disposability prevails, a case which may deserve independent attention. Then, in the second step, the general case will be reduced to the free disposal case. The method of proof is similar to that of Radner, but consists of a more prudent application of the latter.

1   The Radner Turnpike Theorem Reconsidered

1.1   To begin with, for the sake of the reader's convenience, the Radner turnpike theorem, in somewhat modified notation, will be outlined as briefly as possible. The theorem is concerned with optimal paths of growth of an economy whose state is described by an n-dimensional vector x, the components of x standing, e.g., for the amounts of capital stocks. Whenever one finds it convenient to speak of x in explicit reference to a period t, we write $x(t)$.

The economy has a set of possible technologies, which transform $x(t)$ to $x(t + 1)$. These possible pairs of input-output configurations form a technology set T in the nonnegative orthant of a $2n$-dimensional Euclidean space R^{2n}. Radner assumes the following conditions on T.

ASSUMPTION A.1[5] T is a closed convex cone in the nonnegative orthant of a $2n$-dimensional Euclidean space.

ASSUMPTION A.2   If $(0, y)$ is in T, then $y = 0$.

A sequence $\{x(t)\}_{t=0}^{N}$ is said to be feasible, given $x(0) = x^o$, if $(x(t), x(t + 1)) \in T$ for $t = 0, 1, 2, \ldots, N - 1$. Such a sequence describes a mode of economic growth which extends over N periods.

1.2   Moreover, the economy has preferences among feasible sequences. These preferences depend only upon the terminal states $x(N)$ of such sequences. The preference is represented by a numerical function $u(x)$ defined on the nonnegative orthant of an n-dimensional Euclidean space R^n. Radner's assumptions on $u(x)$ are as follow:

ASSUMPTION A.3 $u(x)$ is nonnegative and continuous, and there is an a such that $u(a) > 0$.

ASSUMPTION A.4 $u(x)$ is quasi-homogeneous.[6]

Given N, the span of programming periods, and $x(0) = x^o$, the initial state, a u-optimal sequence is a feasible sequence that maximizes $u(x(N))$ among all feasible sequences $\{x(t)\}_{t=0}^{N}$ of span N.

1.3   For any vectors x and y in R^n, $x'y$ stands for the inner product given by $\sum_{i=1}^{n} x_i y_i$. The norm $\|x\|$ of a vector x in R^n is $(x'x)^{1/2}$. Frequent use will be made of these concepts in the sequel. Radner assumes furthermore:

(i)   There are an $\hat{x} \geq 0$, a price vector $p \geq 0$, and an interest factor (growth factor, at the same time) $\rho > 0$ such that

(i.1) $(\hat{x}, \rho\hat{x}) \in T$;

(i.2) $p'(y - \rho x) \leq 0$ for any $(x, y) \in T$;

(ii)[7] $p'(y - \rho x) < 0$ for all $(x, y) \in T$ that are not proportional to $(\hat{x}, \rho\hat{x})$;

(iii)   there is a number $K > 0$ such that $u(x) \leq Kp'x$ for all $x \geq 0$;

(iv)[8]   an initial vector x^o is given such that for some $L > 0$, and N_o, there is a feasible sequence from x^o to $L\hat{x}$ in N_o periods;

(v)   for some numbers $\hat{u} > 0$ and N_1, and some vector y for which $u(y) = \hat{u}$, there is a feasible sequence from $\hat{x}$ to y in N_1 periods.

1.4 It has been proved by Radner in a very elegant way that under Assumptions A.1–A.4 and (i)–(v) the following theorem holds.

RADNER'S TURNPIKE THEOREM   For any $\varepsilon > 0$ there is a number k such that, for any programming span N and any u-optimal sequence $\{x(t)\}_{t=0}^{N}$ with $x(0) = x^o$, the number of periods in which

$$\left\| \frac{x(t)}{\|x(t)\|} - \hat{x} \right\| \geq \varepsilon \tag{1}$$

holds can not exceed k, provided $\|\hat{x}\| = 1$.

The implication of the theorem is obvious.[9] It states the important result that any u-optimal sequence lies in the ε-neighbouring cone $\{x \mid \|x/\|x\| - \hat{x}\| < \varepsilon\}$ of the balanced growth path $\{\rho^t \hat{x}\}$ except possibly for k periods.

1.5 As was pointed out in the introductory discussion, however, these exceptional periods are not assured to be concentrated about initial periods and terminal periods. Some of them may possibly be intermediate periods which are far from both the starting period 0 and the last period N. Thus it is of some interest to detect further economically meaningufl conditions that exclude this pathological phenomenon of half-way running off. We shall give here some of these conditions, under which Radner's theorem can be restated in the following form:

A STRONG TURNPIKE THEOREM   For any $\varepsilon > 0$ there is a number k such that, for any programming span N and any u-optimal sequence $\{x(t)\}_{t=0}^{N}$ with $x(0) = x^o$ we have, upon the normalization $\|\hat{x}\| = 1$,

$$\left\| \frac{x(t)}{\|x(t)\|} - \hat{x} \right\| < \varepsilon \quad \text{for} \quad k \leq t \leq N - k. \tag{2}$$

This theorem means that any optimal sequence lies entirely in the ε-neighbouring cone of the balanced growth path in all periods extending from k to $N - k$.

1.6 Our *additional assumptions* are as follow:

(α)   For any $x \geq 0$ there is some y such that $(x, y) \in T$.

(β) $\hat{x} > 0$.

(γ)   The preference indicator $u(x)$ satisfies:

$x > y \geq 0$ implies $u(x) > u(y)$.

(α) implies that any combination of goods at any proportion can be transformed into some output. Note that in (α) it does not matter whether or not $y = 0$. (β) is self-explanatory. (γ) slightly strengthens A.3, but not too much from the economic point of view.

In the following two sections we shall prove that, if (α), (β), and (γ) are assumed in addition to Radner's basic assumptions A.1–A.4 and (i)–(v), the strong turnpike theorem also holds.

2   Proof for the Case of Free Disposability

2.1   Assumption (α) is closely related to, but weaker than, the following assumption of free disposability, as given by Radner himself:

ASSUMPTION A.5   If $x^* \geq x$, $y \geq y^* \geq 0$ and $(x, y) \in T$, then $(x^*, y^*) \in T$.

In order to make the crucial points of our proof as clear as possible and to bring into relief the role played by free disposability in the proof, the discussion will be done in two steps. In this section, the proof will be given first for the case of free disposability. Then, in the following section, the general case will be reduced to the free disposal case. Thus, A.5 is assumed in this section. It is noted, however, that one needs A.5 only when proving Lemma 4.

2.2   The proof begins by noting some simple results on the norm $\| \cdot \|$.

Take $\hat{x}$ and p in (i), (ii), and (β). We may assume, without loss of generality, that

$$\|\hat{x}\| = 1, \quad p'\hat{x} = 1. \tag{3}$$

As is well known, any vector x in R^n can be uniquely decomposed to a sum of its orthogonal projection $\theta(x)\hat{x}$ on the straight line spanned by $\hat{x}$ and its orthogonal complement $e(x)$. Explicitly, we have

$$x = \theta(x)\hat{x} + e(x), \tag{4}$$

where

$$\theta(x) = \hat{x}'x. \tag{5}$$

Then, we have

LEMMA 1 $x \neq 0$, $\|(x/\|x\|) - \hat{x}\| < \delta$, $\delta > 0$ imply $\|e(x)\| < \delta\|x\|$.

Proof By decomposing $x/\|x\|$ to the sum $\theta(x/\|x\|)\hat{x} + e(x/\|x\|)$ and noting that $e(x/\|x\|)$ is orthogonal to $\theta(x/\|x\|)\hat{x} - \hat{x}$, we see

$$\delta^2 > \left\| \frac{x}{\|x\|} - \hat{x} \right\|^2 = \left\| \theta\left(\frac{x}{\|x\|}\right)\hat{x} - \hat{x} \right\|^2 + \left\| e\left(\frac{x}{\|x\|}\right) \right\|^2 \geq \left\| e\left(\frac{x}{\|x\|}\right) \right\|^2$$

$$= \|e(x)\|^2/\|x\|^2.$$

This proves the lemma.

2.3   Consider any feasible sequences $\{x(t)\}_{t=0}^N$, with $x(0) = x^o$.

LEMMA 2

(I)   For each of these sequences,

$$p'x(t+1)/\rho^{t+1} \leq p'x(t)/\rho^t \quad (t = 0, 1, \ldots, N-1).$$

(II) $p > 0$.

(III)   There is a number $\Delta > 0$ such that

$$\|x(t)/\rho^t\| \leq \Delta \quad (t = 0, 1, \ldots, N)$$

holds uniformly for all of these sequences of any span N.

(IV)   There is a number $\Gamma > 0$ such that

$$p'x(N)/\rho^N \geq \Gamma$$

holds uniformly for all u-optimal sequences starting at x^o with $N \geq N_o + N_1$.

Proof

(I)   Since $(x(t), x(t+1)) \in T$, we have, by (i.2), $p'x(t+1) \leq \rho p'x(t)$, which, if divided by ρ^{t+1}, yields (I)

(II)   If some components of p vanish, there is some $x \geq 0$ such that $p'x = 0$. By (α), there exists some $y \geq 0$ such that $(x, y) \in T$ for this x. Then, by (i.2), $p'(y - \rho x) \leq 0$. But, since $p'y \geq 0$ and $p'x = 0$, we have $p'(y - \rho x) = 0$. This implies, in view of (ii), (x, y) is proportional to $(\hat{x}, \rho\hat{x})$, so that $p'\hat{x}$ must also vanish, contradicting assumption (β).

(III) By (I), $p'x(t)/\rho^t \leq p'x(0)$. Since $p' > 0$ by (II) and $x(t)/\rho^t$ is non-negative, this implies the desired uniform boundedness.

(IV) As was shown by Radner,[10] there is, in view of (iv) and (v), a feasible sequence $\{\bar{x}(t)\}_{t=0}^N$ with $\bar{x}(0) = x^o$ such that $u(\bar{x}(N)) = L\rho^{N-N_0-N_1}\hat{u} > 0$. Because of the u-optimality of $\{x(t)\}_{t=0}^N$ and in view of (iii), it follows that $Kp'x(N) \geq u(x(N)) \geq u(\bar{x}(N)) = L\rho^{N-N_0-N_1}\hat{u} > 0$. Hence $p'x(N)/\rho^N \geq L\hat{u}/K\rho^{N_0+N_1} = \Gamma > 0$, which holds uniformly for all u-optimal sequences at issue.

An immediate consequence of these two lemmas is

LEMMA 3   Let $\{x(t)\}_{t=0}^N$ be any feasible sequence with $x(0) = x^o$. If $x(t) \neq 0$ and $\|(x(t)/\|x(t)\|) - \hat{x}\| < \delta$ for some t, then $\|e(x(t)/\rho^t\| < \delta\Delta$ for the same t.

The proof is immediate, so that it may be omitted.

2.4   The following lemma is very important to our proof.

LEMMA 4.   Let $\{x(t)\}_{t=0}^N$ be any u-optimal sequence with $x(0) = x^o$. If $\|e(x(r)/\rho^r)\| < \eta$ and $\|e(x(s)/\rho^s)\| < \eta$ for some r, s and $\eta > 0$, then

$$\left| \theta\left(\frac{x(r)}{\rho^r}\right) - \theta\left(\frac{x(s)}{\rho^s}\right) \right| < 2\eta \max_i [\|p\|, 1/\lim \hat{x}_i]$$

for the same r and s.

Proof   Without loss of generality, we may assume that $r < s$. Using (I) of Lemma 2, $p'x(s)/\rho^s \leq p'x(r)/\rho^r$, so that

$$p'\left(\theta\left(\frac{x(s)}{\rho^s}\right)\hat{x} + e\left(\frac{x(s)}{\rho^s}\right)\right) \leq p'\left(\theta\left(\frac{x(r)}{\rho^r}\right)\hat{x} + e\left(\frac{x(r)}{\rho^r}\right)\right).$$

Hence, by rearrangement, and in view of $p'\hat{x} = 1$,

$$\theta\left(\frac{x(s)}{\rho^s}\right) - \theta\left(\frac{x(r)}{\rho^r}\right) = \left(\theta\left(\frac{x(s)}{\rho^s}\right) - \theta\left(\frac{x(r)}{\rho^r}\right)\right)p'\hat{x} \leq p'e\left(\frac{x(r)}{\rho^r}\right) - p'e\left(\frac{x(s)}{\rho^s}\right)$$

$$\leq \|p\|\left(\left\|e\left(\frac{x(r)}{\rho^r}\right)\right\| + \left\|e\left(\frac{x(s)}{\rho^s}\right)\right\|\right) < 2\eta\|p\|.$$

On the other hand, we wish to show that

$$\theta\left(\frac{x(r)}{\rho^r}\right) - \theta\left(\frac{x(s)}{\rho^s}\right) = \omega < \max_i \frac{2\eta}{\hat{x}_i}.$$

Suppose that $\omega \geqq \max 2\eta/\hat{x}_i$. Let

$$\hat{w} = \frac{1}{2}\left(\theta\left(\frac{x(r)}{\rho^r}\right) + \theta\left(\frac{x(s)}{\rho^s}\right)\right)\hat{x}.$$

Since $\dfrac{\omega}{2}\hat{x}_i \geqq \eta > \left\|e\left(\dfrac{x(r)}{\rho^r}\right)\right\| \geqq -e_i\left(\dfrac{x(r)}{\rho^r}\right)$ and $\dfrac{\omega}{2}\hat{x}_i \geqq \eta > \left\|e\left(\dfrac{x(s)}{\rho^s}\right)\right\| \geqq$
$e_i\left(\dfrac{x(s)}{\rho^s}\right)$ for all the components $i = 1, 2, \ldots, n$, we have

$$\frac{x(r)}{\rho^r} = \theta\left(\frac{x(r)}{\rho^r}\right)\hat{x} + e\left(\frac{x(r)}{\rho^r}\right) > \left(\theta\left(\frac{x(r)}{\rho^r}\right) - \frac{\omega}{2}\right)\hat{x} = \hat{w},$$

$$\frac{x(s)}{\rho^s} = \theta\left(\frac{x(s)}{\rho^s}\right)\hat{x} + e\left(\frac{x(s)}{\rho^s}\right) < \left(\theta\left(\frac{x(s)}{\rho^s}\right) + \frac{\omega}{2}\right)\hat{x} = \hat{w}.$$

Note that $(\hat{w}, \rho\hat{w}) \in T$. Therefore, $\hat{w} < x(r)/\rho^r$ implies, by free disposability A.5, that $(x(r)/\rho^r, \rho\hat{w}) \in T$. Hence, $(x(r), \rho^{r+1}\hat{w}) \in T$. On the other hand, because $x(s)/\rho^s < \hat{w}$, we can choose a positive vector $\hat{v}$ such that $x(s) + \rho^s\hat{v} < \rho^s\hat{w}$ and $\hat{v}$ is proportional to $\hat{x}$. But, as $(\rho^{s-1}\hat{w}, \rho^s\hat{w}) \in T$, free disposability A.5 implies that $(\rho^{s-1}\hat{w}, x(s) + \rho^s\hat{v}) \in T$. These results mean that the sequence of span N

$$x(0), \ldots, x(r), \rho^{r+1}\hat{w}, \rho^{r+2}\hat{w}, \ldots, \rho^{s-1}\hat{w}, x(s) + \rho^s\hat{v}, \ldots, x(N) + \rho^N\hat{v}$$

is feasible. Then applying (γ) to $x(N) + \rho^N\hat{v}$ and $x(N)$ entails $u(x(N) + \rho^N\hat{v}) > u(x(N))$, which contradicts the u-optimality of $\{x(t)\}_{t=0}^N$. The desired inequality will readily be obtained by combining these results together.

LEMMA 5   Under the same assumptions as in Lemma 4, we have

$$0 \leqq p'\frac{x(t)}{\rho^t} - p'\frac{x(t+1)}{\rho^{t+1}} < 4\eta \max_i[\|p\|, 1/\min \hat{x}_i]$$

for any t such that $r \leqq t \leqq s - 1$.

Proof   A simple evaluation of upper bounds, based on Lemma 4, gives, for r and s, with $r < s$,

$$0 \leqq p' \frac{x(r)}{\rho^r} - p' \frac{x(s)}{\rho^s} = \theta\left(\frac{x(r)}{\rho^r}\right) - \theta\left(\frac{x(s)}{\rho^s}\right) + p'\left(e\left(\frac{x(r)}{\rho^r}\right) - e\left(\frac{x(s)}{\rho^s}\right)\right)$$

$$\leqq \left|\theta\left(\frac{x(r)}{\rho^r}\right) - \theta\left(\frac{x(s)}{\rho^s}\right)\right| + \|p\|\left(\left\|e\left(\frac{x(r)}{\rho^r}\right)\right\| + \left\|e\left(\frac{x(s)}{\rho^s}\right)\right\|\right)$$

$$< 2\eta \max_i [\|p\|, 1/\min \hat{x}_i] + 2\eta\|p\| \leqq 4\eta \max_i [\|p\|, 1/\min \hat{x}_i].$$

Therefore, in view of (I) in Lemma 2, we finally have

$$0 \leqq p' \frac{x(t)}{\rho^t} - p' \frac{x(t+1)}{\rho^{t+1}} \leqq p' \frac{x(r)}{\rho^r} - p' \frac{x(s)}{\rho^s} < 4\eta \max_i [\|p\|, 1/\min \hat{x}_i]$$

for any t between r and $s - 1$.

2.5 We are now ready to prove the strong turnpike theorem.

Proof of the Theorem   As was proved by Radner,[11] for any $\varepsilon > 0$ we can choose a positive τ with $\rho > \tau$ such that $x \neq 0$, $(x, y) \in T$ and $\|x/\|x\| - \hat{x}\| \geqq \varepsilon$ imply $p'y \leqq \tau p'x$.

Now choose $\eta > 0$ and $\delta > 0$ in such a fashion that

$$4\eta \max_i [\|p\|, 1/\min \hat{x}_i] < \left(1 - \frac{\tau}{\rho}\right)\Gamma, \qquad (6)$$

$$\delta\Delta < \eta, \qquad (7)$$

$$\delta \leqq \varepsilon. \qquad (8)$$

Since A.1.–A.4. and (i)–(v) are assumed, the original Radner Turnpike Theorem holds, so that for this δ there is a number $k = k(\delta)$ such that

$$\left\|\frac{x(t)}{\|x(t)\|} - \hat{x}\right\| < \delta \qquad (9)$$

for any u-optimal sequences with $x(0) = x^o$ except for k periods. In view of (IV) in Lemma 2, it is noted that $\|x(t)\| > 0$ in (9). Now, suppose that $N > k$, and for each of these sequences let r and s be the first and last periods in which (9) is valid. Then,

$$\left\|\frac{x(r)}{\|x(r)\|} - \hat{x}\right\| < \delta \quad \text{and} \quad \left\|\frac{x(s)}{\|x(s)\|} - \hat{x}\right\| < \delta.$$

Accordingly, in view of (6), (7) and Lemmas 3 and 5, we have, for $r \leq t \leq s - 1$,

$$0 \leq p' \frac{x(t)}{\rho^t} - p' \frac{x(t+1)}{\rho^{t+1}} < (1 - \tau/\rho)\Gamma. \tag{10}$$

Suppose that for some t between r and $s - 1$ we would have $\|(x(t)/\|x(t)\|) - \hat{x}\| \geq \varepsilon$. Then, $p'x(t+1) \leq \tau p'x(t)$, so that

$$p' \frac{x(t)}{\rho^t} - p' \frac{x(t+1)}{\rho^{t+1}} \geq \left(1 - \frac{\tau}{\rho}\right) p' \frac{x(t)}{\rho^t} \geq \left(1 - \frac{\tau}{\rho}\right)\Gamma,$$

in the light of (I) and (IV) in Lemma 2. But this contradicts (10). Taking (8) into account, we have thereby shown that

$$\left\| \frac{x(t)}{\|x(t)\|} - \hat{x} \right\| < \varepsilon \quad (r \leq t \leq s).$$

Note that r and s may vary with the u-optimal sequence in question. But it is sure that $r + (N - s) \leq k$ by the very result due to Radner. Therefore, we have, *a fortiori*,

$$\left\| \frac{x(t)}{\|x(t)\|} - \hat{x} \right\| < \varepsilon \quad (k \leq t \leq N - k)$$

for any u-optimal sequences with $x(0) = x^o$ whenever $N \geq 2k$, as was to be shown.

3   Proof of the General Case

3.1   The general case in which A.5 holds no longer, but (α) is valid will be dealt with by imbedding the given system in an extended system where free disposability A.5 prevails. This will begin with enlarging the technology set T by means of the addition of all the conceivable disposal processes. Then it will be easy to show that the strong turnpike theorem holds in the enlarged system. The final necessary step of the argument will be to see that u-optimal sequences in the original system still remain u-optimal in the enlarged system.

3.2   The enlarged technology set, which will be called the *disposal hull* of T and designated by $\tilde{T}$, is defined by

$\tilde{T} = \{(\tilde{x}, \tilde{y}) | \tilde{x} \geq x, y \geq \tilde{y} \geq 0 \text{ for some } (x, y) \in T\}.$

An important, but immediate fact is that $\tilde{T}$ admits free disposability A.5.

3.3 We consider, for the time being, an economy having $\tilde{T}$ as a technology set but having the same preference indicator $u(x)$ as in the original system.

LEMMA 6   If A.1–A.4 and (i)–(v) together with (α), (β), and (γ) are assumed on T, the strong turnpike theorem holds for any u-optimal sequences in $\tilde{T}$, starting at x^o.

Proof If A.1–A.5 and (i)–(v) together with (β) and (γ) are shown to be satisfied in $\tilde{T}$, the lemma will be true by virtue of the result for the free disposal case proved in Section 2. To begin with, let us check on A.1 and A.2. The convexity, nonnegativity, and cone property of $\tilde{T}$ in A.1 as well as the impossibility of the land of Cockaigne, A.2, under the technology set $\tilde{T}$ are immediately seen, so that the proof may be omitted. We shall prove, however, the rather non-evident fact that $\tilde{T}$ is closed. In fact, let $(\tilde{x}^v, \tilde{y}^v) \in \tilde{T}$ $(v = 1, 2, \ldots)$ and $\lim \tilde{x}^v = \tilde{x}$, $\lim \tilde{y}^v = \tilde{y}$. There exist, by definition, $(x^v, y^v) \in T$ $(v = 1, 2, \ldots)$ such that $\tilde{x}^v \geq x^v \geq 0$, $y^v \geq \tilde{y}^v \geq 0$ $(v = 1, 2, \ldots)$. Since $\{\tilde{x}^v\}$ is convergent, $\{x^v\}$ is bounded. Then, the corresponding $\{y^v\}$ must be bounded,[12] by A.1 and A.2. Hence, we may assume, without loss of generality, that $\{x^v\}$ and $\{y^v\}$ converge to some x and y, respectively. Since T is closed, we have, in the limit, $\tilde{x} \geq x \geq 0$, $y \geq \tilde{y} \geq 0$ and $(x, y) \in T$, which proves that $(\tilde{x}, \tilde{y}) \in \tilde{T}$. Therefore $\tilde{T}$ is closed. Thus, A.1 and A.2 are also true for $\tilde{T}$. On the other hand, A.3 and A.4 are trivial, because they have no bearing on the technology set, whereas the prevalence of A.5 in $\tilde{T}$ was already noted. To see the prevalence of the remaining conditions (i)–(v), (β), and (γ), however, it suffices to note that the same $\hat{x}$, p, and ρ which served as von Neumann configurations for T can play the corresponding role for $\tilde{T}$. Indeed, take the same $\hat{x}$, p, and ρ. Then, (iii), (iv), (v), (β), and (γ), which are assumed to hold for T, automatically hold *a fortiori* in $\tilde{T}$, a super set of T. Let us show the validity of (i) and (ii) in $\tilde{T}$. First, (i.1) is trivially true. Next, for any $(\tilde{x}, \tilde{y}) \in \tilde{T}$, there is, by definition, some $(x, y) \in T$ such that $\tilde{x} \geq x$, $y \geq \tilde{y}$. In consequence, we have $p'(\tilde{y} - \rho\tilde{x}) \leq p'(y - \rho x) \leq 0$, proving (i.2). If, furthermore, $p'(\tilde{y} - \rho\tilde{x}) = 0$, then $\tilde{x} = x$, $\tilde{y} = y$, and $p'(y - \rho x) = 0$, because p is positive by Lemma 2. Therefore, by virtue of (ii) for T, $(\tilde{x}, \tilde{y})$ must be proportional to $(\hat{x}, \rho\hat{x})$, which proves (ii) for $\tilde{T}$. We have thereby shown that A.1–A.5, (i)–(v), together with (β) and (γ), are valid in $\tilde{T}$.

3.4 We now proceed to the next step of our argument. From a general point of view, an optimal sequence in the original technology set may cease to be optimal in a larger technology set. However, if (α) is assumed, and if the technology set is enlarged by the addition of disposal processes, it can be shown that no such possibility arises. To prove this plausible, yet non-evident fact, let us introduce the concept of additivity A.0, a structural property of the technology set which is weaker than A.1.

ASSUMPTION A.0   If (x^1, y^1) and (x^2, y^2) are in T, then $(x^1 + x^2, y^1 + y^2)$ is in T.

We shall prove

LEMMA 7   If T satisfies A.0, (α) and if $u(x)$ is nondecreasing, then any u-optimal sequence in T, starting at an x^o, remains to be u-optimal even in $\tilde{T}$.

Proof   Suppose that a u-optimal sequence $\{x(t)\}_{t=0}^N$ with $x(0) = x^o$ were not u-optimal in $\tilde{T}$. Then there would exist a feasible sequence $\{\tilde{x}(t)\}_{t=0}^N$ in $\tilde{T}$, with $\tilde{x}(0) = x^o$, such that

$$u(\tilde{x}(N)) > u(x(N)). \tag{11}$$

By definition, there are N pairs of input-output configurations (z^t, y^{t+1}) such that

$$(z^t, y^{t+1}) \in T \quad (t = 0, 1, \ldots, N - 1), \tag{12}$$

$$x^o = \tilde{x}(0) \geq z^o, \quad y^N \geq \tilde{x}(N), \quad y^t \geq \tilde{x}(t) \geq z^t \quad (t = 1, 2, \ldots, N - 1). \tag{13}$$

Since $x^o - z^o \geq 0$, there is, by (α), some v^1 such that $(x^o - z^o, v^1) \in T$. Then, in view of (13), $y^1 + v^1 - z^1 \geq 0$, so that, again by (α), there is some v^2 satisfying $(y^1 + v^1 - z^1, v^2) \in T$. Repeating this procedure we can obtain N pairs of input-output configurations in T, that is, $(x^o - z^o, v^1)$, $(y^t + v^t - z^t, v^{t+1})$ $(t = 1, 2, \ldots, N - 1)$. Thus, adding them to the corresponding configurations in (12), respectively, based on A.0, we finally get a feasible sequence in T of span N, starting at x^o,

$$x^o, y^1 + v^1, y^2 + v^2, \ldots, y^{N-1} + v^{N-1}, y^N + v^N.$$

But, in view of the nondecreasingness of $u(x)$, (11) and (13) imply $u(y^N + v^N) \geqq u(y^N) \geqq u(\tilde{x}(N)) > u(x(N))$, which contradicts the u-optimality of $\{x(t)\}_{t=0}^N$. This completes the proof.

3.5   We are now in a position to prove the Strong Turnpike Theorem under additional assumptions (α), (β), and (γ). In fact, by Lemma 7, any u-optimal sequence in T, starting at x^o, does not lose its u-optimality in $\tilde{T}$. And, by Lemma 6, the Strong Turnpike Theorem holds for u-optimal sequences in $\tilde{T}$. Therefore, it holds in particular for such sequences in T.

Notes

1. This research was based on a grant from the Ministry of Education, Japan. An earlier version of this paper was circulated as ISER Discussion Paper No. 27, June, 1962, The Institute of Social and Economic Research, Osaka University. The writer should like to acknowledge the stimulus he received upon reading the draft of a paper by Dr. J. Tsukui (1962) on a turnpike theorem for a Leontief type model. It was because of this paper that the writer was led to conjecture and prove the present results. He also benefited from valuable comments by D. Gale, N. Georgescu-Roegen, S. Ichimura, M. Morishima, and a referee of this paper.

2. For general expositions of the turnpike problem see Dorfman-Samuelson-Solow 1958 and Hicks 1961.

3. McKenzie 1963 and Tsukui 1962 are more recent contributions to the problem. They prove turnpike theorems for some Leontief-type models in the explicit presence of a capital coefficient matrix, but on some stringent assumptions.

4. Professor Inada was the first to point out this peculiar feature of the Radner turnpike theorem. Cf. McKenzie 1963. However. he also freed it from this peculiarity later in Inada 1964 independently of the present writer.

5. Radner did not assume convexity in proving his weak turnpike theorem. Our A.1 is just his assumption A1' in Radner 1961, p. 101.

6. See Radner 1961. The concept of quasi-homogeneity is irrelevant to our discussion, and so its definition may be omitted.

7. We follow Radner in assuming (ii), though, as he noted, it implicitly postulates some sort of strict convexity and therefore is not met by the Leontief type models, nor the original von Neumann model. See the introduction and Remark 1 of Radner 1961.

8. Regarding (iv) and (v), see Radner's Remarks 3 and 4 in Radner 1961.

9. Cf. Dorfman–Samuelson–Solow 1958 and Hicks 1961.

10. See Remarks 3 and 4 in Radner 1961.

11. See Lemma in Radner 1961, p. 102.

12. If $\|x^\nu\| \leqq \alpha$, $(x^\nu, y^\nu) \in T$ and $\lim \|y^\nu\| = \infty$, then we may assume that $(x^\nu/\|y^\nu\|, y^\nu/\|y^\nu\|)$ converges to some $(0, y) \in T$ with $y \neq 0$. This contradicts A.2.

References

Dorfman, R., P. A. Samuelson, and R. M. Solow (1958): *Linear Programming and Economic Analysis*, New York: McGraw-Hill.

Hicks, J. R. (1961): Prices and the Turnpike I: The Story of a Mare's Nest, *Review of Economic Studies*, Vol. XXVIII.

Inada, K. (1964): Some Structural Characteristics of Turnpike Theorems, *Review of Economic Studies*, Vol. XXXI.

McKenzie, L. W. (1963): Turnpike Theorems for a Generalized Leontief Model, *Econometrica*, Vol. 31.

Morishima, M. (1961): Proof of a Turnpike Theorem: The No Joint Production Case, *Review of Economic Studies*, Vol. XXVIII.

Radner, R. (1961): Paths of Economic Growth That Are Optimal with Regard Only to Final States: A Turnpike Theorem, *Review of Economic Studies*, Vol. XXVIII.

Tsukui, J. (1962): Efficient and Balanced Growth Paths in Dynamic Input-Output Systems —A Turnpike Theorem, *Rironkeizaigaku*, Vol. XIII.

8 Income Distribution and Growth in a Monopolist Economy

with Hiroshi Atsumi

1 Introduction

It may safely be presumed that the working of competitive economies, whether static or dynamic, and in a greater or less degree of aggregation, has been well explored. In particular, the existing price theory provides us with well-posed theories of income distribution in competitive economies in various degrees of aggregation, from the extremely disaggregative Walrasian general equilibrium model (Walras 1954) to the Solovian aggregate model of neoclassical type (Solow 1956). On the other hand, little has been known about the income distribution aspects of a national economy involving noncompetitive features. The traditional theory of imperfect competition can shed little light on this problem, although its primal objective seems to be a revision of the classical price theory by paying attention to market imperfection and thereby making the classical theory applicable to noncompetitive economies. However, the traditional oligopoly theorist has indulged in partial equilibrium theoretic analyses of a single firm's behavior or a market involving several or many firms. Indeed, his theory has come to get a flavor of realism. But, it has degenerated to a theory of market structures, rather than a theory of income distribution on a national economy basis.

Information about the inter-relations between the behaviors of firms in a specific market alone can hardly give us insight into the income distribution aspects of a national economy. Such information is expected to be obtainable only if interdependence between all economic agents' shares to national income is taken into explicit account, as is the case with all the existing income distribution theories for competitive equilibria. Typical examples are the Walrasian general equilibrium theory (Walras 1954), the Solovian growth theory (Solow 1956), a theory of income distribution in the long-run and its variants, e.g. Uzawa (1962). In sharp contrast to our fairly satisfactory knowledge about the mechanisms of income distribution under competitive pricing, there is no competent counterpart knowledge about noncompetitive situations. One of the reasons why we have few income distribution theories for noncompetitive situations may be that it is generally difficult to obtain a well-posed inter-relations between all economic agents' shares to national income in a noncompetitive situation.

With Hiroshi Atsumi. Reprinted from *Zeitschrift für Nationalökonomie* 28 (1968): 399–416.

The oligopoly theorist analyses firms' behaviors in terms of perceived demand functions. These functions are a source of grave difficulty. Their interdependence in a national economy as a whole is not known to him, so that he can not conceive income distribution. In order to build a theory of income distribution in a noncompetitive economy, it is necessary either to explore the submerged part of the existing oligopoly theory, namely, the interdependence of the relevant perceived demand functions or to invent alternative constructions replacing demand and supply functions.

Nevertheless there is an exceptional case in this regard, which we can meet with the existing analytical machinery. This is a counterpart case under monopolistic pricing of the Solovian neoclassical growth, and our principal purpose in this paper is to consider income distribution and growth in this counterpart situation, including the comparison of the long-run equilibrium real wage rate under monopolistic pricing with that under competitive pricing.

It should also be emphasized that both the model and behavioral principles in this paper by no means claim for realism. They are intended to be only normative constructions and are posed to conceive a hypothetical situation in an extreme opposite direction to perfect competition, another hypothetical situation.

The Model and Income Distribution in the Short-run

The two basic postulates are the technological possibilities representable by a neoclassical type production function and the existence of a supply function of labor. We are concerned with a one-sector model in which GNP as an aggregate magnitude is produced and allocated to both consumption and investment. Let

K = capital stock,

L = labor supply,

ω = real wage rate.

Assumptions $(F.1)$–$(F.6)$ on technological possibilities are premised:

$(F.1)$ There is a neoclassical production function $F(K, L)$, which represents GNP in real terms produced when K units of capital stock and L units of labor service are employed. Mathematically, this function is continuous for $K \geq 0$ and $L \geq 0$, and has continuous partial derivatives up to the second order for $K > 0$ and $L > 0$.

(F.2) $F(0, L) = F(K, 0) = 0$. That is, both capital and labor are indispensable in production.

(F.3)   Constant returns to scale prevail. In other words, $F(K, L)$ is homogeneous of the first degree.

(F.4)   Marginal productivities $F_K(K, L)$ and $F_L(K, L)$ are positive for $K > 0$ and $L > 0$.

(F.5) $F_K(K, L)$ is strictly decreasing with respect to K for each fixed level of L and

$$\lim_{K \to 0} F_K(K, L) = +\infty, \tag{1}$$

$$\lim_{K \to +\infty} F_K(K, L) = 0. \tag{2}$$

(F.6) $F_L(K, L)$ is strictly decreasing with respect to L for each fixed level of K and

$$\lim_{L \to 0} F_L(K, L) = +\infty, \tag{3}$$

$$\lim_{L \to +\infty} F_L(K, L) = 0. \tag{4}$$

Assumptions (L.1)–(L.3) are imposed on the supply function of labor.

(L.1)   The supply function of labor $\omega(L)$ is a continuous function which represents the real wage rate claimed by workers when L units of labor service $L \geq 0$ are supplied. It has a continuous second derivative for $L > 0$.

(L.2) $\omega(0) = 0$. That is, there is no substistence minimum level of real wage rate.

(L.3) $\omega'(L)$ is positive for $L > 0$.

(L.4) $\omega'(L)$ is strictly increasing for $L > 0$.

A few words will be in order here about some of the above assumptions that might cause doubt among the readers. First, there may be objections to assuming constant returns to scale (F.3) and diminishing marginal productivities (F.5) and (F.6) in a noncompetitive situation. In an orthodox

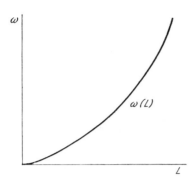

Figure 8.1

formulation a production function in a macroscopic sense should represent a mixture of the technological possibilities and the characteristics of the market structure. But, here we conceive the production function to present only purely technological possibilities, while isolating market imperfections as a specific noncompetitive mode of pricing. This is necessitated by our not accepting the orthodox constructions based on the concept of a perceived demand function in the oligopoly theory.

Second, one who knows the familiar shape of a short-run labor supply function like Fig. 8.2 in a discussion along with the orthodox line, might be out of tune with the shape of a labor supply function given in Fig. 8.1 illustrating assumptions $(L.1)$–$(L.4)$. The shape of the function in Fig. 8.1 differs in two features from that in Fig. 8.2. That is, both the existence of a substistence minimum level of real wage rate and presence of backward-bending. These two points will be touched on in the supplementary remarks in the final section. Here, we just point out that the absence of a substistence minimum level of real wage rate is assumed as a sufficient condition to ensure a steady growth state as in Solow's result, and that the presence of backward-bending phenomena causes no serious trouble, so that we can obtain the same results for a backward-bending labor supply function.

Now, we presume that the short-run determination of the level of GNP and its distribution between two classes of economic agents, namely, capitalists and workers, are worked out in the following simple way. All capitalists cooperate against workers and jointly maximize their total profits in *real* terms

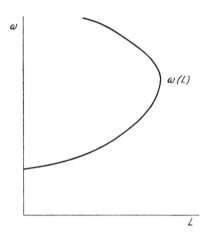

Figure 8.2

$$F(K, L) - \omega(L)L \tag{5}$$

by controlling the volume of employment L for a given amount of capital stock K. This is a situation where capitalists are so powerful that they jointly secure a maximum possible level of real output.

For any positive level of K, the maximand (5) takes on a maximum for a unique positive level of L,[1] so that the following well-known condition holds at this maximizing L:

$$F_L(K, L) = \omega(L) + \omega'(L)L. \tag{6}$$

3   The Dynamic Process of Capital Accumulation

Assuming Equ. (6) as the fundamental principle governing the short-run temporary equilibrium, we shall consider the dynamic process of capital accumulation generated by interweaving these temporary equilibria.

It is now assumed that the labor supply function is a function not only of the labor supply L but also of the time t. Explicitly, the labor supply function is assumed to take the form

$$\omega(e^{-nt}L), \tag{7}$$

where n is interpreted as a rate of population growth. As a matter of fact, the function $\omega(L)$ used to define (7) is assumed to fulfill conditions (L.1)–(L.4).

At each moment of time t, capitalists maximize jointly their total profits

$$F[K(t), L] - \omega(e^{-nt}L)L \tag{8}$$

by controlling the volume of employment L. The condition for a maximum of (8), a counterpart of (6) is

$$F_L[K(t), L] = \omega(e^{-nt}L) + \omega'(e^{-nt}L)e^{-nt}L. \tag{9}$$

Equ. (9) determines the level of employment at time t as a function of both $K(t)$ and t, obtaining

$$L[K(t), t]. \tag{10}$$

Now, let us introduce two new variables k and l, which are defined by

$$k = Ke^{-nt}, \quad l = Le^{-nt}. \tag{11}$$

Then, in terms of these new variables, Equ. (9) reduces to

$$F_L[k(t), l] = \omega(l) + \omega'(l)l, \tag{12}$$

because of the zeroth degree homogeneity of $F_L(K, L)$. Equ. (12) can be immediately obtained by replacing K and L in Equ. (6) by $k(t)$ and l, so that both equations are essentially the same. Equ. (12) determines the level of l for a given level of k, so that we have a function $l(k)$, which has a continuous derivative because of $(F.1)$ and $(L.1)$. Therefore, the level of employment at time t, (10), is in actuality a function of a simple form, written as

$$L[K(t), t] = l[k(t)]e^{nt}. \tag{13}$$

Now that the level of GNP and its distribution to both classes, capitalists and workers, at time t are determined, let their consumption-saving patterns come into the picture. We assume that workers only consume but never save, whereas capitalists may both consume and save. This peculiar spending pattern of workers, which is classical, is assumed just because we are concerned with a special situation where the ownership of capital is exclusively monopolized by capitalists.

Let s and μ be the aggregate propensity to save of capitalists and the rate of depreciation, which are assumed to be constant. Then we have

$$\frac{dK}{dt} = s\{F[K, L(K, t)] - \omega[e^{-nt}L(K, t)]L(K, t)\} - \mu K, \tag{14}$$

the differential equation governing the process of capital accumulation. Equ. (14) can be transformed into the corresponding differential equation in the variable k. In fact, upon differentiating $k = Ke^{-nt}$ with respect to time t, we obtain

$$\frac{dk}{dt} = \frac{dK}{dt}e^{-nt} - nk. \tag{15}$$

Thus, Equs. (14) and (15), combined with the first degree homogeneity of the production function (F.3), together yield

$$\frac{dk}{dt} = s\{F[k, l(k)] - \omega[l(k)]l(k)\} - \lambda k, \tag{16}$$

where

$$\lambda = n + \mu.$$

Equ. (16) is our basic equation, whose solution traces out economic growth under monopolistic pricing.

4   The Steady Growth State

The purpose of this section is to show the possibility, uniqueness and global asymptotic stability of steady growth state in the capital accumulation process under monopolistic pricing, which is depicted by the differential Equ. (16).

The statement of the main results and their demonstration will be preceded by a simple consideration of the behavior of the capital labor ratio $k/l(k)$ as a function of k.

LEMMA   The reciprocal $l(k)/k$ of the capital labor ratio possesses the following two properties (i) and (ii):

(i) $\lim\limits_{k \to +\infty} l(k)/k = 0.$

(ii) $\lim\limits_{k \to 0} l(k)/k = +\infty,$

Proof

(i)   Suppose the contrary and assume that there is a subsequence (k_v) fulfilling

$$\lim_{\nu \to +\infty} k_\nu = +\infty, \tag{17}$$

$$l(k_\nu)/k_\nu \geqq \varepsilon \quad (\nu = 1, 2, \ldots) \tag{18}$$

for a positive number $\varepsilon > 0$.

The function $l(k)$ is defined by Equ. (12), whence we have

$$F_L[k_\nu, l(k_\nu)] = \omega[l(k_\nu)] + \omega'[l(k_\nu)]l(k_\nu). \tag{19}$$

Equ. (19) implies, in the light of (18),

$$F_L(1, \varepsilon) \geqq \omega[l(k_\nu)] + \omega'[l(k_\nu)]l(k_\nu), \tag{20}$$

since $F_L(K, L)$ is homogeneous of degree zero by $(F.3)$, the first degree homogeneity of $F(K, L)$, and is decreasing with respect to L for a fixed level of K by $(F.6)$. Therefore, the right-hand side of (20) must be bounded. On the other hand, (18) can be rearranged to

$$l(k_\nu) \geqq \varepsilon k_\nu \quad (\nu = 1, 2, \ldots)$$

which yields

$$\lim_{\nu \to +\infty} l(k_\nu) = +\infty. \tag{21}$$

We recall that $\omega'(L)$ is positive and increasing by $(L.3)$ and $(L.4)$ and that $\omega(L)$ is also nonnegative. Hence, (21) lets the right-hand side of (20) tend to infinity, which contradicts the boundedness of the right-hand side of (20) established before.

(ii)   The proof is similar, and supposition of the existence of a subsequence (k_ν) fulfilling

$$\lim_{\nu \to +\infty} k_\nu = 0, \tag{22}$$

$$l(k_\nu)/k_\nu \leqq M \quad (\nu = 1, 2, \ldots) \tag{23}$$

for a positive bound $M > 0$ will lead to

$$F_L(1, M) \leqq \omega[l(k_\nu)] + \omega'[l(k_\nu)]l(k_\nu), \tag{24}$$

a counterpart of (20). The right-hand side of (24) must be bounded from below by a positive bound, because of the positive marginal productivity $F_L(1, M) > 0$. On the other hand, (23) can be rearranged to

$$l(k_\nu) \leqq M k_\nu \quad (\nu = 1, 2, \ldots),$$

ensuring

$$\lim_{v \to +\infty} l(k_v) = 0. \tag{25}$$

Therefore we must have

$$\lim_{v \to +\infty} \omega[l(k_v)] = \omega\left[\lim_{v \to +\infty} l(k_v)\right] = \omega(0) = 0 \tag{26}$$

by (25), (L.1) and (L.2). Moreover, by (25) and (L.4), we also have

$$\lim_{v \to +\infty} \omega'[l(k_v)]l(k_v) = 0. \tag{27}$$

Thus, (26) and (27) let the right-hand side of (24) tend to zero, which contradicts its lower boundedness by a positive bound. The proof is thereby complete. It should be noted that proposition (ii) above owes its validity to the absence of a positive substistence minimum level of real wage rate, and that it may fail to hold in the reverse situation. On the other hand, Proposition (i) does not rely on the specific shape of our labor supply function, but remains to be true even for a backward-bending labor supply function of the customary type, as will be considered later in section 6.

Propositions (i) and (ii) in the foregoing lemma are crucial in establishing the possibility of a steady growth state, which may justify the detailed statement of their mathematical demonstration above. We are now in a position to establish the existence of a steady growth state.

THEOREM 1   There is a steady growth solution

$$k(t) = k^* \tag{28}$$

of Equ. (16), where k^* is a positive constant; that is, there is a long-run equilibrium.

Proof   As is well known, a positive number k^* defines a steady growth solution (28) of Equ. (16), if and only if k^* lets the right-hand side of (16) vanish, that is to say, k^* is a solution of the equation

$$s\{F[k, l(k)] - \omega[l(k)]l(k)\} - \lambda k = 0. \tag{29}$$

Let $\Phi(k)$ denote the function on the left-hand side of Equ. (29). In order to see that the function $\Phi(k)$ vanishes for a positive value of k, we shall first establish the following two facts: α) $\Phi(k)$ is negative for large values of k, and β) $\Phi(k)$ is positive for very small values of k. Once these two facts are established, the vanishingness of $\Phi(k)$ somewhere in between is automatically ensured by the continuity of the function. Therefore, it suffices to prove α) and β).

α)   is seen as follows. Taking the first degree homogeneity of $F(K, L)$ and the positivity of $\omega[l(k)]l(k)$ into account, we observe

$$\Phi(k) \leqq sF[k, l(k)] - \lambda k = k\{sF[1, l(k)/k] - \lambda\}. \tag{30}$$

On the other hand,

$$\lim_{k \to +\infty} l(k)/k = 0$$

by Proposition (i) in the foregoing lemma, so that

$$\lim_{k \to +\infty} F[1, l(k)/k] = F(1, 0) = 0$$

by the continuity of $F(K, L)$ and the indispensability of labor. Hence the second factor of the formula on the extreme right-hand side of (30) approaches $-\lambda$ as k tends to infinity. Whence the right-hand side of (30) becomes negative for large values of k. From the majorization (30) it is now clear that $\Phi(k)$ becomes negative for large values of k.

β)   is seen as follows. In the light of Euler's theorem as applied to $F(K, L)$, a homogeneous function of the first degree, the function $\Phi(k)$ can be rearranged to

$$\Phi(k) = s(\{F_K[k, l(k)] - \lambda/s\}k + \{F_L[k, l(k)] - \omega[l(k)]\}l(k)). \tag{31}$$

The second term of the expression in the parentheses is always positive, because the marginal productivity of labor $F_L[k, l(k)]$ exceeds the real wage rate $\omega(k)$ by (12), and $l(k)$ is positive. The first term, too, becomes positive, as k approaches zero, for the following reason. In fact, by Proposition (ii) in the foregoing lemma, we have

$$\lim_{k \to 0} l(k)/k = +\infty,$$

so that

$$\lim_{k \to 0} F_K[k, l(k)] = \lim_{k \to 0} F_K[k/l(k), 1] = +\infty \tag{32}$$

by the zeroth degree homogeneity of $F_K(K, L)$ and (1) in assumption $(F.5)$ on the marginal productivity of capital. (32) ensures that the first term of the expression in the parentheses in (31) becomes positive for small positive values of k. Hence (31) becomes positive for small positive values of k. This completes the proof.

Now that the existence of a steady growth solution is established, we shall consider its uniqueness and global asymptotic stability in the remaining part of the present section.

THEOREM 2   (i) The steady growth level k^* of k is uniquely determined. (ii) The unique steady growth state is asymptotically globally stable; i.e., if k^* is the unique steady growth level of k, for any solution $k(t)$ of Equ. (16), starting at any historically given initial position $k(0) > 0$, we have

$$\lim_{t \to +\infty} k(t) = k^*. \tag{33}$$

Proof   Both propositions (i) and (ii) follow from a simple property of the function $\Phi(k)$ given by the left-hand side of Equ. (29).

To observe this property, we first note the derivative $\Phi'(k)$ of $\Phi(k)$ is given by

$$\Phi'(k) = sF_K[k, l(k)] - \lambda. \tag{34}$$

In fact, upon differentiation, we obtain

$$\Phi'(k) = sF_K[k, l(k)] - \lambda$$
$$+ s\{F_L[k, l(k)] - \omega[l(k)] - \omega'[l(k)]l(k)\}l'(k). \tag{35}$$

But the expression in the braces on the right-hand side of (35) vanishes by (12), so that (35) reduces to (34).

Next, let k^* be a steady growth level of k. Then, by the expression of $\Phi(k)$ in (31), we have

$$\Phi(k^*) = s(\{F_K[k^*, l(k^*)] - \lambda/s\}k^*$$
$$+ \{F_L[k^*, l(k^*)] - \omega[l(k^*)]\}l(k^*)) = 0. \tag{36}$$

As was already noted in the consideration of (31), the second term of the expression in the braces in (36) is positive by virtue of the exceeding marginal productivity of labor over the real wage rate. Whence its first term must be negative, so long as both terms add up to zero in (36). Hence we have

$$\Phi'(k^*) = sF_K[k^*, l(k^*)] - \lambda < 0. \tag{37}$$

It should be noted that the truth of (37) is valid for any steady growth level k^* of k. Geometrically, this means that the graph of the function $\Phi(k)$ must have a negative slope at any point at which it crosses the k-axis, and therefore rules out its multiple crossings with the k-axis for $k > 0$. For such a crossing must be from the region $\Phi > 0$ to the opposite one $\Phi < 0$, and if two crossings occurred, there would be a third crossing at some point in between from the region $\Phi < 0$ to the other $\Phi > 0$, which is a contradiction. We have thereby proved proposition (i). Now let k^* be the unique steady growth level of k. We recall that the function $\Phi(k)$ is positive for small positive values of k and negative for large positive values of k, a fact noted in the course of the proof of Theorem 1. This implies that the function $\Phi(k)$ must be positive for positive levels of k less than k^* and negative for levels of k larger than k^*. For otherwise, the function would be either negative for some positive level k' less than k^* or positive for some level k'' larger than k^*. In the former case $\Phi(k)$ must vanish at some positive level of k still less than k^* by its continuity, because it becomes positive for very small positive values of k. This contradicts the uniqueness of steady growth level, and hence the former case is ruled out. Likewise the latter case is ruled out. Thus there must be the convergence toward k^* of the solution of Equ. (16) in the direction marked with the arrows in Fig. 8.3. This proves proposition (ii).

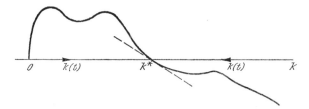

Figure 8.3

5 Comparison to the Solovian Competitive Growth

The preceding sections have established that there is a unique stable steady growth even under monopolistic pricing, such that the movements of the relevant variables are given by

$$K(t) = k^* e^{nt}, \tag{38}$$

$$L(t) = l(k^*) e^{nt}, \tag{39}$$

$$\omega = \omega[l(k^*)], \tag{40}$$

where k^* is the unique solution of Equ. (29). The dynamic performance of the economy is therefore very similar to that of the Solovian competitive economy in the presence of a labor supply function. The reader may wonder how economic growth under monopolistic pricing differs from the competitive one, and may argue that the results in the preceding sections are not too much informative unless comparison is made between the magnitudes of the relevant variables in both situations such as the real wage rates, capital labor ratios and volumes of employment. This section will be devoted to this important issue.

To this end, let us first formulate a steady growth state in the Solovian competitive economy in the presence of a labor supply function, with which the steady growth state under monopolistic pricing will be compared. We are concerned principally with comparison between two economies which are endowed with the same technologies and labor supply function but differ from each other only in the mode of pricing.

Suppose now that capitalists behave as price-takers in the economy endowed with the same production function satisfying (F.1)–(F.6) and the same labor supply function satisfying (L.1)–(L.4). Capitalists adapt themselves to a given real wage rate so as to achieve their maximum profits. Thus a demand function for labor emerges, and the level of real wage rate is determined in such a way that the demand for labor equals the supply of labor. Therefore, at time t when the labor supply function is given by (7), the short-run volume of employment l relative to e^{nt} for a given capital stock level $k(t)$ relative to e^{nt} is determined by

$$F_L[k(t), l] = \omega(l), \tag{41}$$

stated in terms of the variables k and l in (11). Equ. (41) is a counterpart in the competitive situation of Equ. (12) in the monopolistic case.

As a matter of course, the value of l determined by Equ. (41) differs from that determined by Equ. (12), even if the given level of k is the same. Therefore we shall henceforth denote the competitive level of employment determined by (41) by $l_c(k)$ to distinguish it from the $l(k)$ determined by (12).

If we retain the assumptions on the consumption-saving patterns of capitalists and workers, the corresponding differential equation depicting the capital accumulation process in the competitive situation is

$$\frac{dk}{dt} = s\{F[k, l_c(k)] - \omega[l_c(k)]l_c(k)\} - \lambda k, \tag{42}$$

a counterpart of Equ. (16).

Equ. (42) differs only in the employment function $l_c(k)$ from Equ. (16), and we can readily establish a unique stable steady growth solution of Equ. (42) as in the monopolistic case. Therefore let us denote by k_c^* the corresponding unique steady growth level of k in the competitive situation.

We have now the four relevant values

$$k^*/l(k^*)\{= k^*e^{nt}/l(k^*)e^{nt} = K^*(t)/L^*[K^*(t), t]\}$$

   = the long-run capital labor ratio in the monopolistic case,

$$\omega^* = \omega[l(k^*)]$$

   = the long-run real wage rate in the monopolistic case,

$$k_c^*/l_c(k_c^*)\{= k_c^*e^{nt}/l_c(k_c^*)e^{nt} = K_c^*(t)/L_c^*[K_c^*(t), t]\}$$

   = the long-run capital labor ratio in the competitive case,

$$\omega_c^* = \omega[l_c(k_c^*)]$$

   = the long-run real wage rate in the competitive case,

and are particularly interested in comparing $k^*/l(k^*)$ with $k_c^*/l_c(k_c^*)$ and $\omega[l(k^*)]$ with $\omega[l_c(k_c^*)]$.

From both Equs. (12) and (41), it is clear that for a given level of k, the employment $l(k)$ under monopolistic pricing is always less than the employment $l_c(k)$ in the competitive situation, and hence the corresponding real wage rate $\omega[l(k)]$ is lower than the competitive real wage rate $\omega[l_c(k)]$. This comparison is, however, for a common level of k. In the actual dynamic processes, $k(t)$ under monopolistic pricing differs generally from $k(t)$ in the competitive situation. On this ground, what is more important is the comparison of both long-run equilibrium states.

Let us recall the mode of monopolistic pricing. In each temporary equilibrium the real wage rate is priced so as to secure a maximum real output for capitalists, whose constant portion, that is, its 100s percent, is invested. It is anticipated that this mechanism will result in a more intensive capital accumulation than in the competitive situation, and will achieve a long-run capital labor ratio greater than that in the competitive situation. In the long-run, therefore, the marginal productivity of labor is higher in the monopolistic situation than that in the competitive situation. One might therefore surmise that even if the real wage rate falls short of the marginal productivity of labor in the long-run equilibrium under monopoly, it can possibly still exceed the long-run competitive real wage rate. Of these conjectures, the first one for a higher capital labor ratio under monopoly is true, whereas the second one for a higher real wage rate under monopoly is false. These results will be stated and demonstrated below.

THEOREM 3   In the long-run comparison we have:

(i)   The capital labor ratio $k^*/l(k^*)$ under monopoly is greater than the corresponding ratio $k_c^*/l_c(k_c^*)$ in the competitive situation, that is,

$$k^*/l(k^*) > k_c^*/l_c(k_c^*). \tag{43}$$

(ii)   The real wage rate $\omega[l(k^*)]$ under monopoly is lower than the corresponding rate $\omega[l_c(k_c^*)]$ in the competitive situation, that is,

$$\omega[l(k^*)] < \omega[l_c(k_c^*)]. \tag{44}$$

Proof   By definition, k^* satisfies Equ. (29). Likewise k_c^* satisfies

$$s\{F[k, l_c(k)] - \omega[l_c(k)]l_c(k)\} - \lambda k = 0. \tag{29c}$$

From these facts, combined with the first degree homogeneity of the production function, it follows that both long-run real wage rates ω^* and ω_c^* can be expressed as

$$\omega^* = F[k^*/l(k^*), 1] - \frac{\lambda}{s}k^*/l(k^*),$$

$$\omega_c^* = F[k_c^*/l_c(k_c^*), 1] - \frac{\lambda}{s}k_c^*/l_c(k_c^*).$$

Whence, if we let

$$\Omega(\theta) = F(\theta, 1) - \frac{\lambda}{s}\theta, \tag{45}$$

ω^* and ω_c^* are given by

$$\omega^* = \Omega[k^*/l(k^*)], \tag{46}$$

$$\omega_c^* = \Omega[k_c^*/l_c(k_c^*)]. \tag{46c}$$

On the other hand, k^* fulfills (37), and therefore also the following condition

$$F_K[k^*/l(k^*), 1] < \frac{\lambda}{s} \tag{47}$$

by virtue of the zeroth degree homogeneity of the marginal productivity of capital. As a counterpart condition for $k_c^*/l_c(k_c^*)$ we can derive

$$F_K[k_c^*/l_c(k_c^*), 1] = \frac{\lambda}{s} \tag{47c}$$

as will be shown below. In fact, if we denote by $\Phi_c(k)$ the right-hand side of Equ. (42), then we obtain, as a counterpart relation of (36),

$$\Phi_c(k_c^*) = s(\{F_K[k_c^*, l_c(k_c^*)] - \lambda/s\}k_c^*$$
$$+ \{F_L[k_c^*, l_c(k_c^*)] - \omega[l_c(k_c^*)]\}l_c(k_c^*)) = 0. \tag{36c}$$

However, in the competitive case we have the equality of the marginal productivity of labor to the real wage rate, so that the second term in the braces in (36c) vanishes. Hence the first term also vanishes. Thus, we can derive (47c) from

$$F_k[k_c^*, l_c(k_c^*)] - \lambda/s = 0$$

by virtue of the zeroth degree homogeneity of the marginal productivity of capital.

Now, in the light of the strict concavity of the function $\Omega(\theta)$ given by (45), we observe that condition (47c) implies that the function $\Omega(\theta)$ is maximized at $\theta = k_c^*/l_c(k_c^*)$, whereas $\Omega[k^*/l(k^*)]$ does not afford a maximum because of condition (47). Hence, in view of (46) and (46c), we have

$$\omega^* < \omega_c^*,$$

proving proposition (ii). Moreover, by virtue of the diminishing marginal productivity of capital, conditions (47) and (47c) ensure

$$k^*/l(k^*) > k_c^*/l_c(k_c^*),$$

which establishes proposition (i).

Fig. 8.4 illustrates the assertion of Theorem 3 as well as the situation that lets the theorem hold, and that is discussed formally in the proof above. It is thereby realized that there is an overaccumulation of capital in the long-run equilibrium under monopoly that exceeds the socalled Golden Age level of capital accumulation in the competitive situation, while the corresponding real wage rate under monopoly being lower than the Golden Age rate. Moreover, from Proposition (ii) and the monotone property of the labor supply function it is also clear that $l(k^*) < l_c(k_c^*)$.

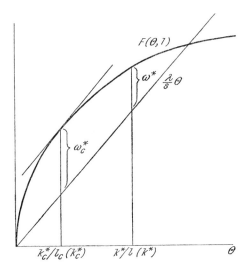

Figure 8.4

Therefore, the total wage bill $\omega[l(k^*)]l(k^*)e^{nt}$ in the steady growth under monopoly also falls short of $\omega[l_c(k_c^*)]l_c(k_c^*)e^{nt}$, that in the Golden Age.

Let us turn to the consideration of the reward to capital. From the definition of a steady growth state, λ/s is the common rate of reward to capital in both situations. However, there is a difference in total rewards due to the inequality between the levels of capital stock in both steady growth states. More explicitly, the total reward to capital in the steady growth under monopoly is greater than that in the competitive steady growth, as can be justified by the following:

THEOREM 4   In the long-run equilibrium the level of capital stock under monopoly always exceeds that in the competitive situation, that is,

$$k^*e^{nt} > k_c^*e^{nt}$$

over time.

Proof   Let us compare the function $\Phi(k)$, the right-hand side of Equ. (16), to the function $\Phi_c(k)$, the right-hand side of Equ. (42). For easier reference, it is convenient to have their explicit forms again here, i.e.,

$$\Phi(k) = s\{F[k, l(k)] - \omega[l(k)]l(k)\} - \lambda k,$$

$$\Phi_c(k) = s\{F[k, l_c(k)] - \omega[l_c(k)]l_c(k)\} - \lambda k.$$

k^* is a unique solution of the equation $\Phi(k) = 0$, whereas k_c^* is a unique solution of the equation $\Phi_c(k) = 0$. Now, both functions $\Phi(k)$ and $\Phi_c(k)$ have the same second term $-\lambda k$, and differ only in the first terms. If we recall the mode of the short-run pricing under monopoly, namely, the maximization of the profit $F(k, l) - \omega(l)l$ for a given k over all l, we must have

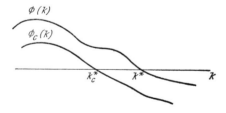

Figure 8.5

$$F[k, l(k)] - \omega[l(k)]l(k) > F[k, l_c(k)] - \omega[l_c(k)]l_c(k)$$

for any level of k. Hence

$$\Phi(k) > \Phi_c(k)$$

for any level of k. In other words, the graph of $\Phi(k)$ lies over that of $\Phi_c(k)$, as is illustrated in Fig. 8.5. In such a situation, k^*, at which the graph of $\Phi(k)$ crosses the k-axis, must lie to the right of k_c^*, at which the graph of $\Phi_c(k)$ crosses the k-axis. Whence $k^* > k_c^*$, proving the theorem.

6 Remarks on the Shape of the Labor Supply Function

The purpose of this supplementary section is to observe what will happen when the labor supply function like that in Fig. 8.1 is replaced by a function of the orthodox type like that in Fig. 8.2, which bends back and has a subsistence minimum level of real wage rate. Of these two peculiar properties, the first one, the presence of a subsistence minimum level of real wage rate, affects the above results, while the second one, a bending-back phenomenon, causes no influence on them.

Let us begin with checking the second property, a bending-back phenomenon. It is quite readily seen that this second property alone can not cause any trouble. In fact, more concretely, let us consider a situation where the labor supply function illustrated in Fig. 8.1 is replaced by a function like that in Fig. 8.6, which bends backward but has no positive subsistence minimum level of real wage rate. Then all the results in the foregoing sections remain to be true *mutatis mutandis*, for the following reasons. First of all, if two levels of real wage rate may correspond to a level of employment, monopoly capitalists are interested only in the lower level. Therefore it is obvious that the bent back part of the labor supply function in Fig. 8.6 is irreveant to them and only its remaining lower part is important. Hence, in substance, they are. assumed to be confronted with a labor supply function as illustrated in Fig. 8.7, which is obtained by removing the bent back portion from the function in Fig. 8.6. Then, it turns out that capitalists maximize their total profits by controlling the level of employment just over the interval between zero and the highest possible level of employment N. Since this interval is closed and bounded, the total profits can be maximized somewhere in this interval because of continuity. Moreover, maximization occurs at some interior point of the

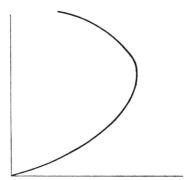

Figure 8.6

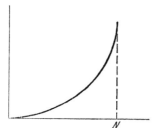

Figure 8.7

interval, because the marginal productivity of labor tends to infinity at
zero, the left endpoint of the interval, and the labor supply function has a
vertical tangent at N, the right endpoint of the interval. Therefore, we
obtain still Equ. (6) as the basic relation defining the short-run level of
employment.

We recall the importance of the lemma in Section 4 for all the subsequent discussion, in particular, for the consolidation of a unique stable
steady growth state. It should be emphasized that the lemma remains to
be true for a labor supply function as illustrated in Fig. 8.7. In fact,
Proposition (i) can be proved more easily this time than for a function as
illustrated in Fig. 8.1, for the following reason. $l(k)$ is defined by Equ. (12)
as before. However, $l(k)$ satisfies $N > l(k) > 0$ for any level of k this time.
From this boundedness of $l(k)$ proposition (i) follows immediately. On the
other hand, the proof of proposition (ii) can be worked out in completely
the same way as before, since the behavior of the labor supply function in

question in the vicinity of zero is unchanged. This argument is also applicable to the discussion of the competitive growth with a labor supply function as illustrated in Fig. 8.7 *mutatis mutandis*. Thus, the comparative results in Section 5 also remain to hold for a labor supply function like that in Fig. 8.7.

Next, we consider the second of the two peculiar properties of the labor supply function in question. If we review the proof of proposition (ii) in the lemma in Section 4, then we realize how heavily the truth of the proposition relies on the convergence toward zero of $\omega(l)$ with the convergence toward zero of l. When there is a positive subsistence minimum level of real wage rate, which implies the limit of $\omega(l)$ as $l \to 0$ is positive, Proposition (ii) may fail to hold. In such a situation it may be possible that the function $\Phi(k)$, the right-hand side of Equ. (16), never vanishes, but is identically negative. Thus, there will be no steady growth, and the economy will decline relative to e^{nt}. Still worse, in the presence of a positive subsistence minimum level of real wage rate, too high relative to the productivity ensured by the existing level of capital stock and technologies, even the maximum total profits of monopoly capitalists are negative, so that the economy may not be workable even in the short-run.

Finally, it should be emphasized that the above argument by no means implies that the presence of a positive subsistence minimum level of real wage rate necessarily rules out the possibility of a unique stable steady growth state. In spite of such wage rigidity, steady growth is possible under circumstances, and once it is possible, it must be uniquely determinate as well as stable. For Theorem 2 is valid for any possible steady growth level of k.

Notes

For the valuable comments and criticism given to the earlier version of this paper the authors wish to thank Professor K. Saito of Osaka University as well as to the participants in research seminars at University of California, Berkeley and Cowles Foundation for Research in Economics, New Haven. As a matter of course, the authors assume sole responsibility for any remaining errors.

1. A brief sketch of mathematical justification of this statement is as follows. The maximand takes negative values for large L, because $F(K, L) - \omega(L) L = L[F(K/L, 1) - \omega(L)]$, and $F(K/L, 1)$ tends to zero as $L \to +\infty$. Let L^* be a large positive number such that $F(K, L) - \omega(L) L < 0$ for $L > L^*$. The maximand takes on a Maximum in the closed bounded interval between zero and L^* by virtue of continuity. This maximum must be nonnegative, since the

value of the maximand is zero at $L = 0$, a member of the interval. Hence this maximum turns out to be a maximum over all $L \geq 0$. Moreover, in view of its first degree homogeneity the maximand can be rearranged as $F_K(K, L)K + [F_L(K, L) - \omega(L)]L$, of which the first term is always positive and the second term becomes positive as $L \to 0$. Whence the maximand certainly takes on positive values for some values of L, so that the aforementioned maximization must occur at some positive L. Finally, the uniqueness of maximizing L is ensured by the strict concavity of the maximand with respect to L.

References

Solow, R. (1956): A Contribution to the Theory of Economic Growth, *Quarterly Journal of Economics*, LXX.

Uzawa, H. (1962): On a Two-Sector Model of Economic Growth, *Review of Economic Studies*, XXIX.

Walras, L. (1954): *Elements of Pure Economics*, W. Jaffe. trans., Homewood, Ill.: Richard D. Irwin.

9 Factor Substitution and Harrod's Knife-Edge

1 Unresolved Knife-Edge

Despite the careful reservations for the modern Keynesian difficulties and rigidities in Solow's monumental work on neoclassical growth (Solow 1956, Section VII), unfortunately it has much contributed to establish the presumption that flexible smooth factor substitution rules out Harrod's knife-edge.

However, the stability of the Solovian neoclassical growth equilibrium heavily relies upon its particular investment habits of capitalists in which investment automatically equals savings, rather than factor substitution.

On the other hand, one of the most crucial points in Harrod's analysis (1939, 1956) is that the investment behaviors of capitalists are primarily responsible for the growth equilibrium balanced on a knife-edge. Thus instability is likely to occur even under flexible smooth factor substitution, depending on the investment habit. This is the case when intended investment increases or decreases relative to the current level of capital stock according as the capitalists are confronted with capital shortage or excess capacity. This note is intended to call attention to possible instability under neoclassical flexible factor substitution[1] by illustrating such a typical unstable situation.

2 The Model

Let $F(K, L)$ be a smooth production function of the standard neoclassical type, where K is capital stock and L is labor input. L is assumed to grow at an exogenously given constant rate n, so that

$$\dot{L}/L = n. \tag{1}$$

Let I be the intended level of investment. If s is the community's average propensity to save, which is assumed to be constant for simplicity, the corresponding ex ante level of national income is I/s. I/s may be larger or smaller than, or equal to the current potential full employment level of national income $F(K, L)$.

Reprinted from *Zeitschrift für Nationalökonomie* 35 (1975): 149–154. © 1975 Springer-Verlag. Reprinted by permission.

The current actual level of national income y at the moment of time t is determined as follows. If the intended level of investment is so high that I/s exceeds the potential full employment level of national income $F(K, L)$, then $y = F(K, L)$. Otherwise $y = I/s$. In symbols y can be defined as

$$y = \min [I/s, F(K, L)]. \tag{2}$$

The intended level of investment is not necessarily equal to the realized level of investment, i.e. the increment of capital stock $\dot{K}$. The latter equals $sF(K, L)$ if $I/s > F(K, L)$,[2] while $\dot{K} = I$ otherwise. In the light of (2) this means

$$\dot{K} = sy. \tag{3}$$

It remains to determine the dynamic behavior of the intended investment I. As was remarked, the ex ante level of national income I/s need not equal its full employment level. Thus, if θ is the ratio of I/s to $F(K, L)$, then

$$I/s = \theta F(K, L) = F(\theta K, \theta L). \tag{4}$$

If the capitalists are so disposed that they build production plans on the basis of the current capital-labor ratio K/L, θ indicates the current level of capital shortage or excess capacity. In fact, $\theta > 1$ means capital shortage, whereas $\theta < 1$ means excess capacity. The investment habit stated in the introductory section means that I/K varies in the direction of the discrepancy between θ and 1. Analytically, the investment habit can be formulated as

$$\frac{d}{dt}(I/K) = \phi(\theta - 1), \tag{5}$$

where $\phi(x)$ is a smooth sign-preserving function in the sense that $\phi(x)$ is positive, negative or zero according as x is positive, negative or zero.

It is also noted that the discrepancy between θ and 1 is always in the same direction of that between the ex ante level of national income I/s and its full employment level $F(K, L)$, i.e. the sign of

$$I/s - F(K, L). \tag{6}$$

Eqs. (1)–(5) altogether determine the complete dynamic paths[3] of L, K, y, θ and I.

3   Instability under Flexible Factor Substitution

If at a moment of time τ capitalists happen to be so bearish that

$$I/s < F(K, L), \tag{7}$$

and furthermore, also at τ,

$$\dot{K}/K \leqq \dot{L}/L = n, \tag{8}$$

(7) will continue to persist forever from τ on. This permanently accelerates the decrease of intended investment through the investment habit (5), and the deficient intended investment will generate enlarged excess capacity and unemployment.

This downward instability will be proved below. In fact, since (7) holds at $t = \tau$, it continues to hold in a time interval $[\tau, \varrho)$, where $\varrho > \tau$. We try to make ϱ for such an interval as large as possible. To this end let ω be the least upper bound of ϱ. If ω proves $+\infty$, then (7) will have been shown to hold over time from τ on.

Suppose now that ω were a finite number. Upon differentiation and rearrangement, we see

$$\frac{d}{dt}\left[\frac{I}{sK} - \frac{F(K, L)}{K}\right] = \frac{1}{s}\frac{d}{dt}\left(\frac{I}{K}\right) - \left(\frac{L}{K}\right)\left(n - \frac{\dot{K}}{K}\right)\frac{\partial}{\partial(L/K)}F(1, L/K). \tag{9}$$

Let us determine the sign of (9) on the right-hand side. The first term is negative in the time interval $[\tau, \omega)$ by (5) and the validity of (7) in this interval. On the other hand, $I = \dot{K}$ by (2) and (3) so long as (7) holds. $\dot{K}/K = I/K$ is not larger at τ than n, and is decreasing in the time interval $[\tau, \omega)$, whence $\dot{K}/K < n$ in the interval. This implies the negativity of the second term of (9) in the time interval $[\tau, \omega)$. From these results it follows that

$$\frac{I}{sK} - \frac{F(K, L)}{K} \tag{10}$$

is decreasing in $[\tau, \omega)$. Moreover, (10) is negative at $t = \tau$. Hence (10) remains to be negative not only in $[\tau, \omega)$ but also at $t = \omega$. Since $K > 0$, this implies that (7) holds even at $t = \omega$. Then we can extend the interval $[\tau, \omega)$ beyond ω while retaining (7). This contradicts the supposition of a finite least upper bound ω. Therefore ω must be $+\infty$.

As is well-known, the Solovian neoclassical growth

$$\dot{K} = sF(K, L) \tag{11}$$

has a unique stable steady state growth, whose equilibrium capital-labor ratio is determined by

$$sF(1, L/K) = n. \tag{12}$$

On this steady state growth path the relevant magnitudes grow at the rate n, in particular $\dot{K}/K = n$. The system determined by (1)–(5) admits this steady state growth path, on which I is set equal to $\dot{K}$. Suppose that the economy has been growing on this path up to now $t = \tau$, and that the intended investment happens to slip down off the steady growth. Then, (7) and $\dot{K}/K = n$ at τ, and there will be enlarged excess capacity and unemployment forever, as was proved.

4   The Enlargement of Excess Capacity and Unemployment

It can readily be shown that in the course of this downward divergence from the steady state growth path, $1 - \theta$, the common ratio of the idle capacity to the potential capacity and the unemployed to the total labor force is increasing.

In fact, from the definition of θ in (4) follows

$$\frac{I}{sK} = \theta \frac{F(K, L)}{K}. \tag{13}$$

I/sK is decreasing on the left-hand side of (13), while $F(K, L)/K$ is increasing on its right-hand side, as was shown in Section 3. Hence θ must be decreasing.

At the same time, if the current full employment level of national income $F(K, L)$ is denoted by y_f, then

$$y = \theta y_f \tag{14}$$

and therefore

$$\frac{\dot{y}}{y} = \frac{\dot{y}_f}{y_f} + \frac{\dot{\theta}}{\theta} < \frac{\dot{y}_f}{y_f}. \tag{15}$$

It can also be shown that

$$\frac{\dot{y}}{y} < \frac{\dot{K}}{K} \tag{16}$$

In fact, by dividing (3) by K, we obtain

$$\frac{\dot{K}}{K} = s\frac{y}{K}, \tag{17}$$

whose left-hand side is decreasing during the downward divergence from the steady state growth path. Hence y/K, too, is decreasing and its derivative is negative. Upon differentiation and rearrangement

$$\left(\frac{\dot{y}}{y} - \frac{\dot{K}}{K}\right)\frac{y}{K} = \frac{d}{dt}\left(\frac{y}{K}\right) < 0, \tag{18}$$

which implies (16) because of the positivity of y/K.

5 Sustaining of the Solovian Growth

What will slight momentary bullishness in the psychology of capitalists generate? If they happen to be so bullish at a moment of time τ as

$$I/s > F(K,L) \tag{19}$$

and moreover the current capital-labor ratio at τ lies in the region determined by

$$sF(1, L/K) \geqq n, \tag{20}$$

(19) will continue to prevail forever from τ on, so that the Solovian growth process (11) will be sustained permanently but possibly with a prolonged inflation.

The proof of this presumption will be outlined briefly below. In fact, the Solovian growth is sustained in the region (20), so long as (19) prevails. During the sustained growth I/sK is increasing, but $F(1, L/K)$ remains to be n or is decreasing towards n,[4] so that (10) is increasing from its positive level at τ. Therefore (10) can neither vanish nor become negative and (19) holds permanently. Then the ex post investment governed by (2), (3) actually conforms to the Solovian rule (11). But at the same time so vigorous an animal spirit is generated and accelerated that the discrepancy between the intended and actual levels of investment is getting enlarged.

6 Concluding Remarks

Although flexible smooth factor substitution enables the economy to admit an equilibrium growth in which the warranted rate of growth is adjusted to the natural rate of growth, it is not powerful enough to wipe out divergence of the growth path from the steady state equilibrium growth path which may be caused by a violent investment behavior. Whether factor proportion is variable or fixed, the stability property is most crucially dependent on the behavior of investment.

Thus the Solovian neoclassical growth process is not spontaneously stable, but can persist only when it is either driven by a vigorous animal spirit or guided by means of appropriate stimulating measures.[5]

Notes

This research is supported by a grant from Japan Economic Research Foundation. The author is indebted to Professor H. Atsumi, M. Fukuoka, H. Kumagai, and S. Wada for suggestions and criticism. Any remaining error is his sole responsibility.

1. This point was already put forward by Eisner (1958). Nonetheless, in pointing out possible instability under flexible factor substitution, aside from his appeal to intuition rather than analytical demonstration, he relies on limited factor substitution due to a certain kind of rigidity in the monetary part of the economy, that prevents capital-labor ratio from becoming too large with a too low level of marginal productivity of capital.

2. It is assumed here just for the sake of simplicity, that forced saving does not take place even in the presence of an inflationary gap.

3. If y is eliminated from (2) and (3), and differentiation is performed in (5), we obtain a system of three differential equations in L, K and I,

$$\dot{L}/L = n$$

$$\dot{K} = s \min [I/s, F(K, L)]$$

$$\dot{I} = (sI/K) \min [I/s, F(K, L)] + K\phi(\theta - 1)$$

where θ is determined by (4).

4. This is just due to the dynamic performance of the Solovian growth process elucidiated in Solow (1956).

5. Nonetheless these stimulating measures must be so carefully implemented that (3) persists for the ex ante propensity to save s without forced saving.

References

Eisner, R. (1958): On Growth Models and the Neo-classical Resurgence, *Economic Journal*, LXVIII.

Harrod R. F. (1939): An Essay in Dynamic Theory, *Economic Journal*, XLIX; errata, June 1939.

——— (1956): Towards a Dynamic Economics, London: Macmillan,

Solow R. (1956): A Contribution to the Theory of Economic Growth, *Quarterly Journal of Economics*, LXX.

10 Harrodian Pathology of Neoclassical Growth: The Irrelevance of Smooth Factor Substitution [1980]

1 Introduction

O41

Smooth factor substitution implies well-behaved marginal productivities upon which the fine edifice of the neoclassical income distribution and capital theories is erected, whereas fixed factor proportions do not go together with it well. Both smooth factor substitution and fixed factor proportions share the convexity of isoquants toward the origin as well as constant returns to scale, both basic crude properties of technology.

Nonetheless, one of them, a fine technological property, supports the edifice which is alien to the other. Then, how can the edifice be more relevant to the economic reality than another which might be built on more fundamental, though less subtle, crude technological properties? Something similar seems to be true with the emphasis of smooth factor substitution in neoclassical growth.

Smooth factor substitution, reinforced by the price mechanism's perfect adjusting functioning to clear markets at each moment of time, can keep the economy on the track of equilibrium growth toward steady state growth, as is most beautifully elucidated in Solow's monumental work (1956). If the economy produces $F(K,L)$ output of an all-purpose good available for consumption and investment with capital stock K (a stock of the same good) and labor input L, the capital labor ratio $r = K/L$ in the well-known neoclassical equilibrium growth with full employment evolves according to the differential equation

$$\dot{r} = sF(r,1) - nr, \tag{1}$$

where n and s are a given growth rate of labor force and a community's propensity to save. The economy, starting at an arbitrary initial position, approaches a unique steady state growth situation corresponding to a stationary level of capital labor ratio r^* characterized as a solution of the equation

$$sF(r,1) = nr. \tag{2}$$

Now, if factor substitution is smooth and allows the average productivity of capital to decrease from infinity to zero with the increase of

Reprinted from *Zeitschrift für Nationalökonomie* 40, nos. 1–2 (1980): 111–134. © 1980 Springer-Verlag. Reprinted by permission.

capital, there is a unique capital labor ratio r^* satisfying (2), at which the economy enjoys steady growth with capital fully utilized.

However, the dynamics of the system (1) is dictated by a crude property of the production function $F(r, 1)$, such as the decreasing average productivity of capital, whether it be smooth or kinky. The same qualitative result also holds, but should be interpreted in a drastically different way under fixed proportions

$$F(K, L) = \min [aK, bL]. \tag{3}$$

In fact, if $sa > n$, Eq. (3) gives rise to a unique capital labor ratio $r^* = sb/n$, at which steady state growth persists with $sb/n - b/a$ units of capital stock per capita remaining idle, a situation with which Harrod is alleged to be seriously concerned. However, how can both entrepreneurs and Harrod remain so indifferent to the idle capacity growing at rate n that investment continues to keep in pace with the community's thriftiness? If the warranted rate of growth sa is higher than the natural rate of growth n, at which the economy is presumed to continue to grow, something else, even unemployment, may eventually take place (Harrod, 1939, 1956, 1973). His insight is principally in the line of disequilibrium dynamics and beyond the reach of neoclassical equilibrium dynamics. He is seriously concerned with where disequilibrium will drive the economy, whereas any possibility of the economy ever slipping off the track of equilibrium growth is ignored in neoclassical growth. Harrod's knife-edge is a disequilibrium phenomenon which neoclassical equilibrium growth, rather than smooth factor substitution, presumes to rule out at the outset.

How then can smooth factor substitution be operative in a disequilibrium situation such as a possible knife-edge? Is not what substantially matters in governing the dynamic behavior of the economy in the situation, again, a basic crude, rather than fine, property of technology, such as smooth factor substitution? As will be elucidated, substantially crucial to such a disequilibrium situation as Harrod's knife-edge is a crude property of technology, namely, the decreasing average productivity of capital regardless of factor substituability.

These are the issues to be discussed in this paper[1] by pushing further the line which was set forth but not thoroughly worked out in my previous paper (Nikaido 1975).

2   The Growth Process

The economy produces one single all-purpose good, available for consumption and investment with capital, K, (a stock of the good) and homogeneous labor, L, by means of a production function

$$F(K, L), \tag{4}$$

which admits constant returns to scale. The production function need not be of the standard neoclassical type with smooth factor substitution, but may be of broader category, including fixed factor proportion (3). It is assumed to be continuous.

The potential level of supply of output is $F(K, L)$, where K and L are the existing levels at a moment of time. Supply is infinitely elastic and adjusts itself instantaneously to demand up to the potential level, beyond which it is perfectly inelastic, at the moment.

For simplicity, the community's average propensity to save is presumed to be stable and a positive constant s less than unity. Let I be the intended level of investment which need not equal its realized level and as will be explained, is determinate in the growth process.

If the demand I/s does not exceed the potential level of supply, the level of income Y is determined as

$$Y = I/s, \tag{5}$$

to which output is instantaneously supplied with the existing capital and labor either fully employed or one or both of them underemployed, depending on the level of income and entrepreneurial behaviors. In this situation I coincides with the realized level of investment $\dot{K}$. On the other hand, if I/s exceeds the potential level of supply, output is instantaneously supplied at the level $F(K, L)$, which is the level of income Y in this case, leaving $I/s - F(K, L)$ as excess demand. Then the intended level of investment exceeds its realized one $\dot{K} = sF(K, L)$.

Accordingly, the level of income is determined as

$$Y = \min \left[I/s, F(K, L) \right] \tag{6}$$

and the realized level of investment always satisfies

$$\dot{K} = sY \tag{7}$$

whether demand is deficient or not.

Labor force is assumed to grow at an exogenously given constant rate n, so that L conforms to

$$\dot{L}/L = n. \tag{8}$$

Naturally, the intended investment is governed by entrepreneurs who are presumed here to be concerned mostly with the demand-supply situation of markets and the degree of utilization of capital. They are so disposed that I/K, the ratio of intended investment to the existing capital, is dictated by

$$(\dot{I}/K) = \Phi(\lambda, \mu) \tag{9}$$

where $\Phi(\lambda, \mu)$ is a continuous function of two variables λ, μ. λ is a variable indicating the demand-supply situation of markets and μ is a variable indicating how idle the existing capital remains. λ, μ are further represented as continuous functions of K, L, I.

Thus we have a dynamic growth process generated by a system of differential Eqs. (7), (8), (9) with (6) in the variables K, L, I, provided the relevant functions are well-behaved enough to let the formulation make sense.

λ, μ will be specified in the following sections, whereas we leave them unspecified in this section. Generally, $\lambda = 0$ corresponds to the situation where just the potential level of output is demanded and therefore where at least one of capital and labor is fully employed (possibly with underutilization of the other due to technological rigidities such as fixed factor proportions). $\lambda > 0$ corresponds to a situation where I/s exceeds the potential level of supply so that excess demand prevails in the commodity market. $\lambda < 0$ corresponds to a situation where I/s is below the potential level of supply, so that from the presumption of instantaneous adjustment of supply to demand within the supply potential, the commodity market is in equilibrium with excess supply prevailing in the labor market. On the other hand, $\mu = 0$ corresponds to full utilization of capital, whereas $\mu > 0$ indicates the degree of underutilization of capital measured in a certain way. μ does not take on any negative value.

A situation corresponding to a positive value of λ stimulates investment, whereas that corresponding to its negative value depresses investment. On the other hand, a positive value of μ depresses investment. Nonetheless, it is assumed that a depressing effect of μ on investment can be offset by a stimulating effect of λ on investment. Analytically, there is a function $g(\mu)$, nonnegative-valued, continuous, defined for $\mu \geq 0$ such that

$$g(\mu) = 0 \quad \text{if and only if} \quad \mu = 0 \tag{10}$$

$$\Phi(\lambda, \mu) \begin{cases} > 0 & \lambda > g(\mu) \\ = 0 & \lambda = g(\mu) \\ < 0 & \lambda < g(\mu) \end{cases} \tag{11}$$

The more specific state of entrepreneurs' minds underlying the function $\Phi(\lambda, \mu)$ will be touched on in the following sections.

3   Instability Under Smooth Factor Substitution

Let us assume that the production function has smooth factor substitutability of the standard neoclassical type and we have a specification of λ as

$$\lambda = \frac{I}{sK} - \frac{F(K, L)}{K} \tag{12}$$

Entrepreneurs can try to meet the demand resulting from the current intended level of investment at a moment of time by carrying out production in a capital labor ratio chosen from among all possible ones available to them within the existing level of capital. Moreover, there is no possibility for excess capacity due to technological rigidities when output is supplied at its potential level. Thus, under the very assumption of neoclassical smooth factor substitution entrepreneurs are likely to always utilize capital in its full capacity and to achieve the level of current production by solely adjusting the level of employment of labor.

Accordingly, if the intended level of investment is so deficient that the demand is short of the potential level of supply, N units of labor determined by $I/s = F(K, N)$ are fully employed to utilize the existing capital, while $L - N$ units of labor remain unemployed. As a matter of course the existing capital and labor are fully employed when there is enough or more than enough demand. Thus, capital is always fully utilized so that there is no idle capital and μ is then specified as

$$\mu = 0 \quad \text{(identically).} \tag{13}$$

Letting

$$\phi(\lambda) = \Phi(\lambda, 0), \tag{14}$$

we can reduce (9) to a specified form

$$(\dot{I}/K) = \phi\left(\frac{I}{sK} - \frac{F(K,L)}{K}\right), \tag{15}$$

and the system (7), (8), (15) with (6) generates a growth process under neoclassical smooth factor substitution.

Then, what is the state of entrepreneurs' minds underlying the investment habits (15)? Capital is always fully utilized. When $I/sK > F(K,L)/K$, excess demand prevails in both commodity and labor markets. In such a situation entrepreneurs are very likely to accelerate investment so as to meet the labor shortage by substituting more capital for labor in virtue of its very smooth factor substitutability, while in an opposite situation they are very likely to decelerate investment by the same token. They are satisfied and have no inducement to change the rate of investment in case demand equals the potential level of supply, so that both commodity and labor markets are in equilibrium.

Now, to explore the most crucial, dynamic nature of the economy, let us proceed in terms of capital labor ratio

$$k = K/L, \tag{16}$$

which coincides with Solow's r in a full employment situation but is defined in an underemployment situation simply as the ratio of the existing capital (which is always fully employed) to the existing labor force.

Then under the assumed constant returns to scale the system (7), (8), (15) with (6) reduces to a system of two differential equations.

$$\frac{\dot{k}}{k} = \min\left[\frac{I}{K}, \frac{sf(k)}{k}\right] - n \tag{17}$$

$$\left(\frac{\dot{i}}{K}\right) = \phi\left(\frac{I}{sK} - \frac{f(k)}{k}\right), \tag{18}$$

where

$$f(k) = F(k, 1) \tag{19}$$

in the two variables k and I/K.

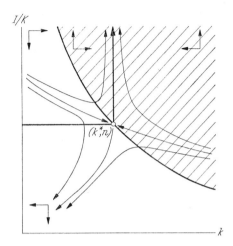

Figure 10.1

Since the production function admits average productivity continuously diminishing from infinity to zero under the neoclassical presumption, the system of equations

$$\frac{sf(k)}{k} = \frac{I}{K} = n \qquad (20)$$

has a unique solution, (k^*, n), which is the neoclassical state of steady growth.

The corresponding phase diagram is given in Fig. 10.1. The locus $\dot{k} = 0$ is given by the equation

$$\min\left[\frac{I}{K}, \frac{sf(k)}{k}\right] - n = 0 \qquad (21)$$

and looks like a reversely L-shaped rectangular curve on whose upper left-hand side $\dot{k}$ is positive and on the other side, is negative. This is because the function on the left-hand side of (21) is increasing with respect to I/K and decreasing with respect to k. The locus $(\dot{I/K}) = 0$ is nothing but the graph of the decreasing average productivity of capital multiplied by s

$$\frac{I}{K} = \frac{sf(k)}{k}, \qquad (22)$$

on whose upper and lower sides (I/K) is positive and negative, respectively.

Thus, the critical point (k^*, n), the Solovian neoclassical state of steady growth, is a saddle point in the phase diagram. All trajectories eventually depart away from the steady growth except for two approaching it (which will be referred to as critical trajectories), thus allowing instability to prevail.

Note that labor is fully employed in and only in the shaded area in the phase diagram where Eq. (17) becomes

$$\frac{\dot{k}}{k} = \frac{sf(k)}{k} - n, \tag{23}$$

the Solovian equation of neoclassical growth (1).

The shaded and unshaded areas will be dubbed the boom and slump regions, respectively, for self-explanatory reasons. Full employment of labor accompanied by excess demand in both commodity and labor markets prevails in the boom region, while under-employment with excess supply in the labor market prevails in the slump region. On the curve (22) just in between both regions, the economy enjoys equilibrium in all the markets with both factors fully employed. But no economic growth persists along the curve, except at the Solovian steady state growth. A trajectory either fails to reach the curve or at best crosses it just once at a moment.

A trajectory lying below the two critical trajectories either continues to stay in the slump region from the outset or eventually reaches from the boom region to stay continually in the slump region. Likewise, a trajectory lying above the two critical trajectories either continues to stay in the boom region from the outset or eventually reaches from the slump region to continually stay in the boom region.

Neoclassical growth persists for a while after the economy starts at an initial position in the boom region below the critical trajectories. But the moment must come when it slips off the track of neoclassical growth and continually moves away from the steady state growth in the slump region.

On the other hand neoclassical growth persists, either from the outset or eventually above the critical trajectories, so that the capital labor ratio k monotonically tends to its equilibrium level k^*. All these take place at the cost of prolonged inflation accompanying an ever-growing excess demand for commodities and labor in a capitalist economy. The process

(23), even when it persists, gives the appearance of an iceberg above sea level.

4 Harrodian Situations

One can not necessarily presume that Harrod assumes fixed factor proportions. In fact, his insight into the fragility of capitalist economic growth reveals itself as enlightening in the very presence of smooth factor substitution, as was seen in the foregoing section. Nonetheless it is interesting to see from Harrod's insight what will result from the typical discrepancies among the relevant rates of growth under extreme rigidities such as fixed factor proportions.

Let us now assume the economy to have a production function (3) under fixed factor proportions. There is a possibility for under-utilization of capital due to fixed factor proportions. μ, the variable indicating this technological under-utilization is here specified as

$$\mu = a - \frac{\min [aK, bL]}{K} \tag{24}$$

that is,

$$\mu = a - \frac{\min [ak, b]}{k} \tag{25}$$

in terms of the capital labor ratio k. On the other hand we retain (12). However, the stimulating effect of $\lambda > 0$ on investment does not come from entrepreneurs' efforts to substitute capital for labor (which is impossible under fixed factor proportion) but originates with their bullish state of mind in a boom situation. The same is true for the depressing effect $\lambda < 0$ on investment.

Thus the system of differential equations governing the movements of k and I/K, a counterpart to the system (17), (18) is

$$\frac{\dot{k}}{k} = \min \left[\frac{I}{K}, \frac{sf(k)}{k} \right] - n \tag{26}$$

$$\left(\frac{\dot{I}}{K} \right) = \Phi \left(\frac{I}{sK} - \frac{f(k)}{k}, a - \frac{f(k)}{k} \right), \tag{27}$$

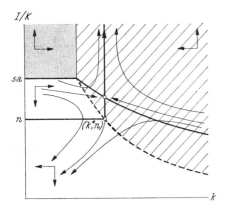

Figure 10.2

where

$$f(k) = \min \, [ak, b]. \tag{28}$$

The corresponding phase diagram slightly differs depending on the relationship among the key parameters a, s, n. Nonetheless, what most vitally dictates the dynamics of the system and builds in instability is again the decreasing average productivity of capital, a crude property of technology shared by smooth factor substitution as well.

Figs. 10.2, 3, and 4 are the phase diagrams for three cases (i) $sa > n$, (ii) $sa < n$, (iii) $sa = n$, respectively, where, needless to say, sa is the warranted rate of growth and n is the natural rate of growth.

A little complication arises from the fact that the average productivity of capital does not decrease but remains at a constant level, a, with the increase of capital labor ratio up to b/a, and then decreases toward zero. This gives rise to alternative situations as to the critical points of the system (26), (27), that is, the solution of the system of equations

$$\min \left[\frac{I}{K}, \frac{sf(k)}{k} \right] - n = 0, \tag{29}$$

$$\Phi \left(\frac{I}{sK} - \frac{f(k)}{k}, a - \frac{f(k)}{k} \right) = 0 \tag{30}$$

Now, from the basic assumption of the offsetting relationship between the stimulating effects of a boom and the depressing effects of under-

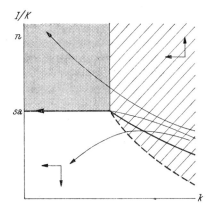

Figure 10.3

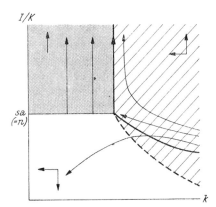

Figure 10.4

utilization of capital on investment, Eq. (30) is transformed to

$$\frac{I}{K} = \frac{sf(k)}{k} + sg\left(a - \frac{f(k)}{k}\right) \tag{31}$$

in terms of the function $g(\mu)$. (31) is the average productivity curve lowered by 100 s percent and shifted upward by $sg(a - f(k)/k)$.

In case (i) there is a unique critical point $(sb/n, (I/K)^*)$ where $(I/K)^* = n + sg(a - n/s)$, because the average productivity is equated once and only once to n/s at $k = k^* = sb/n$. In case (ii) the left-hand side of (29) is identically negative, so that there is no critical point. In case (iii) infinitely many critical points fill out the segment with the endpoints (o, n) and $(b/a, n)$.

In all the three phase diagrams capital is fully utilized, in and only in the darkened area and labor is fully employed in and only in the shaded area. The boom and slump regions are characterized as the regions above and below the curve (31), respectively.

Instability inherent in the system due to the decreasing average productivity of capital reveals itself in all the cases. In particular, case (i) has essentially the same phase diagram as Fig. 10.1. The point $(sb/n, n)$, which is alleged to depict a situation that Harrod has in mind, lies on a trajectory departing downward away from the critical point, a steady state growth sustained by a higher rate of intendend investment just enough to offset the depressing effect of idle capacity in capital and just balanced on a knife-edge.

It is well-known, and formally presented (Alexander 1950, Baumol 1959, Jorgenson 1960, Tokita 1976, Ch. 6, and others) that in Harrod's insight a discrepancy between the actual and warranted rates of growth causes instability. However, under fixed factor proportions no upward discrepancy of the former from the latter can occur, except in a situation of underemployment of both factors, since a realized investment can raise the level of output at the rate sa at most when labor is not binding production and at a lower rate than sa when labor is binding. What can actually grow at a higher rate than sa and drive the economy away from the warranted growth is demand for output I/s. In fact, by performing differentiation of I/K we have

$$\text{growth rate of } I/s = \left(\frac{\dot{i}}{K}\right)\bigg/\frac{I}{K} + \frac{sY}{K},$$

which is higher in the darkened area than sa.

In Fig. 10.2 a slight downward slip off the warranted growth above the critical trajectories eventually sends the economy upward toward a prolonged boom. This contradicts Harrod's contention that a downward slip off the warranted growth sends the economy further downward away from it and an upward one sends the economy further upward away from it. Actually what occurs specifically, though not qualitatively, depends on how bullish entrepreneurs are, that is, the specific shape of the offsetting function $g(\mu)$. In fact, for a special offsetting function

$$g(\mu) = \mu,$$

the curve (31) becomes a horizontal straight line

$$\frac{I}{K} = sa \tag{32}$$

and the corresponding phase diagram, in which (32) coincides with the two critical trajectories, is compatible with the contention.

5   Alternative Investment Habits

The investment habit (15) is an accelerator type in the boom region, where $F(K, L) = \dot{K}/s$, and I/K varies in the direction toward the discrepancy between the intended I and actual $\dot{K}$ levels of investment. But it responds in a depressing situation more sensitively than an accelerator would. One

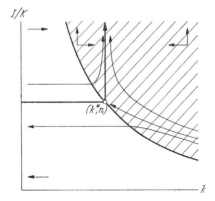

Figure 10.5

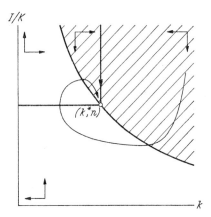

Figure 10.6

may have an alternative system by replacing (15) by

$$\left(\frac{\dot{I}}{K}\right) = \phi\left(\frac{I}{sK} - \frac{\dot{K}}{sK}\right) \tag{33}$$

which is of an accelerator type in both upward and downward positions. Thus, in view of (6), (7), we have a counterpart

$$\frac{\dot{k}}{k} = \min\left[\frac{I}{K}, \frac{sf(k)}{k}\right] - n \tag{17}$$

$$\left(\frac{\dot{I}}{K}\right) = \phi\left(\frac{I}{sK} - \min\left[\frac{I}{sK}, \frac{f(k)}{k}\right]\right) \tag{34}$$

to the system (17), (18).

The phase diagram of the alternative system is given in Fig. 10.5. It has infinitely many critical points filling out the segment with endpoints (o, n) and (k^*, n) and reveals instability again. An accelerator of this type can also be built in to the Harrodian situations without causing any essential effects on the inherent instability.

Admittedly, the built-in investment habits of the system are exclusively myopic and do not incorporate other aspects such as long-run expectations. Nonetheless, entrepreneurs here behave in plausible ways peculiar to a capitalist economy. These habits are mainly responsible for instability under a crude technological property such as the decreasing average productivity of capital.

To endorse this view further let us consider an experimental situation where entrepreneurs' states of mind would be still myopic, but completely opposite. They still fully utilize capital under smooth factor substitution. But they depress investment when they face labor shortage, while they accelerate investment when there is under-employment of labor, as if they were Keynesian gospelers. What happens then?

Instead of the system (17), (18) we would have a system

$$\frac{\dot{k}}{k} = \min \left[\frac{I}{K}, \frac{sf(k)}{k} \right] - n \tag{17}$$

$$\left(\frac{\dot{I}}{K} \right) = -\phi \left(\frac{I}{sK} - \frac{f(k)}{k} \right). \tag{35}$$

The corresponding phase diagram in Fig. 10.6 reveals the Solovian steady state growth as a unique stable critical point.

6   Prices as Stabilizer?

If the price mechanism functioned so perfectly that all the markets were instantaneously brought to equilibrium at each moment of time, then entrepreneurs would be maximizing profits to supply output at the current potential level just enough to meet demand. If they continued to keep pace with community's thriftiness in investment in this lucky situation, they would never be motivated for extra-acceleration or deceleration of investment, so that the inherent instability would not reveal itself and neoclassical equilibrium growth would persist.

In all the situations considered here market disequilibrium does not instantaneously let prices adjust themselves toward equilibrium. Prices are momentarily inflexible but vary over time responding to market disequilibrium. On the other hand, quantity adjustments are instantaneous toward effective, rather than notional, levels and transactions are actually made on the short side at each moment of time.

Thus, at each moment of time entrepreneurs are maximizing profits subject to quantity constraints by adjusting supply to the shorter side of demand and the potential level of supply, as in Patinkin's (1965, Ch. 13) and his recent followers' (Barro and Grossman 1971, 1976, Ch. 2) contention. This situation exists provided prices change over time while keeping the rate of real wage not exceeding the marginal productivity of employed labor under smooth factor substitution or the output labor ratio b under fixed proportions.

All our discussion is based on this presumed mode of price change during the dynamic movement of the system along a trajectory. It may be supported by intuition but needs an analytical endorsement. This will be obtained by reformulating the growth process in a system of differential equations in prices as endogenous variables in addition to quantity variables.

Price level p and money wage rate w, the price variables to be incorporated, change in response to the demand-supply situations of the commodity and labor markets, respectively, and thereby govern the change of the rate of real wage ω over time.

When the rate of real wage ω is so high that entrepreneurs will not increase supply beyond the notional profit-maximizing level (in spite of excess demand for commodities and excess supply of labor) this level determines the realized level of national income Y as the shortest among the three quantities, namely, demand I/s, the potential level of supply $F(K, L)$ and this level $F(K, N)$ at the moment, where N is the notional profit-maximizing level of employment at which the marginal productivity of employed labor $F_L(K, N)$ is equated to ω. Letting

$$m = \frac{K}{N} \tag{36}$$

in view of the o-th degree homogeneity of the marginal productivity, we have m as a smooth increasing function

$$m(\omega) \tag{37}$$

of ω.

Then a counterpart of the system (17), (18) will be

$$\frac{\dot{k}}{k} = \min\left[\frac{I}{K}, \frac{sf(k)}{k}, \frac{sf(m(\omega))}{m(\omega)}\right] - n \tag{38}$$

$$\left(\frac{\dot{I}}{K}\right) = \phi\left(\min\left[\frac{I}{sK}, \frac{f(m(\omega))}{m(\omega)}\right] - \min\left[\frac{f(k)}{k}, \frac{f(m(\omega))}{m(\omega)}\right]\right) \tag{39}$$

$$\frac{\dot{p}}{p} = \alpha\left(\frac{I}{sK} - \min\left[\frac{f(k)}{k}, \frac{f(m(\omega))}{m(\omega)}\right]\right) \tag{40}$$

$$\frac{\dot{w}}{w} = \beta\left(\min\left[\frac{I}{sK}, \frac{f(m(\omega))}{m(\omega)}\right] - \frac{f(k)}{k}\right)$$ (41)

where $\omega = w/p$. In the above formulation we have

$$\min\left[\frac{I}{sK}, \frac{f(m(\omega))}{m(\omega)}\right] = \text{demand-constrained plan of supply,}$$

$$\min\left[\frac{f(k)}{k}, \frac{f(m(\omega))}{m(\omega)}\right] = \text{labor-constrained plan of supply}$$

per unit of capital.

Entrepreneurs never want to supply beyond the current notional profit-maximizing level of output even in the presence of much current demand. Thus, in view of this entrepreneurial psychology, the excess of the demand-constrained plan of supply over the labor-constrained one per unit of capital

$$\min\left[\frac{I}{sK}, \frac{f(m(\omega))}{m(\omega)}\right] - \min\left[\frac{f(k)}{k}, \frac{f(m(\omega))}{m(\omega)}\right]$$ (42)

is a good proxy measure of the entrepreneurial motivation for investment.

Thus, investment is accelerated or decelerated in the direction of (42) in (39) so as to substitute capital for labor or labor for capital. At the same time the rate of money wage goes up or down in response to the excess of the demand-constrained plan of supply over the potential level of supply per unit of capital

$$\min\left[\frac{I}{sK}, \frac{f(m(\omega))}{m(\omega)}\right] - \frac{f(k)}{k}$$ (43)

in (41) (a good proxy measure of the excess demand for labor) while the price level responds to the excess demand for output per unit of capital

$$\frac{I}{sK} - \min\left[\frac{f(k)}{k}, \frac{f(m(\omega))}{m(\omega)}\right]$$ (44)

in (40).

In a depressing situation when (44) is negative the commodity market is in equilibrium from the assumed instantaneous supply equal to demand, so that the function $\alpha(x)$ is assumed to satisfy

$$\alpha(x) \begin{cases} = 0 & \text{if } x \le 0 \\ \text{is strictly increasing for } x \ge 0. \end{cases} \tag{45}$$

The function $\beta(x)$ is so responsive to the demand-supply situation that it is strictly increasing everywhere and vanishes just at $x = 0$.

One can not tell on any a priori ground how rapidly p and w rise relative to each other, when $\dot{p}$ and $\dot{w}$ are positive. Nonetheless, a case where p and w potentially go up at the same pace in a boom situation in such a sense that

$$\alpha(x) = \beta(x) \quad \text{for } x \ge 0 \tag{46}$$

deserves attention.

Now, what happens in the growth process generated by (38)–(41)? It is generally hard to have a complete phase diagram of a four-variable system like the present one. But fairly useful information is available.

First of all, let us see the very simple mode of change in the rate of real wage ω. Note that p never falls. When (43) is negative, w is falling, so that ω is falling. When (43) is not negative, from (46), the increasingness of $\alpha(x)$ in (45) and the inequality $(44) \ge (43) \ge 0$ in this situation give us

$$\frac{\dot{\omega}}{\omega} = \alpha((43)) - \alpha((44)) \le 0.$$

Hence the rate of real wage is always falling, or more exactly, never rising. Let ω^* be the rate of real wage corresponding to the Solovian steady state growth, and suppose that the economy starts at an initial rate of real wage ω_0 lower than ω^*. The result is that ω never rises and the economy goes on staying in the region $\omega \le \omega_0 \le \omega^*$. Then closer examination tells us that the projection of this region of the phase diagram on the $(k, I/K)$ plane essentially looks like Fig. 10.1 in the portion southeast of the point $P_0 = (m(\omega_0), sf(m(\omega_0))/m(\omega_0))$ as in Fig. 10.7. For $f(m(\omega))/m(\omega)$, not falling over time, never becomes operative in the system and the system is substantially (17), (18) with

$$\frac{\dot{\omega}}{\omega} = \beta\left(\frac{I}{sK} - \frac{f(k)}{k}\right) - \alpha\left(\frac{I}{sK} - \frac{f(k)}{k}\right).$$

On the other hand, suppose that the economy starts at a higher rate of real wage ω_0 than ω^*. Because it is ever-falling, ω tends to ω_∞ and possibly (though not necessarily) $\omega_\infty = 0$, the situation eventually becomes Fig.

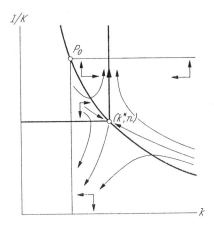

Figure 10.7

10.7 from a moment of time when a lower rate of real wage ω_1 than ω^* is actually reached, with P_0 replaced by the point P_1 corresponding to ω_1. From this moment of time on the economy will or will not lie in the portion southeast of P_1. But once it is there at a subsequent moment of time, it moves on a trajectory in Fig. 10.7, with P_0 replaced by P_1.

What happens if $\omega_\infty > \omega^*$? The economy never lies in the interior of the portion northwest of the point $P_\infty = (m(\omega_\infty), sf(m(\omega_\infty))/m(\omega_\infty))$ including the Solow point where the system would be subjected to

$$\frac{\dot{k}}{k} \leq \frac{sf(m(\omega_\infty))}{m(\omega_\infty)} - n < 0, \tag{47}$$

$$\left(\frac{i}{K}\right) = 0, \tag{48}$$

$$\frac{\dot{\omega}}{\omega} \leq \beta\left(\frac{f(m(\omega_\infty))}{m(\omega_\infty)} - \frac{f(k)}{k}\right) < 0. \tag{49}$$

In fact, if the economy ever reached this area it could not leave the area because of its persistent leftward horizontal movement from (47), (48). However, this would result in the rate of real wage falling less slowly than at a positive constant rate from (48), (49), which contradicts its convergence to a finite ω_∞.

In case $\omega_\infty = \omega^*$, reasoning in the same line as above rules out the presence of the economy in the interior of the portion northwest of the Solow point.

Now, consider the case where ω remains higher in the course of its convergence to ω^* than ω^*. From the information above, the economy must stay in the region characterized by

$$\min\left[\frac{I}{sK}, \frac{f(k)}{k}\right] \leq \frac{n}{s} \tag{50}$$

Clearly, $\dot{k} < o$ from $sf(m(\omega))/m(\omega) < n$.

Let us now locate the part of the trajectory lying in the subregion defined by

$$\frac{I}{sK} \leq \frac{f(k)}{k} \tag{51}$$

To this end suppose that

$$\frac{I}{sK} < \frac{f(m(\omega))}{m(\omega)} \tag{52}$$

at a moment of time. I/K is decreasing by (39), (51), (52) from that moment on, because both $f(k)/k$ and $f(m(\omega))/m(\omega)$ are increasing. Then $\dot{p} = 0$, and

$$\frac{\dot{\omega}}{\omega} = \beta\left(\frac{I}{sK} - \frac{f(k)}{k}\right)$$

is nonpositive and decreasing, which contradicts the convergence of ω to a finite limit. Hence

$$\frac{I}{sK} \geq \frac{f(m(\omega))}{m(\omega)} \tag{53}$$

always holds. Then (39), (51) and (53) imply that I/K is a constant which must be n from the relation $n \geq I/K \geq sf(m(\omega))/m(\omega)$ over time with the rightmost term tending to n. Thus the part of the trajectory lying in the subregion is the horizontal ray emanating leftward from the Solow point.

An analogous reasoning rules out the presence of any part of the trajectory in another subregion characterized by $I/K > n$. Hence, the remaining part of the trajectory must lie in the subregion defined by

$$\frac{n}{s} \ge \frac{I}{sK} > \frac{f(k)}{k}, \tag{54}$$

where I/K is increasing from (39), (54). Therefore, the part of the trajectory in question is a curve in the subregion with its tangent vector pointing northwestward on which the economy moves toward the Solow point. It should be noted that the economy need not converge to the Solow point while moving on this part of the trajectory, but it can possibly reach the point at a moment of time from which onward it continues moving further leftward on the horizontal part of the trajectory, depending on the initial conditions.

Consider the case where ω reaches ω^* at a moment of time so that ω and $\dot\omega$ remain ω^* and zero from that moment on, respectively. $\dot p$ always being not negative, then $\dot w$ must not be negative, otherwise $\dot\omega$ would be negative. Hence, (43) must not be negative. Now if $I/sK > f(m(\omega))/m(\omega)$, we would have (44) larger than (43), making $\dot\omega$ negative. Therefore, the trajectory must stay from that moment on, in the subregion defined by

$$n = \frac{sf(m(\omega^*))}{m(\omega^*)} \ge \frac{I}{K} \ge \frac{sf(k)}{k}$$

where the price variables are inoperative in the system which substantially functions as the system (17), (18). Thus, in the light of the phase diagram in Fig. 10.1, there are just two trajectories persistently lying in the sub-region, namely, the Solovian neoclassical steady state growth and the critical trajectory on the right approaching it.

7 Variable Thriftiness Due to Forced Saving

As is elucidated in Section 3, the excess demand for output is evergrowing in the economy's upward departure away from the neoclassical steady state growth. In spite of, or what is more, rather driven by, possible prolonged inflation, the Solovian growth process persists and the capital labor ratio is approaching the neoclassical equilibrium level k^*. One might realize, therefore, that after all, nothing anomalous happens in the real side of the economy on the upswing[2].

Nonetheless, the economy owes this lucky destiny to the presumed stable thriftiness of the community. If the Solovian growth process persisted, with equilibrium sustained over time in all the markets, the community's thriftiness would also be stable. The everlasting upswing is driven by the self-perpetuating intended investment exceeding the realized investment from which originates a growing excess demand for commodities likely to force the community to save more in favor of more of the realized investment at the cost of reduced consumption. If the prolonged inflation influences the real side of the economy in this way, the Solovian growth process will not persist even in the upswing, and the economy's dynamic destiny will be different.

To endorse this intuition analytically, let us reformulate the growth process (17), (18) so as to have a variable propensity to save s exclusively due to forced saving by inflationary pressure.

Assume that s is a continuous, nondecreasing function $h(x)$ of the variable x indicating the excess of the intended level of investment over the realized investment per unit of the existing capital such that it is defined on all reals and

$$1 > h(x) > 0, \tag{55}$$

$$\lim_{x \to +\infty} h(x) = s_\infty > s_0 = h(0). \tag{56}$$

The function $h(x)$ indicates the potential influence of excess investment demand on s. s_0 is the community's spontaneous propensity to save and (56) means a forced rise of s due to a higher level of excess investment demand. $h(x)$ may or may not remain unchanged for negative x's.

Now substitute $I/K - sf(k)/k$ for x in $s = h(x)$, where k and I/K are arbitrary and positive, so as to obtain

$$s = h\left(\frac{I}{K} - \frac{sf(k)}{k}\right), \tag{57}$$

an equation which s has to fulfill. The solution of (57) is uniquely determined. In fact, let

$$\theta\left(k, \frac{I}{K}, s\right) = \text{right-hand side of (57)}. \tag{58}$$

Then,

$$s = o < s_0 = h(0) \leq h(I/K) = \theta(k, I/K, o)$$

if $s = o$, and

$$s \geq 1 > \theta(I/K, k, s)$$

if $s \geq 1$, in the light of the assumptions on $h(x)$. Hence, s is equated to (58) at some value of it by continuity. Clearly the solution is unique because (58) is not increasing with s.

Thus, the solution s is a continuous function

$$s(k, I/K) \tag{59}$$

of the positive variables k, I/K. It is important to bear in mind the identically holding relation obtained by substituting (59) for s in (57).

This variable propensity to save (59) has the following interesting properties.

(a) It is nondecreasing with respect to both k and I/K. For an increase in k or I/K shifts the function θ upward, so that the corresponding solution of (57) generally becomes higher.

(b) We have by definition

$$s(k, I/K) = s_0, \tag{60}$$

if

$$I/K = s(k, I/K)f(k)/k. \tag{61}$$

(c) The magnitude

$$\frac{s(k, I/K)f(k)}{k} \tag{62}$$

is decreasing, as k is increasing. For, if (62) does not decrease, s must increase because of the decreasing average productivity of capital. But at the same time, s must not increase since $I/K - sf(k)/k$ does not increase in (57), a contradiction.

Now, by incorporating this variable propensity to save into the system, we have

$$\frac{\dot{k}}{k} = \min\left[\frac{I}{K}, \frac{s(k, I/K)f(k)}{k}\right] - n \tag{63}$$

$$\left(\frac{\dot{I}}{K}\right) = \phi\left(\frac{I}{s(k, I/K)K} - \frac{f(k)}{k}\right). \tag{64}$$

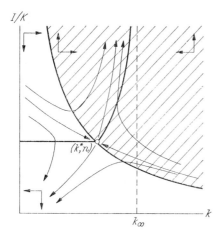

Figure 10.8

The corresponding phase diagram looks like Fig. 10.8. It is remarkable that just because of the property (b) the locus $(I/K) = o$ and both boom and slump regions are exactly the same as in Fig. 10.1 in which s is presumed to be stable at the spontaneous level s_0. As to the locus $\dot{k} = o$, the originally vertical part, now determined by

$$\frac{s(k, I/K)f(k)}{k} = n \tag{65}$$

$$\frac{I}{K} \geq n \tag{66}$$

is inclined to lean rightward. In fact, an increased level of the left-hand side of (65) due to a rise in I/K is brought back to the level n by a rise in k because of the property (c). Thus, an inflationary gap gives rise to a more intensive realized capital accumulation than the community would spontaneously desire. Moreover, since k is bounded on the locus because of $1 > s \geq s_0 > 0$ and the decreasing average productivity of capital, the nondecreasing k eventually tends on the locus with the indefinite rise in I/K to a level k_∞, higher than k^*, defined by

$$\frac{s_\infty f(k_\infty)}{k_\infty} = n \tag{67}$$

in the light of (56). The properties (a), (c) also ensure the positivity of $\dot{k}$ in the upper left-hand side of the locus $\dot{k} = o$ and its negativity in the other side.

Therefore, the phase diagram is essentially the same as in Fig. 10.1, revealing again the Solovian steady state growth as a saddle point. The only difference is that in the upswing phase, the economy inevitably approaches a situation where prolonged inflation forces the community to accumulate capital in excess of the intensity which it would spontaneously desire.

8 Concluding Remarks

All the above results seem to support the contended fragility of the capitalist economic growth for which the investment habits of entrepreneurs and a crude property such as the decreasing average productivity of capital are responsible.

The former are too myopic but conceived plausible ones peculiar to the capitalist economic growth. Under constant returns to scale the latter is a mere consequence of a very crude aspect of technology that output increases with the increase of labor input.

Smooth factor substitution makes no distinguishable contribution to stabilize the growth process. It merely enables the economy to admit a steady state growth with capital and labor fully employed, just balanced on a knife-edge.

Notes

1. This research was carried out during my visit at the Department of Economics, University of Southern California, to which many thanks are due for its support of my visit. I owe very much to R. M. Solow for his criticism on my previous note (Nikaido 1975) in correspondence, which considerably motivated this research. I greatly appreciate the valuable suggestions and comments which I received from R. H. Day while preparing the manuscript.

2. This realization was pointed out to me by W. D. Dechert.

References

Alexander, S. S. (1950): Mr. Harrod's Dynamic Model, *Economic Journal 60*.

Barro, R. J. and H. I. Grossman (1971): A General Disequilibrium Model of Income and Employment, *American Economic Review 61*.

——— (1976): Money, Employment and Inflation, Cambridge: Cambridge University Press.

Baumol, W. J. (1949): Formalization of Mr. Harrod's Model, *Economic Journal 59*.

Harrod, R. F. (1939): An Essay in Dynamic Theory, *Economic Journal 49*.

——— (1956): *Towards a Dynamic Economics*, London: Macmillan.

——— (1973): *Economic Dynamics*, London: Macmillan.

Jorgenson, D. W. (1960): On Stability in the Sense of Harrod, *Economica 27*.

Nikaido, H. (1975): Factor Substitution and Harrod's Knife-edge, *Zeitschrift für Nationalökonomie 35*.

Patinkin, D. (1965): *Money, Interest and Prices*, 2nd Edition, New York: Harper & Row.

Solow, R. M. (1956): A Contribution to the Theory of Economic Growth, *Quarterly Journal of Economics 70*.

Tokita, T. (1976): *Macrodynamics*, in Japanese, Tokyo: Toyokeizai Shinposha.

11 No Growth, No Fluctuations

1 An Overview

Arrow (1981, p. 140) quite rightly argues:

The view that only real magnitudes matter can be defended only if it is assumed that the labor market (and all other markets) always clear—that is, that all unemployment is essentially voluntary.... The view that only real magnitudes matter, even over the short periods of the business cycle, can only be defended on this extreme view of smoothly working labor markets. If the contrary view is held, that actual unemployment is to a considerable extent involuntary, then monetary magnitudes retain some of their traditional importance for the analysis of and policy toward short-term economic fluctuations.

The neoclassical world with full price flexibility essentially differs from the intrinsically heterogeneously working capitalist economies, whose working cannot be resolved into the so-called neoclassical synthesis, as is quite appropriately pointed out by Arrow (1967, p. 735). Nor can it be elucidated by the currently fashionable unhappy, peculiar marriage of neoclassical theory with a specific (though important in itself) mode of expectation.

Persistent deficiency of demand or excess of demand relative to supply, that is, disequilibrium is the inevitable destiny of the capitalist economies —one that cannot be substantially cured, though temporarily it might be made less bitter by some allopathic measures.

This destiny is intrinsically dynamic in nature and this cannot be brought to light through the looking glass of static equilibrium. Keynes's ingenuity (1936) penetrated with incisive insight deep into this destiny as a disequilibrium situation. However, he expressed his correct vision of the destiny as an underemployment *static equilibrium* situation—an inadequate formulation, in fact, a *contradictio in adjecto*.

What is more important, the destiny persists not only over short-term fluctuations, but over longer-term economic growth. There is a firmly rooted modern tradition, a dichotomy in separately treating fluctuations as short-term phenomena caused by the imbalance of supply and demand, and growth as an evolution of supply capacity through the interplay of productivity and thrift. Kalecki (1971, p. 165, 1968, p. 263), a well-known independent initiator of Keynesian dynamics, quite rightly remarks:

From G. R. Feiwel, ed., *Arrow and the Foundations of the Theory of Economic Policy* (London: Macmillan, 1987), 421–445. Reprinted by permission.

The contemporary theory of growth of capitalist economies tends to consider this problem in terms of a moving equilibrium rather than adopting an approach similar to that applied in the theory of business cycles. The latter consists of establishing two relations: one based on the impact of the effective demand generated by investment upon profits and the national income, and the other showing the determination of investment decisions by, broadly speaking, the level and the rate of change of economic activity. The first relation does not involve now particularly intricate questions. The second, to my mind, remains the central *pièce de résistance* of economics. I do not see why this approach should be abolished in the face of the problem of long-run growth. In fact, the long-run trend is but a slowly changing component of a chain of short-period situations; it has no independent entity, and the two basic relations mentioned above should be formulated in such a way as to yield the trend cum business-cycle phenomenon. It is true that the task is incomparably more difficult than in the case of another abstraction, that of the 'pure business cycle' and, as will be seen below, the results of such an inquiry are less 'mechanistic'. This, however, is no excuse for dropping this approach, which seems to me the only key to the realistic analysis of the dynamics of a capitalist economy.

Nevertheless, almost all the modern works by eminent authors on either business cycles or growth are within this modern tradition. Hicks (1950) is no exception. His cyclical growth is just a superimposition of a pure cycle on an autonomous growth trend. Notwithstanding a possible unilateral effect from the growth trend to slow down an upswing of the cycle as a ceiling that causes a downturn of the swing, the trend itself is never affected by the cycle. Similarly Kalecki, after making the remarks quoted above, tried to combine cycle and trend by the superimposition.

In a more pioneering way, Smithies (1957) combined cycle and growth to a cyclical growth, but he, too, focused on the superimposition of the former on the latter, taking the basic premise of equality of investment and savings (absence of disequilibrium). Here the only peculiar situation is a special state that occurs for such a specific rate of the autonomous investment as to equal one of the two eigenvalues relevant to the pure cycle that emerges in the absence of the growth trend. After his well-known work on pure business cycles (1951), Goodwin formulated growth cycles (1955, 1967) in ingenious ways. Yet these rested on the basic premise of the automatic equality of savings (all profits saved) to investment; that is, absence of disequilibrium. This system generated growth-rate cycles of a concentric type (trajectories concentric at, concave towards, and around a steady growth state with a vanishing trace of the Jacobian matrix, so not of the familiar limit cycle type emerging from a non-linear accelerator).

It should be emphasized that unlike the other modern cyclical growth theories, this growth trend is not autonomously predetermined but endogenously determined in the interplay between growth and cycle without relying on the superimposition. But the interplay is through the variation of profits that are automatically invested, caused by a trade-off with the real wage rate in the neighbourhood of full employment (a Phillips curve phenomenon, thus without substantial involuntary unemployment, that is, the absence of disequilibrium). Kaldor (1940, 1957; Kaldor and Mirrlees 1962), too, is within this tradition of dichotomy. Last, but not least Arrow, who, from a philosophical point of view, rightly sees through the nature of the Keynesian dynamics (Arrow 1967, p. 735) and is seriously concerned with fluctuations due to disequilibrium (1981), in his actual works, seems to fall within the dichotomy (e.g., 1962, 1968; Arrow and Kurz 1970, and many others).

In the capitalist economies, however, growth and fluctuations are intimately and/or fatefully interrelated. Fluctuations over time govern the *actual* path of the productivity growth, which in turn gives rise to causes of *actual* fluctuations. Growth and fluctuations are mutually causes and effects over both the long and short run. There is only one true exception in this tradition of dichotomy. While he was being criticized by the traditionalists (see Solow 1956, p. 66) for "studying long-run problems with the usual short-term tools," Harrod (1939, 1948, 1973) tried hard to set Keynes in motion and to shed light on the working of capitalist economies. With this one exception, the modern growth theories so far, whether *positive* (descriptive) or *normative* (prescriptive), can hardly be looked upon as a true long-term dynamics of capitalist economies; they can only be considered as certain dynamizations of the Walrasian general equilibrium as a theory of ideal resource allocation. *L'oiseau bleu* of a true long-term dynamics of capitalist economies is still lacking and we should try hard to look for it.

Taking as a point of departure the view that there is no growth without cycles and no cycles without growth, in this chapter I try to consider in an *analytical* model a growth situation accompanied by never-damping fluctuations (almost cyclical, though not necessarily cyclical in the rigorous meaning of the term), with a steadily growing labour force either fully employed or involuntarily unemployed in the various phases of the major and minor fluctuations. The possibility of steady growth is precluded, thus the fluctuations can never be cycles around any steady growth, which is non-existent. These occur in a very simple non-peculiar model of a capitalist economy whose productive potential is given by a familiar very well-known and well-behaved neoclassical production function. The only exogenously given trend parts of the model are a steady rate of growth of the labour force, involving a constant rate of steadily advancing Harrod neutral labour-augmenting technical change, and a constant rate of steady monetary expansion.

Generally, in this model money is not superneutral. The rate of steady monetary expansion crucially affects the destiny of growth and fluctuations in real magnitudes despite the absence of any real money balance effects (or, more generally, any wealth effects) on consumption and savings, deliberately ignored here.

Throughout this model of a capitalist economy the most crucial view is that demand is effective and matters only if it is financed and backed up monetarily (so guaranteed as to be ready for payment by money in the presence of affluent supply, and expressed in nominal magnitudes), and that, when demand meets supply at each moment of time, the prices of goods do not (or, to express more appropriately the intrinsic nature of the state of affairs, cannot) clear the commodity and labour markets, whereas transactions are always carried out on the short side while changes in prices ensue *over* the moment from the disequilibrium.

On the other hand, at each moment of time the rate of interest is instantly adjusted to clear the money market. None the less, in the state of universal disequilibrium between the actual and the demanded levels of output, demand for real money balances depends not only on the rate of interest (negatively on one hand, as usual), but also on the *demanded* level of output (rather than on its *actual* level)—another crucial view.

The model does not pretend to be *un oiseau bleu*; much more modestly I wish that it would turn out to be an *ugly duckling*, so as to shed some light on the generation of major and minor cycles, with the latter occurring in the course of the former, both vitally, mutually interrelated throughout growth within an *analytical*, rather than empirical and/or historical, framework.

2   The Model

A capitalist economy is formulated as a macroeconomic model, where an aggregative homogeneous good Y is produced with the cooperation of capital K (the accumulated stock of the good) and homogeneous labour L by a given familiar well-behaved production function

$$F(K, L) \tag{11.1}$$

of the standard neoclassical type. The good is consumed as well as invested to increase the capital.

The labour force L is steadily growing at a constant rate n, involving a steadily advancing Harrod neutral labour-augmenting technical change. n is therefore a natural rate of growth and

$$\frac{\dot{L}}{L} = n \tag{11.2}$$

Let I be the *intended* real investment, which need not equal the *actual* one. Under a positive constant saving ratio s $(1 > s > 0)$ a multiplier process is assumed to work out instantly to the level of demand for real output I/s. At each moment of time, firms supply just the demanded level of output up to the production capacity represented by (11.1), but cannot supply more beyond it. The actual level Y of output is thus determined as

$$Y = \min\left[F(K, L), \frac{I}{s} \right] \tag{11.3}$$

at each moment of time. If the demand is so deficient that I/s is lower than $F(K, L)$, then Y is determined as $Y = I/s$. Otherwise $Y = F(K, L)$. Firms are presumed always to utilize fully the existing capital K and to adjust supply by changing the level of employment by virtue of the neoclassical smooth flexible factor substitutability. Such a lower amount of labour N than the existing labour force L is thus employed in a situation of deficient demand that

$$\frac{I}{s} = Y = F(K, N) < F(K, L)$$

with $L - N$ being involuntarily unemployed. When demand is sufficient enough to ensure full employment, $Y = F(K, L)$ either with all markets cleared, so that $Y = I/s$ and $N = L$, or with the accompanying excess demand

$$\frac{I}{s} - F(K, L) > 0$$

On the other hand, the firms' idealized instant adjustment of supply to demand (for simplicity) makes overproduction impossible. Thus under the circumstances, these phenomena are occurring behind the determination of the actual level of output (11.3).

At each moment of time the actual level of investment $\dot{K}$ is determined as $100\,s$ per cent of the actual output Y

$$\dot{K} = sY \tag{11.4}$$

(11.4) implies, in the light of (11.3), that $\dot{K} = I$ as a realization of the intended investment when demand is deficient, whereas $\dot{K} = sF(K, L)$ otherwise.

The intended level I of real investment is given as an investment function

$$\frac{\dot{I}}{I} = \varphi(k, R - (r - \pi)) \tag{11.5}$$

where

$$k = \frac{K}{L} \tag{11.6}$$

is the ratio of the existing capital stock to the (not always fully employed) labour force, as it were, a *social* capital–labour ratio; and R, r and π are the rate of profit, the nominal rate of interest and the rate of inflation, respectively.

k affects the intended investment negatively (the partial derivative φ_1 with respect to k being negative) over longer terms, while $R - (r - \pi)$ affects it positively (the partial derivative φ_2 with respect to $R - (r - \pi)$ being positive) over shorter terms.

R can be looked upon as an increasing function of the output–capital ratio

$$R = \psi\left(\frac{Y}{K}\right) \tag{11.7}$$

A very specific instance of the functional form of ψ is provided, when R is the marginal productivity of capital at the moment. In fact, the actual level of output

$$F(K, N)$$

for the actual level of employment N at the moment, which is less than or equal to L under circumstances, determines

$$\frac{Y}{K} = \frac{f(K/N)}{K/N} \tag{11.8}$$

where

$$f\left(\frac{K}{N}\right) = F\left(\frac{K}{N}, 1\right) \tag{11.9}$$

A rising Y/K in (11.8) implies a falling K/N, thereby a rising marginal productivity of capital $f'(K/N)$. Naturally, ψ need not be this specific instance, but can be any more general positive correlation between Y/K and the rate of profit. The economy need thus not be competitive, with the possibility of letting the real wage rate deviate from the marginal productivity of labour.

Let p be the price level, then

$$pK = \text{monetary value of capital stock} \tag{11.10}$$

$$pI = \text{monetary value of intended investment} \tag{11.11}$$

The intended investment in its monetary value is presumed always to be so thoroughly realized that

$$pI = (p\dot{K}) = p\dot{K} + \dot{p}K$$

where $\dot{K}$ is the actual real investment (11.4), thus determining the rate of inflation π as

$$\pi = \frac{\dot{p}}{p} = \frac{I}{K} - \frac{\dot{K}}{K} = \frac{I}{K} - \frac{sY}{K} \tag{11.12}$$

Note that the rate of inflation is always non-negative; it is positive under excess demand, while it is zero in a situation of deficient demand relative to the momentary supply potential (that is, in the case where the intended real investment is realized at the level equal to the actual one $\dot{K}$) by the basic presumption.

In a situation where generally disequilibrium prevails, so that the demanded level I/s for output differs from the actual one, we assume that the demand for real money balances depends not only on the interest rate r

(negatively, as usual), but also on the *demanded* level for output, rather than on the actual one, so that an equilibrium in the money market is

$$\frac{M}{p} = m(r)\frac{I}{s}$$

(11.13)

On the left-hand side of (11.13) M is the level of nominal money stock supplied, and on its right-hand side $m(r)$ is a Marshallian k, positive-valued, but diminishing with the rise of r. The nominal money stock supply is assumed to be steadily expanding at a constant rate θ prescribed by the central bank,

$$\frac{\dot{M}}{M} = \theta$$

(11.14)

In sharp contrast with the commodity and labour markets, which do not always clear (even despite the presumed absence of excess supply of output in a situation of deficient demand relative to the social supply potential), the money market instantly clears at each moment of time by virtue of the adjustment of the interest rate r so as to let (11.13) hold.

From all the basic relations above we formulate a dynamic evolution process of the capitalist economy—that is, a system of three differential equations in the three variables, the social capital–labour ratio k, the rate of the intended investment to the existing capital I/K (that is, the intended rate of capital accumulation), and the interest rate r.

First, from (11.1), (11.2), (11.3), (11.4), (11.6) and (11.9) follows

$$\frac{\dot{k}}{k} = \min\left[\frac{sf(k)}{k}, \frac{I}{K}\right] - n$$

(11.15)

Second, from (11.4), (11.5) and (11.7) follows

$$\frac{(\dot{I/K})}{(I/K)} = \varphi\left(k, \psi\left(\frac{Y}{K}\right) + \pi - r\right) - \frac{sY}{K}$$

(11.16)

Third, by differentiating the logarithm of (11.13) with respect to time and denoting the elasticity of the Marshallian $m(r)$ by $\sigma(r)$, in the light of (11.5), (11.7), (11.12) and (11.14) we have

$$\frac{\dot{r}}{r} = -\frac{1}{\sigma(r)}\left[\frac{I}{K} - \frac{sY}{K} + \varphi\left(k, \psi\left(\frac{Y}{K}\right) + \pi - r\right) - \theta\right]$$

(11.17)

where

$$\frac{Y}{K} = \min\left[\frac{f(k)}{k}, \frac{I}{sK}\right], \frac{\dot{K}}{K} = \frac{sY}{K} \tag{11.18}$$

All the three equations (11.15), (11.16), (11.17) together with (11.12), (11.18) thus form the system of three differential equations in the three variables $k, I/K$ and r (naturally, economically as well as mathematically meaningful only for the positive values of the variables) that generates the evolution over time of the capitalist economy considered here.

3 The Evolution of the Economy

The destiny of the economy crucially hinges on a certain basic relation between the capitalists' propensity to invest on the demand side and the production potential on the supply side.

Let $k*$ be the familiar Solovian full employment steady growth state capital–labour ratio (Solow 1956, p. 69), determined so as to fulfil

$$\frac{sf(k*)}{k*} = n \tag{11.19}$$

An abnormal situation in the capitalist economy—so abnormal that it is possible only incidentally and with luck—is one where the capitalists' investment spirits are so full of vigour that the investment function satisfies

$$\varphi\left(k*, \psi\left(\frac{n}{s}\right) + \theta - n\right) > n \tag{11.20}$$

relative to the natural rate of growth n. In this case, for a positive interest rate $r*$, we have

$$\varphi\left(k*, \psi\left(\frac{n}{s}\right) + \theta - n - r*\right) = n \tag{11.21}$$

so that

$$k = k*, \frac{I}{K} = \theta, r = r* \tag{11.22}$$

determine a long-run full employment steady growth state, with a rate of inflation

$$\pi = \frac{\dot{p}}{p} = \frac{I}{K} - \frac{sY}{K} = \theta - n \tag{11.23}$$

at which money is superneutral, in that θ does not affect any real magnitudes, while the excess of θ over n is completely absorbed by the rate of inflation, except for the level of I/K.

The state need not be stable, as will readily be seen by the inspection of the Jacobian matrix.

When θ is higher than n, the equations (11.15)–(11.17) take in the neighbourhood of the state the form (not the linear approximation)

$$\dot{k} = sf(k) - nk$$

$$\left(\frac{\dot{I}}{K}\right) = \left(\frac{I}{K}\right)\left[\varphi\left(k, \psi\left(\frac{f(k)}{k}\right) + \frac{I}{K} - \frac{sf(k)}{k} - r\right) - \frac{sf(k)}{k}\right]$$

$$\dot{r} = -\frac{r}{\sigma(r)}\left[\frac{I}{K} - \frac{sf(k)}{k} + \varphi\left(k, \psi\left(\frac{f(k)}{k}\right) + \frac{I}{K} - \frac{sf(k)}{k} - r\right) - \theta\right]$$

whose Jacobian matrix evaluated at the state $k = k*$, $I/K = 0$, $r = r*$ is

$$\begin{bmatrix} sf'(k*) - n & 0 & 0 \\ \gamma & \theta\varphi_2^* & -\theta\varphi_2^* \\ \delta & -\dfrac{r*(1 + \varphi_2^*)}{\sigma(r*)} & \dfrac{r*\varphi_2^*}{\sigma(r*)} \end{bmatrix}$$

in which the values of γ and δ are irrelevant to the reasoning below, where

$$\varphi_2^* = \varphi_2\left(k*, \psi\left(\frac{n}{s}\right) + \theta - n - r*\right)$$

The matrix of order 3 is decomposable, and has one real negative eigenvalue $\lambda_1 = sf'(k*) - n$, and two eigenvalues λ_2 and λ_3 obtained as those of the matrix of order 2

$$\begin{bmatrix} \theta\varphi_2^* & -\theta\varphi_2^* \\ -\dfrac{r*(1 + \varphi_2^*)}{\sigma(r*)} & \dfrac{r*\varphi_2^*}{\sigma(r*)} \end{bmatrix}$$

that has a positive determinant

$$-\frac{\theta r^* \varphi_2^*}{\sigma(r^*)}$$

and a trace

$$\left(\theta + \frac{r^*}{\sigma(r^*)}\right)\varphi_2^*$$

whose sign is the same as that of $\theta + r^*/\sigma(r^*)$, which may be positive, negative or zero depending on the relative magnitudes of θ, r^* and $\sigma(r^*)$.

Note the very important fact that the Solovian steady growth state is impossible if θ is lower than n. For in such a situation I/K must be equal to θ, which contradicts the first equation of the Solovian growth state

$$0 = \frac{\dot{k}}{k} = \min\left[\frac{sf(k^*)}{k^*}, \frac{I}{K}\right] - n$$

$$= \min[n, \theta] - n = \theta - n < 0$$

A steady monetary expansion at a rate slower than n thus allows no Solovian steady growth of real magnitude to exist. Furthermore, it must set the economy in motion towards a lower social capital–labour ratio which will eventually make unemployment inevitable.

Now we consider the more important case

$$\varphi\left(k^*, \psi\left(\frac{n}{s}\right) + \theta - n\right) < n \tag{11.24}$$

a situation of deficient demand, a more universal chronic situation of the capitalist economy.

To begin with, let us rearrange the fundamental system (11.15)–(11.17) in the form

$$\dot{k} = \min\left[sf(k), k\frac{I}{K}\right] - nk \tag{11.25}$$

$$\left(\frac{\dot{I}}{K}\right) = \left(\frac{I}{K}\right)\left[\varphi\left(k, \psi\left(\frac{Y}{K}\right) + \pi - r\right) - \frac{sY}{K}\right] \tag{11.26}$$

$$\dot{r} = -\frac{r}{\sigma(r)}\left[\frac{I}{K} - \frac{sY}{K} + \varphi\left(k, \psi\left(\frac{Y}{K}\right) + \pi - r\right) - \theta\right] \tag{11.27}$$

where still

$$\pi = \frac{I}{K} - \frac{sY}{K} \tag{11.12}$$

$$\frac{Y}{K} = \min\left[\frac{f(k)}{k}, \frac{I}{sK}\right], \frac{\dot{K}}{K} = \frac{sY}{K} \tag{11.18}$$

Y/K can be continuous even when k equals zero because $f(k)/k$ tends to plus infinity as k approaches zero. A mathematically fastidious or finical reader may set himself at ease by assuming the continuity of the non-vanishing negative elasticity $\sigma(r)$—e.g., most simply its negative constancy, in the whole real half-line extending from zero to infinity—as he likes. The fundamental system is rearranged and immersed in a more general system (11.25)–(11.27) in order to locate economically meaningful trajectories generated by the fundamental system within the positive orthant in the $(k, I/K, r)$-space.

A special case of the system (11.25)–(11.27) is given for r set equal to zero over time,

$$\dot{k} = \min\left[sf(k), k\frac{I}{K}\right] - nk$$

$$\left(\frac{\dot{I}}{K}\right) = \left(\frac{I}{K}\right)\left[\varphi\left(k, \psi\left(\frac{Y}{K}\right) + \pi\right) - \frac{sY}{K}\right]$$

$$\dot{r} = 0, \text{(always } r = 0),$$

which implies that the non-negative co-ordinate plane orthant formed by all non-negative points $(k, I/K, 0)$ is completely filled out by the trajectories of the system (11.25)–(11.27). By the same token, this fact also applies to the other two non-negative co-ordinate plane orthants obtained by setting k and I/K equal to zero, respectively. Therefore, a trajectory of the system (11.25)–(11.27) passing through a point $(k, I/K, r)$, with the co-ordinates positive, never meets any of the three non-negative co-ordinate plane orthants, so that it remains forever within the positive orthant in the space. For this reason, the fundamental system (11.15)–(11.17) with (11.12), (11.18) generates the evolution of the economy within the positive orthant.

Now let θ, the rate of steady monetary expansion, be higher than the natural rate of growth n. Then we have

PROPOSITION 1   The plane region $k = k^*$ bounded by

$$\frac{I}{K} \geqq \frac{sf(k^*)}{k^*} = s\left(\frac{Y}{K}\right)^* = n$$

is completely filled out by trajectories of the system (11.15)–(11.17).

For, in the region the system (11.15)–(11.17) becomes

$$\frac{\dot{k}}{k} = 0 \text{ (always } k = k^*)$$

$$\frac{(\dot{I/K})}{(I/K)} = \varphi\left(k^*, \psi\left(\frac{n}{s}\right) + \frac{I}{K} - n - r\right) - n$$

$$\frac{\dot{r}}{r} = -\frac{1}{\sigma(r)}\left[\frac{I}{K} - n + \varphi\left(k^*, \psi\left(\frac{n}{s}\right) + \frac{I}{K} - n - r\right) - \theta\right]$$

whose solution trajectories fill out the region, so that any other trajectories of the fundamental system neither meet nor cross the region.

PROPOSITION 2   The phase diagram in the whole region $k = k^*$ looks like Fig. 11.1, where the directions of the movements of I/K and r are shown by arrows as usual, while that of k is shown by an encircled plus sign, minus sign or zero, meaning $\dot{k} > 0$, $\dot{k} < 0$ or $\dot{k} = 0$, respectively.

In Fig. 11.1 the first equation becomes

$$\frac{\dot{k}}{k} = \frac{I}{K} - n < 0$$

for $I/K < n$, thus a minus sign is encircled.

PROPOSITION 3   Always $\dot{k} < 0$ in the space bounded by $k > k^*$.

This is obvious, because $sf(k)/k < n$ for $k > k^*$, so that

$$\frac{\dot{k}}{k} = \min\left[\frac{I}{K}, \frac{sf(k)}{k}\right] - n \leqq \frac{sf(k)}{k} - n < 0$$

Together these three propositions imply that any trajectory generated by the fundamental system (11.15)–(11.17) lies from the beginning (or eventually enters, and never leaves) in the space region Ω bounded by k^* in the positive orthant.

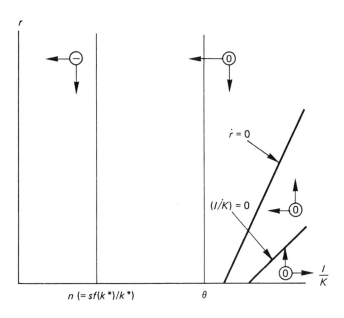

$n \ (= sf(k^*)/k^*)$ θ

$(k = k^*)$

Figure 11.1

PROPOSITION 4   There is no steady growth state whether the labour force is underemployed or fully employed.

For otherwise, $(I/K) = 0$ at such a state would imply

$$\varphi\left(k, \psi\left(\frac{Y}{K}\right) + \pi - r\right) = \frac{sY}{K}$$

so that $I/K = \theta$ by $\dot{r} = 0$. Moreover, $sf(k)/k > n$ always in Ω, and

$$\frac{\dot{k}}{k} = \min\left[\frac{sf(k)}{k}, \frac{I}{K}\right] - n$$

$$> \min\left[n, \theta\right] - n = n - n = 0$$

With all these facts in mind, within the region Ω certain phase diagrams are drawn in the same manner as in Fig. 11.1 for a fixed level of k such as $k^* > k > 0$.[1] Fig. 11.2a and 11.2b are the cases where

$$\theta > \frac{sf(k)}{k} > n \tag{11.28}$$

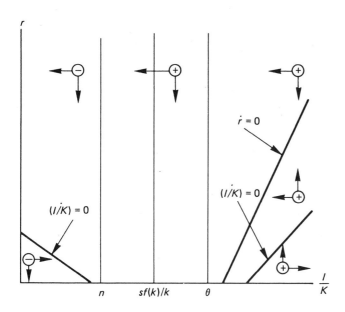

(k close to k^*)

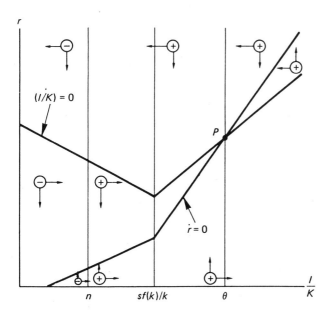

(k intermediate)

Figure 11.2

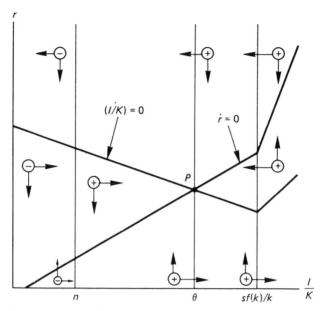

(k very close to zero)

Figure 11.3

and Fig. 11.3 is the case where

$$\frac{sf(k)}{k} > \theta \ (> n \text{ naturally}) \tag{11.29}$$

Regarding the investment function we presume a very plausible short-term stability condition

$$\varphi_2\left(k, \psi\left(\frac{Y}{K}\right) - r\right)\psi'\left(\frac{Y}{K}\right) < s \tag{11.30}$$

which makes the locus $(I/K) = 0$ downward-sloped in the interval $sf(k)/k \gtreqqless I/K \geqq 0$ in the phase diagrams. Obviously it is the counterpart of the lower propensity to invest (with respect to income) than the propensity to save in the 45° line argument.

Note the important fact that in any of the figures, I/K must be θ, when both loci $(I/K) = 0$ and $\dot{r} = 0$ intersect. If we would keep k constant at a level between k^* and zero, the point $P = (\theta, r^0)$, the intersection of both loci, if any, is a critical point of a system of two differential equations

$$\frac{(\dot{I/K})}{(I/K)} = \varphi\left(k, \psi\left(\frac{Y}{K}\right) + \frac{I}{K} - \frac{sY}{K} - r\right) - \frac{sY}{K}$$

$$\frac{\dot{r}}{r} = -\frac{1}{\sigma(r)}\left[\frac{I}{K} - \frac{sY}{K} + \varphi\left(k, \psi\left(\frac{Y}{K}\right) + \pi - r\right) - \theta\right]$$

where still

$$\pi = \frac{I}{K} - \frac{sY}{K}, \frac{Y}{K} = \min\left[\frac{f(k)}{k}, \frac{I}{sK}\right]$$

but with k kept at a constant level, in the two variables I/K and r, naturally a system different from the fundamental one.

The point $P = (\theta, r^0)$ is determined depending on the level of k and shifts with the increase of k in Fig. 11.2b and 11.3. This is due to the shift of both loci caused by the shifting effect of the increase of k on the investment function φ. As k increases towards k^*, the point shifts along the vertical straight line $I/K = \theta$ in the phase diagrams, until it reaches the horizontal axis and then disappears as in Fig. 11.2a.

From all the above results we know that there are cyclical fluctuations of k (the ratio of always fully utilized capital to the not always fully employed labour force) of relatively longer terms and also cyclical fluctuations of I/K (the desired level of investment–capital ratio) and r (the interest rate) of relatively shorter terms mutually and inseparably involved and entangled in their generation. During the fluctuations capital is always utilized, but the labour force is underemployed when I/K is lower than $sf(k)/k$ and fully employed otherwise. In particular, in a situation of full employment of labour with I/K higher than $sf(k)/k$ (that is, accompanied by the excess demand $I/s - F(K, L)$) inflation proceeds at the rate $\pi = I/K - sf(k)/k$, which varies over time. It is also noted that in a full employment situation the economy grows along the ceiling of the production potential, with a falling rate of profit $R = \psi(Y/K)$ resulting from the falling average productivity of capital $Y/K = f(k)/k$, operative in determining Y/K instead of a higher I/sK—a factor that eventually brings about a downturn.

The cyclical fluctuations of k occur in the following way: while k continues to rise with $\dot{k}$ kept positive in the region Ω in which $sf(k)/k$ is always higher than n, the point $(I/K, r)$ remains within the portion $I/K > n$ in the diagrams. The continuous rise of k, however, must eventually bring about a situation such as Fig. 11.2a where $(I/K, r)$ eventually gets in the portion

$I/K < n$, making $\dot{k}$ negative and letting k start falling. While k continues to fall, with $\dot{k}$ kept negative in the region Ω, the point $(I/K, r)$ remains within the portion $I/K < n$ in the phase diagrams. The time must then come when the point $(I/K, r)$ gets in the portion $I/K > n$ such as depicted in Fig. 11.2b or Fig. 11.3, making $\dot{k}$ positive and letting k start rising. k must thus fluctuate cyclically.

A continuous rise or fall of k thereby also causes fluctuations of I/K and r that keep pace with the fluctuations of k. The point $(I/K, r)$ may possibly undergo several rounds of cyclical movement around and near the point (θ, r^0), shifting in the phase diagrams during a phase of continuous rise of k, as is likely to be the case, provided the shift is slowed by a weak effect of the change of k on the investment function.

The fluctuations are never damping, for otherwise, the state of the economy $(k, I/K, r)$ would converge to a non-existent steady growth state. The damp of the fluctuation of k would imply the convergence of k to k^*, so that a situation such as depicted in Fig. 11.2a can persist, sending the point $(I/K, r)$ into the portion $I/K < n$ eventually and letting it remain there some time and thereby bringing about an impossible perpetual fall of k. The fluctuation of $(I/K, r)$ is never damped either, for, otherwise, I/K would converge to θ (higher than n) and k would eventually continue to rise forever in contradiction with the persistence of fluctuations. Thus the capitalist economy must continue to undergo *un retour éternel* within the region Ω.

In the above growth cycles, θ (the constant rate of steady monetary expansion, set at a level higher than n) clearly affects the fluctuations of the real magnitudes, except for the lucky abnormal situation in the capitalist economy, where the investment spirits of capitalists are so full of vigour that (11.20) holds.

A higher level of θ (by causing the downward shift of the function on the right-hand side of (11.17), which decelerates the rise of the interest rate or accelerates the fall of the interest rate, and thereby decelerates the fall of I/K or accelerates the rise of I/K in (11.16)) gives rise to an expansionary effect on the economy. In the phase diagrams raising the level of θ shifts downward the locus $\dot{r} = 0$ and enlarges the portion where r is falling, while keeping the locus $(I\dot{/}K) = 0$ intact. This accelerates the economy in a downswing phase towards the turn to an upswing and prolongs the duration of an upswing. In the fluctuation of k, the upswing phase is likely to get prolonged, whereas the downswing is likely to get shortened.

The inevitability of growth cycle originates in the weak investment spirits of capitalists relative to the natural rate of growth at the capital–labour ratio k^* prevailing in the Solovian neoclassical steady growth as expressed in (11.24). The left-hand side of (11.24) can be increased by raising the level of θ and a situation such as (11.20) may be reached by setting the rate of steady monetary expansion at a sufficiently high level to get the economy on the track of steady growth. But this possibility depends on the investment spirits. While the left-hand side of (11.24) increases with the increase of θ, it never catches up to the right-hand side if the investment spirits are so weak relative to the natural rate of growth that the value of the investment function tails off without reaching n with the increase of θ to infinity. Under such circumstances the growth cycle cannot be eliminated by any high rate of steady monetary expansion.

4   What Happens When θ Is Not Higher Than n

Consider the possibility of a steady growth state when θ equals n. If

$$\varphi\left(k^*, \psi\left(\frac{n}{s}\right)\right) > n$$

then

$$\varphi\left(k^*, \psi\left(\frac{n}{s}\right) - r^*\right) = n$$

for a positive r^*, so that $k = k^*$, $I/K = n$, $r = r^*$ give a steady growth state without inflation. But it is unstable, because once I/K happens to deviate below n, then $\dot{k}/k = I/K - n$ becomes negative and the economy gets into the region Ω where k is lower than k^*, and can never come back to this state.

Next suppose

$$\varphi\left(k^*, \psi\left(\frac{n}{s}\right)\right) \leqq n$$

If pairs (k^0, r^0) such as fulfil

$$\varphi\left(k^0, \psi\left(\frac{n}{s}\right) - r^0\right) = n$$

exist, then all such pairs form a curve in the (k, r)-plane, and a point on it determines a steady growth state at which

$$k = k^0, \frac{I}{K} = n, r = r^0$$

where naturally k^0 is lower than k^*, and without inflation, but with unemployment of labour. There are thus multiple (infinitely many) steady growth states of such a kind. Each of them is, however, unstable for the following reasons.

In fact, in the neighbourhood of such a state the system becomes

$$\frac{\dot{k}}{k} = \frac{I}{K} - n$$

$$\frac{(\dot{I/K})}{(I/K)} = \varphi\left(k, \psi\left(\frac{I}{sK}\right) - r\right) - \frac{I}{K}$$

$$\frac{d}{dt}\log m(r) = n - \varphi\left(k, \psi\left(\frac{I}{sK}\right) - r\right)$$

Then, summing up all three equations above, and integrating them, we have

$$k\frac{I}{K}m(r) = \text{constant} \tag{11.31}$$

In the neighbourhood of such a steady growth state the trajectory lies within the surface above in the $(k, I/K, r)$-space for a specific value of the constant on the right-hand side of (11.31). Hence, if the economy is slightly perturbed to a point on the surface for a different value of the constant, it remains within the new surface, so that it cannot get back to the original steady growth state.

Let us examine what a steady monetary expansion at a slower rate θ than n will cause. The fundamental equations take the form

$$\frac{\dot{k}}{k} = \frac{sY}{K} - n$$

$$\frac{(\dot{I/K})}{(I/K)} = \varphi\left(k, \psi\left(\frac{Y}{K}\right) + \pi - r\right) - \frac{sY}{K}$$

$$\frac{d}{dt}\log m(r) = \theta - \varphi\left(k, \psi\left(\frac{Y}{K}\right) + \pi - r\right) - \pi$$

which add up to

$$\frac{d}{dt} \log\left(k \frac{I}{K} m(r)\right) = \theta - n - \pi$$

$$\leq \theta - n < 0$$

implying that $k(I/K)m(r)$ is steadily diminishing towards zero.

Naturally there is no steady growth state for the same reason mentioned before on the basis of the fact that I/K must be θ in such a state. Moreover, wild fluctuations are caused. They are undamping, as can be seen by inspecting the corresponding phase diagrams, the counterparts of and similar to Fig. 11.1, 11.2a, 11.2b and 11.3.

5 Conclusion

In summary form, the above results show that capitalist economies are capable of evolution over time, but inevitably in the form of cyclical growth. This is not a pure cyclical movement superimposed on an autonomous growth trend, nor is the endogenously determined growth trend without cycles. Rather it ensues from the instability inherent in the workings of the capitalist economies as an entangled complex of growth and fluctuations mutually acting as causes and effects.

As the social capital–labour ratio k is rising, the pair of the rate of intended accumulation I/K and the interest rate r continues to fluctuate around point P (in Fig. 11.2b and 11.3), which shifts to keep pace with the change of k through mutual interaction. If k could be kept unchanged, point P would stop moving and its stability[2] would make the fluctuations around it damped, so that if there were no growth,[3] there would be no fluctuations. Actually, k changes over time and shifts point P, making the fluctuations undamped, until a situation without such a point P (Fig. 11.2a) is reached where the eventually inevitable downward movement of I/K brings about that of k before k can reach the Solovian capital–labour ratio k^*, the barrier level of k inherent in the workings of the systems. The fluctuations that must accompany growth thus eventually hinder growth and must bring about the lowering of the growth rate, thereby triggering a downswing in the cyclical movement of k.

Very likely, the slower and longer lasting is a monotonous change of k (say its rise), the milder are the accompanying fluctuations in I/K and r. By the same token, the more rapid and shorter lasting is the change of k, the wilder are the accompanying fluctuations in I/K and r. Theoretically, however, it is hardly feasible to tell how long the duration of one round of the cycle of k is, but this is a matter of empirical verification.

As a matter of fact, it is not clear here whether a complete limit cycle trajectory exists within the region Ω, on which the triplet $(k, I/K, r)$ moves. But this lack of exact information about the existence of a complete periodic trajectory seems to be rather irrelevant, compared with the main knowledge here that the growth of a capitalist economy must undergo *un retour éternel* even in the complete ignorance of more instability due to such destabilizing factors as uncertainty regarding disequilibrium in the future (see Arrow 1981, especially pp. 142–50) and/or the Schumpeterian creative destruction.

Notes

For permissions to quote I am grateful to the relevant authors, Basic Books Inc., and Cambridge University Press.

1. In Fig. 11.2b and 11.3 each of both loci $(I/K) = 0$ and $\dot{r} = 0$ has a unique kink at which the value of Y/K switches from I/sK to $f(k)/k$. The locus $(I/K) = 0$ is downward-sloped by the short-term stability condition (11.30) on the left of the kink, and a 45° straight line beyond it. The locus $\dot{r} = 0$ is upward-sloped globally, and has a steeper slope than the one on the right of the kink.

2. Point P is locally stable in Fig. 11.3 by virtue of the short-term stability condition (11.30), whereas it need not be stable in Fig. 11.2b.

3. To express it more exactly, "if there were no unsteady growth."

References

Arrow, K. J. (1962): The Economic Implications of Learning by Doing, *Review of Economic Studies*, 29.

———— (1967): Samuelson Collected, *Journal of Political Economy*, 75.

———— (1968): Optimal Capital Policy with Irreversible Investment, in J. N. Wolfe (ed.) *Value, Capital and Growth*, Edinburgh: Edinburgh University Press.

———— (1981): Real and Nominal Magnitudes in Economics, in D. Bell and I. Kristol (eds.) *The Crisis in Economic Theory*, New York: Basic Books.

Arrow, K. J. and M. Kurz (1970): *Public Investment, the Rate of Return, and Optimal Fiscal Policy*, Baltimore: The Johns Hopkins Press.

Goodwin, R. M. (1951): The Nonlinear Accelerator and the Persistence of Business Cycles, *Econometrica*, 19.

———— (1955): A Model of Cyclical Growth, in E. Lundberg (ed.) *The Business Cycle in the Post-War World*, London: Macmillan.

—— (1967): A Growth Cycle, in C. H. Feinstein (ed.) *Socialism, Capitalism and Economic Growth, Essays Presented to Maurice Dobb*, Cambridge: Cambridge University Press.

Harrod, R. F. (1939): An Essay in Dynamic Theory, *Economic Journal*, 49.

—— (1948): *Towards a Dynamic Economics*, London: Macmillan.

—— (1973): *Economic Dynamics*, London: Macmillan.

Hicks, J. R. (1950): *A Contribution to the Theory of the Trade Cycle*, London: Oxford University Press.

Kaldor, N. (1940): A Model of the Trade Cycle, *Economic Journal*, 50.

—— (1957): A Model of Economic Growth, *Review of Economic Studies*, 29.

Kaldor, N. and J. A. Mirrlees (1962): A New Model of Economic Growth, *Review of Economic Studies*, 29.

Kalecki, M. (1968): Trend and Business Cycles Reconsidered, *Economic Journal*, 78.

—— (1971): *Selected Essays on the Capitalist Economy*, Cambridge: Cambridge University Press.

Keynes, J. M. (1936): *The General Theory of Employment, Interest and Money*, London: Macmillan.

Smithies, A. (1957): Economic Fluctuations and Growth, *Econometrica*, 25.

Solow, R. M. (1956): A Contribution to the Theory of Economic Growth, *Quarterly Journal of Economics*, 70.

12 A Genuine Keynesian Growth Cycle

1 Introduction

Monetarists Mark I believe that the capitalist economy is by nature well-behaved, well-workable and stable, unless disturbances from outside—including, naturally, government interventions—are injected into the economy. The economy is equipped with certain filters which work, though not instantly, but gradually and steadily, and are capable of making the effects of disturbances from outside eventually die out.

Monetarists Mark II believe in the well-behavedness, well-workability and stability as well. They believe, furthermore, that the economy is equipped with a special device (rational expectations), which instantly becomes operative to cut off the effects of all disturbances from outside but the unanticipated ones, which are the only causes disturbing the good behaviour and well-workability of the economy.

Both accuse Keynesians for their "activist stance," as the former call it—that is, the intention to control the economy by government intervention—as something disturbing and/or ineffective. Keynesians are not a single monolith, however, and not all of them are activists. Indeed, some (probably a majority) of them, are activists. Nonetheless, some others are pessimists who do not believe in the controllability of the economy just because of their serious view of its ill-behavedness.

What is common to all Keynesians, and which so distinguishes them from monetarists, is their vision that the capitalist economy is ill-behaved, even if it is shielded from exterior disturbances, in sharp contrast to the monetarists' belief in the well-behavedness of the capitalist economy.

This difference in the visions as to the basic structure and performance of the *genuine* capitalist economy, "genuine" in the sense that it is cut off from all exterior disturbances, leads to the essential difference in the business cycle theories. For the Keynesians business cycles are inherent to the genuine capitalist economy, whereas for the monetarists they are the bad effects of disturbances from outside on the geniune capitalist economy which would otherwise work well.

The modern business cycle theories in the Keynesian paradigm have a long history. Among them the most relevant ones are of nonlinear types such as Goodwins (1951, 1955, 1967), Kaldor (1940), Rose (1967),

From Mukul Majumdar, ed., Equilibrium and Dynamics: Essays in Honour of David Gale (London: Macmillan, 1992), 247–258. Reprinted by permission.

Morishima (1958), and Yasui (1961). From the analytical point of view these nonlinear theories, whether verbally or analytically presented, essentially owe the core of their results—that is, the possibility of business cycles—either implicitly or explicitly, to the Poincaré–Bendixon (hereafter P–B) theorem on the existence of a limit cycle, except Goodwin (1967) results, which depend on the Volterra differential equation simulating the symbiosis of prey and predator, that generates infinitely many concentric periodic trajectories.

Benassy (1984) also showed the possibility of a pure business cycle of a short-term duration, based on the P–B theorem in a model of an IS-LM apparatus combined with a Phillips curve.

I myself am allied in spirit with the Keynesian paradigm, and will show in this study the possibility of a long-term growth cycle with explicit consideration of both demand-side and supply-side potential based on the P–B theorem.

The growth cycle considered in this model must inevitably be around a steady growth state with *unemployment* and can never be around the Solovian steady growth state with full employment.

These and other results will be established in a model which is an integration of Kaldor's pure business cycle (1940) and Solow's neoclassical growth (1956), through their mutual interaction, rather than a mere superimposition of the former on the growth trend generated by the latter. To simplify the matter so as to get a complete growth cycle (a periodic trajectory) the monetary factors are deliberately ignored. In a more complex situation involving monetary factors, both growth rate fluctuations of rather longer terms and those of intended investment and interest rate of shorter terms coexist, entangled and interrelated, as elucidated elsewhere (Nikaido, 1987). Ignoring the monetary factors here is just for the sake of obtaining a complete growth cycle based on the P–B theorem.

2 The Growth Process

A capitalist economy is formulated in terms of a macroeconomic model where the output, an aggregative homogeneous good, can be consumed as well as invested in order to increase the existing capital stock. The output is produced with the cooperation of the existing capital K and the employed labour N through a given well-behaved production function of the standard neoclassical type

$$F(K, N) \tag{12.1}$$

under constant returns to scale.

The labour force L is steadily growing at a constant rate n, involving a steadily advancing Harrod-neutral labour-augmenting technical change

$$\frac{\dot{L}}{L} = n \tag{12.2}$$

n is therefore the natural rate of growth. It is important to note that the labour force is not always fully employed, so that N need not equal L.

Let X be the level of sales of output expected by the firms, at the moment, in real terms. If X does not exceed the supply potential $F(K, L)$, they carry through the production of X by employing N units of labour such that $X = F(K, N)$, $N \leq L$. In case N is less than L in such a situation, $L - N$ units of labour are involuntarily unemployed. On the other hand, if X exceeds the supply potential, the output is produced at full capacity with the labour force fully employed. Thus, the *actual* level of output Y at the moment is determined so that

$$Y = \min \left[F(K, L), X \right] \tag{12.3}$$

On the assumption of a constant saving ratio $s(1 > s > 0)$, the actual investment $\dot{K}$ at the moment is determined so that

$$\dot{K} = sY \tag{12.4}$$

Let I be the intended real investment, which is not always equal to the actual one. If all the other things which affect the animal spirit are given and remain unchanged, I/K, the ratio of the intended investment to the existing capital stock, depends on the two factors, the capital–(not always fully employed) labour ratio

$$k = \frac{K}{L} \tag{12.5}$$

as it were, the social capital–labour ratio, and the current rate of profit R. Therefore,

$$\frac{I}{K} = \Phi(k, R) \tag{12.6}$$

in which k and R affect I/K negatively and positively, respectively, so that its partial derivatives fulfil

$$\Phi_1(k, R) < 0 < \Phi_2(k, R) \tag{12.7}$$

R is presumed to be an *increasing* function of the output–capital ratio Y/K,

$$R = \Psi\left(\frac{Y}{K}\right) \tag{12.8}$$

$$\Psi'\left(\frac{Y}{K}\right) > 0 \tag{12.9}$$

A specific example, which is by no means asserted to be universally valid here, is the case where R is the marginal productivity of capital. Since $Y = F(K, N)$ for the current level of employment N, we have

$$\frac{Y}{K} = \frac{f(K/N)}{K/N} \tag{12.10}$$

where

$$f\left(\frac{K}{N}\right) = F\left(\frac{K}{N}, 1\right) \tag{12.11}$$

In equation (12.10) a rise in Y/K implies a fall in K/N, whence a rise in the marginal productivity of capital $f'(K/N)$.

The expected level of sales of output X varies so as to chase the demand, conforming to the multiplier process

$$(X/K) = G\left(\frac{I}{K} + \frac{cY}{K} - \frac{X}{K}\right) \tag{12.12}$$

where G is an increasing function, with a positive derivative and $G(0) = 0$ and $c = 1 - s$ is the propensity to consume.

From the above equations we get the fundamental system of differential equations representing the growth process of the economy. In fact, from (12.1)–(12.5) we have

$$\frac{\dot{k}}{k} = \frac{sY}{K} - n \tag{12.13}$$

with

$$\frac{Y}{K} = \min\left[\frac{f(k)}{k}, \frac{X}{K}\right] \tag{12.14}$$

$$f(k) = F(k, 1) \tag{12.15}$$

From equations (12.6), (12.8), and (12.12) we have

$$(X/K) = G\left(\Phi\left(k, \Psi\left(\frac{Y}{K}\right)\right) + \frac{cY}{K} - \frac{X}{K}\right) \tag{12.16}$$

Equations (12.13), (12.16) with (12.14), (12.15) form the fundamental system of differential equations in the two variables k and X/K representing the growth process. Note that equation (12.13) represents the Solovian neoclassical growth process when $f(k)/k$ is operative in equation (12.14) as in Solow (1956).

3 The Possibility of a Growth Cycle

There are several alternative possibilities as to the shape of the intended investment curve

$$\frac{I}{K} = \Phi\left(k, \Psi\left(\frac{Y}{K}\right)\right) \tag{12.17}$$

with respect to the change of the output–capital ratio Y/K, for a fixed level of the social capital–labour ratio k. It is definitely upward sloping by (12.8), (12.9), and the right-hand part of (12.7). Here, it is assumed to be convex (that is, its second derivative positive), and with a positive level of investment $\Phi(k, \Psi(0))$ even at $Y/K = 0$. The shape looks like that depicted in Fig. 12.1.

Then, for a fixed level of k, the curve

$$\Phi(k, \Psi(Y/K)) + \frac{cY}{K} \tag{12.18}$$

looks like the one in Fig. 12.2a, as the variable X/K varies. Note that by equation (12.14) the value of Y/K in (12.18) switches from (X/K) to $f(k)/k$, which accounts for the kink in the curve. The curve shifts downward as k increases. It is assumed that the curve intersects the 45° line thrice for

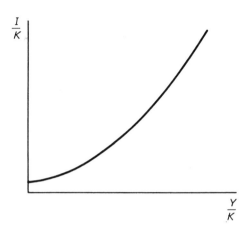

Figure 12.1

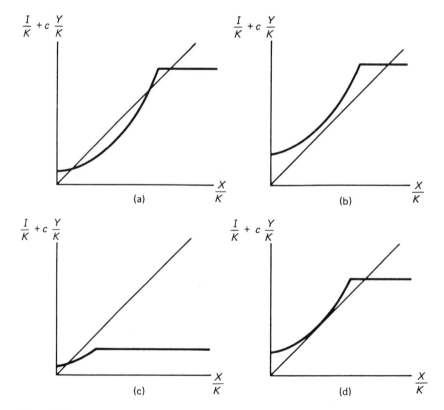

Figure 12.2

intermediate levels of k as in Fig. 12.2a. It is also assumed that the curve intersects the 45° line once for a very low level of k as in Fig. 12.2b and likewise once for a very high level of k as in Fig. 12.2c. Moreover, a unique level of k is assumed to exist such that a border situation as in Fig. 12.2d takes place. In summary, the curve shifts downward as k increases, starting from situations as in Fig. 12.2b via those as in Fig. 12.2d and Fig. 12.2a toward those as in Fig. 12.2c.

Now, let k^* be the capital–labour ratio in the Solovian full employment steady growth state as determined by

$$\frac{f(k^*)}{k^*} = \frac{n}{s} \tag{12.19}$$

(Solow 1956). Note that k^* need not ensure a steady growth in the process considered here.

We consider the case where

$$\Phi\left(k^*, \Psi\left(\frac{n}{s}\right)\right) < n \tag{12.20}$$

a situation of deficient demand relative to the supply potential due to the rather weak propensity to invest.

Fig. 12.3a and 12.3b depict the two possible typical alternative situations of the corresponding phase diagrams. In them, the dashed downward sloping curve represents the average productivity of capital

$$\frac{X}{K} = \frac{f(k)}{k} \tag{12.21}$$

and the upper shaded portion bounded by equation (12.21) is the full employment region, where the labour force is fully employed, while it is underemployed in the other unshaded portion likewise bounded by equation (12.21), the underemployment region.

From the definitions in equations (12.13) and (12.14), the locus $\dot{k} = 0$ is the bold reversely L-shaped rectangular curve on whose north-west side $\dot{k}$ is positive, and negative on the other side, because the function (12.14) is decreasing with respect to k and increasing with respect to X/K.

On the other hand, from the assumptions on the shape of the curve (12.18) and the manner in which it shifts with the change of the level of k, the locus $(\dot{X}/K) = 0$ looks like the other bold curve with a kink in the diagram. (X/K) is positive on the west side of the locus and negative on its east side in the light of the sign-preserving property of the function G.

In the situation now under consideration of the deficient demand relative to the supply potential (12.20), both loci intersect at a point P lying on the horizontal part of the locus $\dot{k} = 0$ where $k^* > k > 0$ and $X/K = n/s$.

The intersection point P of both loci is the critical point representing a steady state growth with underemployment of labor.

In a case as in Fig. 12.3a the locus $(X/K) = 0$ is upward sloping in the neighbourhood of the point P. P is unstable, as can also be shown analytically by evaluating the Jacobian matrix there. In view of the fact that X/K is operative to determine the value of equation (12.14) in the neighbourhood of the point P, the Jacobian matrix is

$$
\begin{bmatrix}
0 & k^0 \\
G'(0)\Phi_1\left(k^0, \Psi\left(\dfrac{n}{s}\right)\right) & G'(0)\left[\Phi_2\left(k^0, \Psi\left(\dfrac{n}{s}\right)\right) - s\right]
\end{bmatrix}
\tag{12.22}
$$

where the coordinates of P are k^0 and n/s. It has

$$
\text{Determinant} = -k^0 G'(0)\Phi_1\left(k^0, \Psi\left(\dfrac{n}{s}\right)\right) > 0
$$

since k^0, $G' > 0 > \Phi_1$, and

$$
\text{Trace} = G'(0)\left[\Phi_2\left(k^0, \Psi\left(\dfrac{n}{s}\right)\right) - s\right] > 0
$$

as P corresponds to the middle of the three points of intersection in Fig. 12.2a, at which $\Phi_2(k^0, \Psi(n/s)) - s > 0$.

Now, from the phase diagram drawn in Fig. 12.3a all the trajectories starting at any point are bounded and eventually wind spirally clockwise, either inward or outward around the unique unstable critical point $P = (k^0, n/s)$. Under these circumstances there is a limit cycle $ABCDEF$ by virtue of the P–B theorem (see, e.g., Pontryagin 1962, pp. 220–31).

The cycle may be bounded entirely within the underemployment region, allowing the economy to grow cyclically without having any phase of full employment. Nonetheless, the cycle must have a phase to travel on the full employment region, provided the firms are bullish enough so as to make the evolution of the economy explosive if unbounded by the supply capacity (that is, in a fictitious situation where X/K is always actively operative

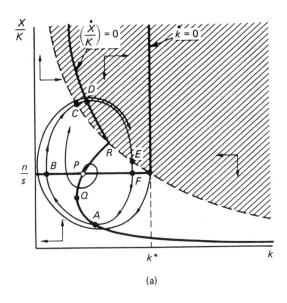

(a)

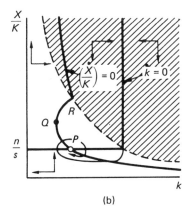

(b)

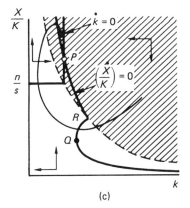

(c)

Figure 12.3

in equation (12.14)), as is likely to be the case. Thus the cycle $ABCDEF$ in Fig. 12.3a is a typical limit cycle.

Let us look at a circuit of the cycle. In the phase AB the economy turns from a downswing to an upswing at A by a low level of the social capital–labour ratio and grows upward, driven by the decreasing social capital–labour ratio, the excess demand for output and the rising rate of profit. In the phase BC, the economy continues to grow accumulating capital relative to the labour force. The growth is driven by the intensified investment due to the excess demand for output and the rising rate of profit, whose effects surpass the depressing effects of the increasing social capital–labour ratio from B to C, until the economy reaches the full employment region at C. But from the moment at which the economy gets into full employment region the rate of profit must fall at the same pace as that of the decreasing average productivity of capital during the boom, making the economy destined for a turn to a downswing. The turn comes at D, and the economy ceases to be in boom at E after continuing to grow in boom, still maintaining full employment of labour, driven by the falling but still high rate of profit. In the phase EF the still increasing social capital–labour ratio and the falling rate of profit severely depress growth. In the phase FA the stagnant investment gives rise to a decrease in the social capital–labour ratio so as to decrease the excess supply of output, allowing an otherwise inevitable dive into stagnation due to the depressing effects of the falling rate of profit to be curbed toward the turn of the downswing to an upswing at A again, completing one circuit of the cycle.

Consider now the other alternative situation in the case of deficient demand (12.20) depicted in Fig. 12.3b. The locus $(X/K) = 0$ is downward sloping in the neighbourhood of the critical point P, which corresponds to the left-most intersection point in Fig. 12.2a. The corresponding Jacobian matrix in (12.22) has a negative trace, while its determinant is still positive. Hence P is locally stable. Nonetheless it need not be globally stable. All the trajectories, starting at any point, are bounded and wind spirally clockwise around P. Hence, either all the trajectories approach the critical point or a periodic trajectory exists, on which the economy cycles around P and which certain trajectories wind spirally around and approach from outside.

Even if P is located at Q, where the trace of the Jacobian matrix vanishes, the same result holds—that is, either all the trajectories approach the critical point or there is a cycle around it.

4   What Happens under Affluent Demand

In the case where

$$\Phi\left(k^*, \Psi\left(\frac{n}{s}\right)\right) > n \tag{12.23}$$

a situation of affluent demand relative to the supply potential, in contrast to (12.20), the critical point P is located on the vertical part of the locus $\dot{k} = 0$, where $k = k^*$, and $X/K > n/s$. At the point P the Solovian neo-classical full employment steady growth persists, while being accompanied by an everlasting excess demand $(X/K)^* - f(k^*)/k^*$. $f(k)/k$ is operative in equation (12.14) in the neighbourhood of the critical point P, and the Jacobian matrix is readily shown to have a positive determinant and a negative trace, so that P is locally stable. Moreover, from the phase diagram drawn in Fig. 12.3c, the point is a globally stable node.

In the very exceptional coincidental case where

$$\Phi\left(k^*, \Psi\left(\frac{n}{s}\right)\right) = n \tag{12.24}$$

both the loci $\dot{k} = 0$ and $(X/K) = 0$ intersect at the point at which their kinks coincide. The corresponding critical point represents the neoclassical full employment steady growth without excess demand and supply, and is a globally stable node.

5   Concluding Remarks

The economy undergoes either growth cycles approaching a limit cycle around a steady state growth with underemployment of labour or con-verges to a stable steady state growth with underemployment of labour or to the Solovian full employment steady state growth accompanied by everlasting excess demand except in a coincidental case where it con-verges to the Solovian full employment steady state growth without excess demand and supply.

What happens crucially hinges on the magnitude of propensity to invest $\Phi(k^*, \Psi(n/s))$ at the Solovian neoclassical steady state growth relative to the natural rate of growth n. The lower is the former relative to the latter, the more stagnant is the economy.

Nonetheless, seemingly paradoxically, the economy becomes less stagnant, and moves toward prosperity, as n gets higher. For, suppose (12.20) holds, and the economy is stagnant. If n increases, the Solovian capital–labour ratio k^* in equation (12.19) falls, so that $\Phi(k^*, \Psi(n/s))$ also increases, and eventually at a faster pace than n, due to the assumed shape of the curve in equation (12.17) (Fig. 12.1), so that $\Phi(k^*, \Psi(n/s))$ catches up and then surpasses n. Hence with the increase of n, the situation changes from (12.20) via (12.24) to (12.23).

The economy owes this seemingly paradoxical state of affairs to the potential strong propensity to invest at higher levels of Y/K assumed to be inherent in it. Otherwise, (e.g., if the slope of the curve in equation (12.17) tails off at higher levels of Y/K, as in Kaldor (1940)), this may not occur, and even a possibility for the locus $(X/K) = 0$ to lie entirely in the underemployment region may arise so as to let (12.20) hold for any level of n.

References

Benassy, J. P. (1984): A Non-Walrasian Model of the Business Cycle, *Journal of Economic Behaviour and Organization*, 5.

Goodwin, R. M. (1951): The Nonlinear Accelerator and the Persistence of Business Cycles, *Econometrica*, 19.

Goodwin, R. M. (1955): A Model of Cyclical Growth, in E. Lundberg, ed., *The Business Cycle in the Post-War World*, London: Macmillan.

Goodwin, R. M. (1967): A Growth Cycle, in C. H. Feinstein, ed., *Socialism, Capitalism and Economic Growth, Essays Presented to Maurice Dobb*, Cambridge: Cambridge University Press.

Kaldor, N. (1940): A Model of the Trade Cycle, *Economic Journal*, 50.

Morishima, M. (1958): A Contribution to the Nonlinear Theory of the Trade Cycle, *Zeitschrift für Nationalökonomie*, 18.

Nikaido, H. (1987): No Growth, No Fluctuations, in G. R. Feiwel, ed., *Arrow and the Foundations of the Theory of Economic Policy*, London: Macmillan.

Pontryagin, L. S. (1962): *Ordinary Differential Equations*, Reading, Mass.: Addison Wesley.

Rose, H. (1967): On the Non-Linear Theory of the Employment Cycle, *Review of Economic Studies*, 34.

Solow, R. M. (1956): A Contribution to the Theory of Economic Growth, *Quarterly Journal of Economics*, 70.

Yasui, T. (1961): Self-excited Oscillations and the Business Cycle (mimeo); a condensed English version of the original paper having the same title in Japanese included in Yasui, *Fundamental Problems of Equilibrium Analysis* (1955) in Japanese, Tokyo: Iwanami-Shoten.

IV CLASSICAL PRICE-QUANTITY DYNAMICS

0235
0322
Δ##, E25, E11
231-57
B31
Marx, Karl
[1983]

13 Marx on Competition

1 Conjecture of Profit Rate Equalization

In Marx's capitalist economic system there are three layers of valuation of goods, viz., labor values, prices of production and market prices. The first valuation is most basic to the system and very instrumental in getting insight into the reality of its working beyond appearances. However, labor values do not manifest themselves as such, but are transformed to the second valuation, in which a positive uniform rate of profit prevails across all sectors of industry, redistributing surplus value evenly among them.

The third valuation, market prices, which differs from both the first and second ones, is actually formed in the markets subject to demand and supply and fluctuates around the second. As to how it is related to the others, there is a presumption of Marx, typical of classicals, alleging a centripetal tendency via the effect of competition for market prices to approach prices of production through capital mobility across sectors in pursuit of a higher rate of profit. Market prices, which are determined by the law of demand and supply, need not equalize sectoral rates of profit. Nevertheless, they eventually settle down on prices of production, completely equalizing rates of profit as capital moves from sectors yielding lower rates of profit to those yielding higher ones. It is argued that such capital movements across sectors bring about increased supply in sectors into which capital flows and decreased supply in those which capital exits, and thereby bid down the prices of products in the former sectors and bid up those in the latter, diminishing profit rate differentials toward equalization.

This presumption, which relates the third valuation to the second by asserting the latter as *stable* long-run equilibrium prices, has not admitted any analytical evidence,[1] comparable to that for the transformation of the first to the second valuation.[2]

The purpose of the present paper is to examine this alleged tendency for market prices to converge to prices of production through capital mobility. This will be done by formulating dynamic processes in which capital moves across sectors in pursuit of higher rates of profit so as to cause changes in market prices, and examining where the system eventually tends to go. Of the processes formulated some are disequilibrium

Reprinted from *Zeitschrift für Nationalökonomie* 43, no. 4 (1983): 337–362. © 1983 Springer-Verlag. Reprinted by permission.

dynamic ones in which markets need not clear and quantities adjust and disequilibrium entails changes in prices, and the other is a market clearing dynamic process. In all these processes market price formation is effected by the interplay of supply with demand consisting exclusively of capitalists' and workers' consumption and sectoral investment corresponding to capital movements, while allowing no room for anything else volatile like subjective utility and marginal productivity.

The important findings in the examination are that the dynamic equalization of profit rates vitally hinges on how sectors differ in their organic compositions of capital, ratios of constant to variable capital, and that if the capital good sector (the department producing means of production) has a higher organic composition than the consumption good sector (the department producing wage and luxury goods), market prices tend to diverge from prices of production, as capital moves, disproving profit rate equalization. On the other hand, reversal of organic compositions brings about a potential for convergence to prices of production, which reveals itself as an endorsement of the conjecture in the simplest situations, the case of the movement of money capital alone and the case of the market clearing process, but in general profit rate equalization is conditional on the trajectory of capital movement and not thoroughly ensured.

2   Output and Prices in Marx's Scheme of Reproduction

To examine the conjecture of dynamic equalization of profit rates, let us formulate the standard two-sector circulating capital model of Marx's reproduction scheme within the framework of the Leontief system and make preliminary remarks in this section.

There are two aggregative goods in the economy, a capital good and a consumption good. Production is carried out in two sectors, each of which produces a single good with capital and labor as inputs under constant returns to scale and in fixed factor proportions. The first sector produces the capital good, and the second sector produces the consumption good. The capital good and the sector producing it are referred to by the number 1, and the consumption good and the sector producing it are referred to by the number 2. The inputs per unit output in both sectors are a_{1j} units of the capital good and l_j units of labor ($j = 1, 2$), respectively, all of which are assumed to be positive constants. This given technology is assumed to be capable of producing positive net outputs of both goods, so that

$$a_{11} < 1. \tag{1}$$

On the basis of (1) the labor values σ_1, σ_2 of both goods are defined by the system of equations

$$\sigma_1 = a_{11}\sigma_1 + l_1,$$
$$\sigma_2 = a_{12}\sigma_1 + l_2. \tag{2}$$

Let a_{20} be the amount of the consumption good which workers consume to reproduce one unit of labor, and which is small enough to admit exploitation, so that

$$a_{20}\sigma_2 < 1, \tag{3}$$

that is, the value of one unit of labor is less than one. Then, (2) can be rearranged to

$$\sigma_1 = a_{11}\sigma_1 + a_{21}\sigma_2 + (1 - a_{20}\sigma_2)l_1,$$
$$\sigma_2 = a_{12}\sigma_1 + a_{22}\sigma_2 + (1 - a_{20}\sigma_2)l_2, \tag{4}$$

where we define new input coefficients for labor-feeding

$$a_{2j} = a_{20}l_j. \quad (j = 1, 2) \tag{5}$$

In the Marxist terminology $a_{1j}\sigma_1$, $a_{2j}\sigma_2$, $(1 - a_{20}\sigma_2)l_j$ are the constant capital, variable capital and surplus value per unit output of the jth sector, respectively, all of which are positive. While the rate of surplus value $(1 - a_{20}\sigma_2)l_j/a_{2j}\sigma_2 = (1 - a_{20}\sigma_2)/a_{20}\sigma_2$ is common for both sectors, the rates of profit in value

$$\frac{(1 - a_{20}\sigma_2)l_j}{a_{1j}\sigma_1 + a_{2j}\sigma_2} \quad (j = 1, 2) \tag{6}$$

are not equal unless the organic compositions $a_{1j}\sigma_1/a_{2j}\sigma_2$ $(j = 1, 2)$ are equal. Obviously the organic compositions are equal if and only if the capital labor ratios a_{1j}/l_j are equal.

In light of the well-known results centering around the Frobenius theorem and the Hawkins–Simon conditions on non-negative matrices, the positivity of the surplus values in terms of the positive labor values σ_1, σ_2 in (3) implies, among others, the following facts (α), (β):

(α) There are uniquely determinate special positive relative prices p_j^* ($j = 1, 2$), prices of production at which a positive uniform rate of profit r prevails so that

$$p_j^* = (1 + r)(a_{1j}p_1^* + a_{2j}p_2^*), \quad (j = 1, 2) \tag{7}$$

where $r = 1/\lambda - 1$, and λ is the dominant positive Frobenius eigenvalue of the positive matrix

$$A = \begin{pmatrix} a_{11} & a_{12} \\ a_{21} & a_{22} \end{pmatrix}. \tag{8}$$

(β) $I - A$, where I is the identity matrix, has a positive inverse. Hence in particular, any bill of capitalists' final demand $c_i \geqq 0$ ($i = 1, 2$) is producible, that is, the system of equations

$$x_i = a_{i1}x_1 + a_{i2}x_2 + c_i \quad (i = 1, 2) \tag{9}$$

has uniquely determinate positive solutions x_i ($i = 1, 2$) unless $c_1 = c_2 = 0$, in which case it has $x_1 = x_2 = 0$ as the only possible solution.

In (9) c_1 represents net output of the capital good available for net investment in constant capital, and c_2 represents net output of the consumption good available for net investment in variable capital and capitalists' consumption. The most special situation $c_1 = 0$, $c_2 > 0$ determines configurations x_1, x_2, c_2 in a simple reproduction in which capitalists consume all c_2 but do not invest so that the economy remains stationary.

The rates of profit at a system of prices are

$$r_j = \frac{p_j}{a_{1j}p_1 + a_{2j}p_2} - 1, \quad (j = 1, 2) \tag{10}$$

respectively. In the present simple two-sector case, the rates of profit are continuous monotone functions of the single variable p_1/p_2, specifically r_1 is strictly increasing with range from -1 to $1/a_{11} - 1$, and r_2 is strictly decreasing with range from $1/a_{22} - 1$ to -1, as p_1/p_2 runs from 0 to infinity. Therefore, r_1 is equated to r_2 at a uniquely determinate positive value $\pi^* = p_1^*/p_2^*$ of p_1/p_2. The corresponding uniform rate of profit r satisfies

$$r[(a_{11}p_1^* + a_{21}p_2^*)x_1 + (a_{12}p_1^* + a_{22}p_2^*)x_2] = c_1 p_1^* + c_2 p_2^* \tag{11}$$

for any bill of capitalists' final demand $c_i \geqq 0$ $(i = 1, 2)$ and the corresponding output levels $x_j > 0$ $(j = 1, 2)$, which implies its positivity.

3   How Can Capital Move across Sectors?

When it comes to price changes due to capital movements, we have to take into full account the consideration of how market prices are formed in the current demand–supply situation. We will therefore pay much attention to this aspects in formulating the adjustment processes.

To begin with, it should be noted that the prices of production yielding the positive uniform profit rate are compatible with any bill of capitalists' final demand c_i $(i = 1, 2)$ and the corresponding market-clearing output levels x_j $(j = 1, 2)$ determined in (9), in so far as c_i's possible dependence on prices is left out of account. But, when the dependence cannot be ignored, the compatibility is obtained only with the particular bill of capitalists' final demand determinate under the influence of the prices.

Nonetheless there can be as many alternative bills of capitalists' final demand compatible with the prices as possible modes of their dependence on the prices, allowing either simple or expanded reproduction. In this paper whose main purpose is to examine the contended equalization of profit rates in a not too-complicated situation, we will concentrate on the case of simple reproduction.

Let c_2 be a positive level of capitalists' final demand for the consumption good, which will henceforth be assumed to be constant. If capitalists are not investment-minded, this c_2 determines the market-clearing output levels x_j $(j = 1, 2)$ by (9) for $c_1 = 0$ in the corresponding simple reproduction in which they just consume c_2 while having zero net investment.

Then, what will take place if there are differentials in profit rates at the current prices? The contention asserts that the differentials stimulate capital movements from the sector yielding the lower profit rate to the other. But what kind of capital moves? There may be movements of money and/or real capital, and the ways they move have to be made clear. Real capital is a stock of goods. The real capital of each sector is a stock of both goods in a definite proportion $a_{1j} : a_{2j}$ $(j = 1, 2)$. Therefore real capital cannot move merely from one sector to the other, maintaining its aggregate level at a constant level without nonzero net investments, even if the organic compositions of both sectors are equal. Movement of real capital can occur only through nonzero net real investment.

Thus, the contended movement of real capital amounts to presuming that differentials in profit rates stimulate investment in the sector yielding a higher profit rate and depress it in the other. Now, since the constant and variable capitals are in a definite fixed proportion in each sector, the level of output and its rate of change per unit of time can be regarded as indices of capital stock and investment in each sector, respectively. Then, the level of intended investment in the jth sector, measured in terms of the index, is a function

$$\phi_j(r_1 - r_2) \quad (j = 1, 2) \tag{12}$$

of the difference of the current profit rates r_1, r_2.

These intended investment functions underlie the contended capital movement and must have in the Marxist view the following properties: ϕ_1 is strictly increasing and ϕ_2 is strictly decreasing. Both vanish at $r_1 - r_2 = 0$.

The intended investment (12), which need not equal the actual investment, gives rise to investment demand for both goods

$$a_{i1}\phi_1(r_1 - r_2) + a_{i2}\phi_2(r_1 - r_2) \quad (i = 1, 2) \tag{13}$$

while there is always capitalists' constant demand c_2 for the consumption good. The demand thus resulting

$$
\begin{aligned}
&a_{11}\phi_1(r_1 - r_2) + a_{12}\phi_2(r_1 - r_2) \\
&a_{21}\phi_1(r_1 - r_2) + a_{22}\phi_2(r_1 - r_2) + c_2
\end{aligned}
\tag{14}
$$

has to be momentarily equated to supply in the markets of both goods.

If x_1, x_2 are the current output levels of both goods, their net supplies are

$$x_i - (a_{i1}x_1 + a_{i2}x_2) \quad (i = 1, 2) \tag{15}$$

which equal

$$
\begin{aligned}
&a_{11}\dot{x}_1 + a_{12}\dot{x}_2 \\
&a_{21}\dot{x}_1 + a_{22}\dot{x}_2 + c_2
\end{aligned}
\tag{16}
$$

on the assumption that capital is fully used.

Suppose that markets of both goods are always kept cleared. Then, the intended investment ϕ_j equals $\dot{x}_j$, and (14) equals (16). However, the system

(15) = (16), a system of linear differential equations, alone completely determines trajectories on which the actual investments $\dot{x}_1$, $\dot{x}_2$ are not compatible with the intended ones ϕ_1, ϕ_2, as will be seen below.

The general solution of the system (15) = (16) is a sum of the stationary solution

$$x_i = x_i^* = \text{the } i\text{th component of } (I - A)^{-1} \begin{pmatrix} 0 \\ c_2 \end{pmatrix} \quad (i = 1, 2) \tag{17}$$

and the general solution of the corresponding homogeneous system, which is obtained from (15) = (16) by setting c_2 equal to zero. The solution of the homogeneous system and its properties depend on the difference of both sectors' organic compositions. The sign of the determinant of the input coefficients matrix A completely characterizes how both sectors differ from each other in organic compositions. The first (capital good) sector's organic composition is higher (case I), lower (case II), than that of the second (consumption good) sector, according as it is positive or negative.

In both cases the reciprocals of the eigenvalues of the positive matrix

$$(I - A)^{-1}A \tag{18}$$

and their eigenvectors completely generate the general solution of the homogeneous system. The positive matrix (18) has a positive dominant eigenvalue with an associated positive eigenvector unique up to scalar multiplication and another real eigenvalue, smaller in absolute value than the dominant one, with an associated eigenvector having components of alternating signs, as is readily seen by the Frobenius Theorem. The latter eigenvalue is positive or negative according as case I or case II occurs, since the determinant of (18) equals the product of the two eigenvalues, and the determinant of $(I - A)^{-1}$ is positive by the Hawkins–Simon conditions.

Now, in case I both eigenvalues are positive, so that the unique critical point having coordinates (17) is an unstable node. On a trajectory of the system (15) = (16) emanating from the critical point $\dot{x}_1$ and $\dot{x}_2$ are either of the same sign or of the opposite sign with their absolute values ever increasing. The former situation is incompatible with the opposite-signedness of ϕ_1, ϕ_2, and in the second situation the absolute values of ϕ_1, ϕ_2 increase, enlarging profit rate differentials. In case II there is a positive eigenvalue with an associated positive eigenvector and a negative eigenvalue with an associated eigenvector having components of alternating signs, so that the unique critical point is a saddle. On any trajectory, other than the two separatrixes approaching the critical point, $\dot{x}_1$ and $\dot{x}_2$ eventually become of the same sign, which is incompatible with the opposite-signedness of ϕ_1 and ϕ_2.

The above situation shows that the intended investment cannot always equal the actual one, and that a capital movement process must allow for possible discrepancies between the intended and actual investments, the latter of which has to be somehow determined in the markets within supply capacity of output.

On the other hand, money capital, an indispensable companion of real capital, can move more flexibly across sectors in pursuit of a higher rate of profit via the metamorphosis from money through commodities to money. Money is the unique indispensable carrier of market demand and supply, and mediates between them by forming market prices. Thus intended investment in money capital always materializes in the actual one, which decomposes to the actual real investment and price changes.

The process of capital movement is therefore a process in which either money capital or both money and real capitals move across sectors while momentarily forming market prices.

4 The Capital Movement Process

Let q_j be the price of the jth sector's capital, i.e. the value of one unit of the capital consisting of a_{1j} units of capital good and a_{2j} units of consumption good at their prices,

$$q_j = a_{1j}p_1 + a_{2j}p_2 \quad (j = 1, 2). \tag{19}$$

If M_j and x_j are the existing levels of money and real capitals in the jth sector, they are related by

$$q_j x_j = M_j \quad (j = 1, 2) \tag{20}$$

which determines the prices of sectoral real capital and, thereby, the prices of goods through (19). Variations of M_j and x_j in (20) over time entail changes of q_j and p_i.

The variation in money capital M_j is governed by intended investment in pursuit of a higher rate of profit

$$\dot{M}_j = \psi_j(p_1, p_2) \quad (j = 1, 2), \tag{21}$$

where $\psi_j(p_1, p_2)$ are investment functions in money capital with the prices of goods p_1, p_2 as arguments, such that

$$\psi_1 > 0 > \psi_2 \quad \text{if } p_1/p_2 > \pi^* \tag{22}$$

$$\psi_1 < 0 < \psi_2 \quad \text{if } p_1/p_2 < \pi^* \tag{23}$$

$$\psi_1 = \psi_2 = 0 \quad \text{if } p_1/p_2 = \pi^* \tag{24}$$

π^* = price ratio in the prices of production.

It is remarked that (22), (23) and (24) are situations of positive, negative and vanishing profit rate differentials $r_1 - r_2$, respectively, by the relation (10). The intended investment in money capital always materializes in the actual one in (21).

Specifically, if money capital moves across sectors while maintaining a constant total level

$$M_1 + M_2 = M = \text{constant} \tag{25}$$

the investment functions fulfill identically

$$\psi_1 + \psi_2 = 0. \tag{26}$$

Intended investment in real capital is also represented by functions $\phi_j(p_1, p_2)$ for both sectors $j = 1, 2$, such that

$$\phi_1 \geqq 0 \geqq \phi_2 \quad \text{if } p_1/p_2 > \pi^* \tag{27}$$

$$\phi_1 \leqq 0 \leqq \phi_2 \quad \text{if } p_1/p_2 < \pi^* \tag{28}$$

$$\phi_1 = \phi_2 = 0 \quad \text{if } p_1/p_2 = \pi^*. \tag{29}$$

In the most special case of no intended real investment, both functions ϕ_1, ϕ_2 identically vanish, equality also holding in (27), (28). More generally, however, strict inequality holds in (27), (28).

The intended real investment cannot always materialize in the actual one, unlike investment in money capital, because of the constraints by the current capacity of supply. On the assumption of instantaneous working out of the relevant multiplier process, the actual real investment $\dot{x}_j$ ($j = 1, 2$), together with capitalists' demand for consumption good c_2, gives rise to the actual levels y_j of output of both goods $j = 1, 2$ determined by

$$\begin{pmatrix} y_1 \\ y_2 \end{pmatrix} = A\begin{pmatrix} y_1 \\ y_2 \end{pmatrix} + A\begin{pmatrix} \dot{x}_1 \\ \dot{x}_2 \end{pmatrix} + \begin{pmatrix} 0 \\ c_2 \end{pmatrix}, \tag{30}$$

which do not exceed the current capacity levels x_j ($j = 1, 2$) of output supply, respectively,

$$y_j \leqq x_j \quad (j = 1, 2) \tag{31}$$

(31) gives the constraints subject to which the actual real investment has to be determined,

$$b_{i1}\dot{x}_1 + b_{i2}\dot{x}_2 \leqq x_i - x_i^* \quad (i = 1, 2), \tag{32}$$

where

$$\begin{pmatrix} b_{11} & b_{12} \\ b_{21} & b_{22} \end{pmatrix} = (I - A)^{-1}A = B \tag{33}$$

$$\begin{pmatrix} x_1^* \\ x_2^* \end{pmatrix} = (I - A)^{-1}\begin{pmatrix} 0 \\ c_2 \end{pmatrix} = x^*. \tag{34}$$

The domain of $(\dot{x}_1, \dot{x}_2)$ constrained by (32) is the set of all possible supplies of savings available at the current levels of real capital stock x_1, x_2, from which a pair $(\dot{x}_1, \dot{x}_2)$ of actual levels of investment has to be picked in response to the intended levels of investment ϕ_1, ϕ_2. A manifold of alternative modes of determining actual investment within the potential savings responding to the intended one are conceivable, and each of them generates a distinct dynamic process of capital movement. A very few of the most plausible modes will be considered in the following sections.

If the actual levels of investment $\dot{x}_j$ ($j = 1, 2$) are determined somehow as functions of the current levels of capital stock x_j ($j = 1, 2$) and prices p_i ($i = 1, 2$), the rates of price change $\dot{p}_i$ ($i = 1, 2$) are automatically determined by way of investment in money capital (21) as those derived upon differentiation of (19) and (20). In fact, $\dot{q}_j$ ($j = 1, 2$) are determined so as to fulfill

$$\dot{q}_j x_j + q_j \dot{x}_j = \psi_j \quad (j = 1, 2) \tag{35}$$

and, then $\dot{p}_i$ ($i = 1, 2$) are derived from

$$\dot{q}_j = a_{1j}\dot{p}_1 + a_{2j}\dot{p}_2. \quad (j = 1, 2). \tag{36}$$

Thus, the dynamic process of movement of either money capital or both money and real capitals across sectors is formulated as a system of differential equations in the eight unknowns M_j, x_j, q_j ($j = 1, 2$), p_i ($i = 1, 2$), provided that the relevant functions, namely, ψ_j, ϕ_j, and those determining the levels of actual investment $\dot{x}_j$ ($j = 1, 2$) are continuous. The process is a true dynamic one in which capital moves gradually over time, but not instantaneously, and thereby rules out the obvious, trivial equalization of profit rates through instantaneous capital movement once and for all.

During the working out of the process, the existing capital is likely to be under-utilized. At the output levels y_j ($j = 1, 2$) determined in (30), $a_{1j}y_j$ units of constant capital and $a_{2j}y_j$ units of variable capital are used up in production and replaced by investment from current gross output y_j, while $a_{1j}(x_j - y_j)$ units of constant capital and $a_{2j}(x_j - y_j)$ units of variable capital remain idle in the jth sector. Whence sectoral capitals x_j grow at the rate of net investment $\dot{x}_j$ ($j = 1, 2$).

Price-weighted summation of current output y_j ($j = 1, 2$) determined in (30), in view of (10), (19), leads to

$$r_1 q_1 y_1 + r_2 q_2 y_2 = q_1 \dot{x}_1 + q_2 \dot{x}_2 + p_2 c_2, \tag{37}$$

the equality of total profit on the left-hand side to the sum of monetary values of actual investment and consumption on the right-hand side in terms of current prices. Corresponding to the under-utilization of real capital, $q_j(x_j - y_j)$ units of sectoral money capital remain idle, and only $q_j y_j$ units earn profit at the rates r_1, r_2, respectively.

5   The Case where Money Capital Alone Moves

In this section we will examine the conjecture of equalization of profit rates through movement of money capital alone, by considering an extremely special case of the dynamic process.

The intendend investment functions in real capital in this case are

$$\phi_j(p_1, p_2) = 0 \quad \text{identically } (j = 1, 2). \tag{38}$$

For an arbitrary level x_j^0 ($j = 1, 2$) of real capital stock fulfilling $x_j^0 \geqq x_j^*$, the domain constrained by (32) includes the origin and therefore can accommodate the identically vanishing intended real investment, so that the process is represented by (20), (21), (36) and

$$x_j = x_j^0 = \text{constant} \quad (j = 1, 2) \tag{39}$$

$$\dot{q}_j x_j^0 = \psi_j(p_1, p_2) \quad (j = 1, 2) \tag{40}$$

resulting from (35) for $\dot{x}_j = \phi_j(p_1, p_2) = 0 \ (j = 1, 2)$.

From (36), (40) follows a system of two differential equations

$$\dot{p}_j = \Psi_j(p_1, p_2)/\Delta \quad (j = 1, 2) \tag{41}$$

with good prices as unknowns, where

$$\Psi_1(p_1, p_2) = a_{22}\psi_1(p_1, p_2)/x_1^0 - a_{21}\psi_2(p_1, p_2)/x_2^0 \tag{42}$$

$$\Psi_2(p_1, p_2) = -a_{12}\psi_1(p_1, p_2)/x_1^0 + a_{11}\psi_2(p_1, p_2)/x_2^0 \tag{43}$$

Δ = determinant of A.

Now suppose that the capital good sector is higher in organic composition than the consumption good sector so that Δ is positive. If currently $r_1 > r_2$ and hence $p_1/p_2 > \pi^*$, condition (22) on ψ_1, ψ_2 implies by way of (42), (43) with all a_{ij} positive

$$\dot{p}_1 = \Psi_1/\Delta > 0 > \Psi_2/\Delta = \dot{p}_2,$$

whence p_1/p_2 deviates farther from π^* to widen the profit rate differentials. If currently $r_1 < r_2$ and hence $p_1/p_2 < \pi^*$, condition (23) on ψ_1, ψ_2 implies further deviation downward of p_1/p_2 away from π^* to widen the profit rate differentials.

Suppose next that the capital good sector is lower in organic composition than the consumption good sector, so that Δ is negative. Then, the signs of $\dot{p}_j$ and Ψ_j are opposite in (41). Hence the prices change in the direction to lessen the deviation from π^* toward equalization of profit rates, until they converge to the prices of production.

The truth of the conjecture of profit rate equalization therefore vitally hinges on how both sectors differ in organic composition of capital, and is disproved if the capital good sector has a higher organic composition, and proved if it has a lower organic composition. This fact reveals itself quite transparently in this case of no real capital movement.

In the above results the assumption of a constant level of total money capital (25), (26) is not needed, though the most typical situation in which the results hold is the case of movement of money capital while retaining it at a constant level.

6   The Case where Both Capitals Move

Suppose that both capitals move across sectors. The total level of money capital is now explicitly assumed to be constant. Thus its movement across sectors is effected by the actual investment (21) always being equal to the intended investment determined by investment functions in money capital ψ_j fulfilling (22) through (26).

As to the movement of real capital, capitalists are presumed to intend to carry out ϕ_j units of net investment in real capital worth the monetary value of investment in money capital ψ_j in current prices. The intended investment functions ϕ_j in real capital are therefore related to those in money capital ψ_j in such a way that

$$\psi_j(p_1, p_2) = q_j \phi_j(p_1, p_2) \quad (j = 1, 2) \tag{44}$$

and thereby fulfill identically

$$q_1 \phi_1 + q_2 \phi_2 = 0 \tag{45}$$

by (26).

ϕ_j ($j = 1, 2$) are assumed to satisfy the conditions that they are functions of the single variable p_1/p_2, the price ratio, ϕ_1 strictly increasing, ϕ_2 strictly decreasing, and both vanishing at $p_1/p_2 = \pi^*$, which are more stringent than (27), (28), (29). Because of the basic relations (10) between prices and profit rates, ϕ_j are equivalent functions of the profit rate differentials $r_1 - r_2$ with the same monotone properties, vanishing at $r_1 - r_2 = 0$.

At the moment there are the savings opportunities characterized by (32), from which a point $(\dot{x}_1, \dot{x}_2)$ has to be chosen in the markets so as to determine the levels of actual investment in real capital. The choice is made in the following way. First, if the point (ϕ_1, ϕ_2) is included in the opportunities, it is picked, so that the intended investment materializes in the actual one. Second, if the point (ϕ_1, ϕ_2) is excluded from the opportunities, but the straight line

$$q_1 \dot{x}_1 + q_2 \dot{x}_2 = 0 \tag{46}$$

in the $(\dot{x}_1, \dot{x}_2)$ plane intersects the opportunities set, capitalists make such dual decisions as to pick the uniquely determinate point $(\dot{x}_1, \dot{x}_2)$ in the shortest distance to (ϕ_1, ϕ_2) among all points in the opportunities set satisfying (46). Third, if the straight line (46) does not intersect the opportunities set, the vertex $(\dot{x}_1, \dot{x}_2)$ of the set determined as the solution of

$$b_{i1}\dot{x}_1 + b_{i2}\dot{x}_2 = x_i - x_i^* \quad (i = 1, 2) \tag{47}$$

is picked. Determination of the levels of actual real investment is coincident in any possible overlapping situation of the three cases, and depends continuously on the current capacity levels x_1, x_2 ($=$ current levels of capital stock) and the price ratio p_1/p_2. This continuous dependence is ensured by the fact that the normal vector (q_1, q_2) of the straight line (46) is a linear combination of both rows of the matrix B in (33) with positive weights $r_1 q_1, r_2 q_2$ so long as prices and profit rates are positive, and therefore the straight line can intersect either facet of the savings opportunities set at most once. Thus $\dot{x}_j$ ($j = 1, 2$) are determined as continuous functions

$$\dot{x}_j = f_j(x_1, x_2, p_1/p_2, \phi_1(p_1/p_2), \phi_2(p_1/p_2)) \quad (j = 1, 2). \tag{48}$$

The dynamic process of capital movement is thereby formulated as a specific instance of the basic framework in section 4, which generates the evolution of the relevant magnitudes, money capital levels M_j, real capital stock levels x_j, and prices p_j, q_j ($j = 1, 2$).

Let us examine the behaviors of the variables, focusing special attention on the validity of the conjecture of equalization of profit rates. To this end the system will be reduced to a system of three differential equations in three variables, the heart of it, by eliminating certain of the eight variables.

Obviously M_j can readily be eliminated by (20). Next the basic relation (19) implies

$$q_1/q_2 = g(p_1/p_2) = \frac{a_{11}p_1/p_2 + a_{21}}{a_{12}p_1/p_2 + a_{22}}. \tag{49}$$

The continuous function g has the following readily verifiable properties:

(i)   It is strictly increasing if $\Delta > 0$, that is, the capital good sector has a higher organic composition than the consumption good sector.

(ii)   It is strictly decreasing if $\Delta < 0$, that is, the capital good sector has a lower organic composition than the consumption good sector.

(iii) $p_1/p_2 = g(p_1/p_2)$ if and only if $p_1/p_2 = \pi^*$, that is, prices of production prevail.

Therefore, the inverse function g^{-1} of g also has the same properties, and p_1/p_2 can be eliminated by

$$p_1/p_2 = g^{-1}(q_1/q_2). \tag{50}$$

Whence (48) takes the form

$$\dot{x}_j = f_j(x_1, x_2, g^{-1}(\pi), \phi_1(g^{-1}(\pi)), \phi_2(g^{-1}(\pi))) \quad (j = 1, 2) \tag{51}$$

where

$$\pi = q_1/q_2. \tag{52}$$

From (35), (44) follow

$$\dot{q}_j/q_j = (\phi_j - \dot{x}_j)/x_j \quad (j = 1, 2) \tag{53}$$

which, combined together, lead to

$$\dot{\pi}/\pi = (\phi_1(g^{-1}(\pi)) - \dot{x}_1)/x_1 - (\phi_2(g^{-1}(\pi)) - \dot{x}_2)/x_2. \tag{54}$$

Thus we have arrived at the system of three differential equations, $j = 1, 2$ in (51) and (54), in the three variables x_j ($j = 1, 2$) and π, the heart of the capital movement process.

Let us examine the trajectories of the system in the (x_1, x_2, π)-space to see what will take place along them, as time tends to infinity. This will be done by inspecting phase diagrams drawn in a special way.

The system has infinitely many critical points which fill out the portion of the space characterized by

$$\begin{array}{l} x_i \geq x_i^* \\ \quad (i = 1, 2) \\ \pi = \pi^* \end{array} \tag{55}$$

In fact, the savings opportunities set (32) includes the point $(\phi_1, \phi_2) = (0, 0)$ at any point of the portion (55) so that $\dot{x}_j = 0$ ($j = 1, 2$), $\dot{\pi} = 0$ by definition, and vice versa because ϕ_j ($j = 1, 2$) are nonvanishing and of the opposite sign at $\pi \neq \pi^*$. The portion consists of the situation of simple reproduction without idle capital (x_1^*, x_2^*, π^*) and all those with idle capital.

From now on the examination will be worked out separately for the case of positive Δ where the capital good sector has a higher organic composition than the consumption good sector and the case of negative Δ where the capital good sector has a lower organic composition than the consumption good sector.

(I) Case of positive Δ. In order for good prices to remain positive, π must remain in the interval

$$a_{11}/a_{12} > \pi > a_{21}/a_{22}, \tag{56}$$

and for profit rates to remain positive, π must remain in the interval

$$[a_{11}(1 - a_{22}) + a_{12}a_{21}]/a_{12} > \pi > a_{21}/[(1 - a_{11})a_{22} + a_{12}a_{21}]. \tag{57}$$

However, because the interval (57) is included in the interval (56), as is readily verified, in order for good prices and profit rates to remain positive, π must remain in the interval (57). The system of differential equations is therefore meaningful and well-behaved only in the region Ω constrained by (57) and

$$x_i > 0 \quad (i = 1, 2). \tag{58}$$

Let us now draw phase diagrams of the system in Ω in the following special way. In Fig. 13.1a, corresponding to a point (x_1, x_2, π) in Ω, the savings opportunities set (32) and the point (ϕ_1, ϕ_2) are depicted in the $(\dot{x}_1, \dot{x}_2)$-plane to know the sign of $\dot{\pi}$. In detecting the sign the following facts must be taken into account.

(I-1)   As functions of π, ϕ_1 is strictly increasing, and ϕ_2 is strictly decreasing, both vanishing at $\pi = \pi^*$.

(I-2)   All coefficients b_{ij} being positive, both facets of the savings opportunities set are downward sloping, and the facet characterized by equality holding for $i = 1$ in (32) is steeper than the other one characterized by holding of equality for $i = 2$ in (32), because the determinant of B is positive.

(I-3)   The slope of the straight line (46), on which the point (ϕ_1, ϕ_2) lies by (45), is between those of both facets of the savings opportunities set, because (q_1, q_2) is a linear combination of the rows of B with positive weights $r_1 q_1, r_2 q_2$.

In Fig. 13.1b, 1c, 1d the signs of $\dot{x}_1$, $\dot{x}_2$, $\dot{\pi}$ are given on the plane section of Ω corresponding to a common level of π, those of $\dot{x}_1$, $\dot{x}_2$ by directions of arrows and that of $\dot{\pi}$ by an encircled one of $+$, $-$, 0 or ?. The broken straight line parallel to the x_2 axis is the locus of

$$b_{11}\phi_1 + b_{12}\phi_2 = x_1 - x_1^* \tag{59}$$

in the section, and the broken straight line parallel to the x_1 axis is the locus of

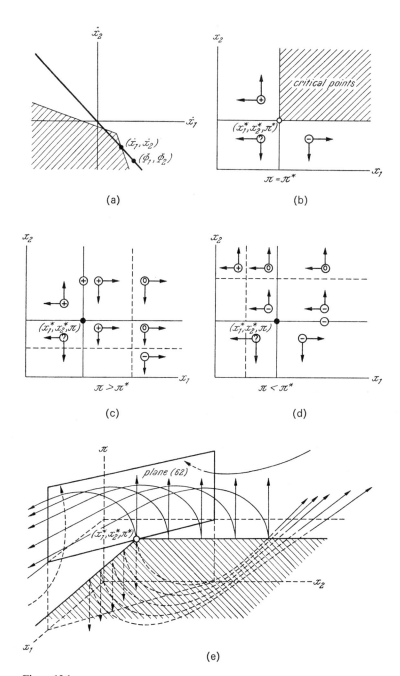

Figure 13.1

$$b_{21}\phi_1 + b_{22}\phi_2 = x_2 - x_2^* \tag{60}$$

in the section.

In the portion of Ω constrained by

$$p_1^* x_1 + p_2^* x_2 < p_1^* x_1^* + p_2^* x_2^* \tag{61}$$

the point (x_1, x_2, π) moves along a trajectory farther away from the plane

$$p_1^* x_1 + p_2^* x_2 = p_1^* x_1^* + p_2^* x_2^* \tag{62}$$

toward the boundary of Ω, thereby never toward a critical point. In fact, summation of both inequalities in (32) with prices of production p_i^* $(i = 1, 2)$ as weights leads to

$$v \leqq v(t_0) \exp r(t - t_0), \tag{63}$$

where r is the uniform profit rate and

$$v = p_1^* x_1 + p_2^* x_2 - (p_1^* x_1^* + p_2^* x_2^*), \quad v(t_0) < 0.$$

The right-hand side of (63) must tend to minus infinity.

Fig. 13.1c shows that the portion of Ω constrained by $x_1 = x_1^*$, $x_2 > x_2^*$, $\pi > \pi^*$ is completely filled by upward moving vertical trajectories. Fig. 13.1d shows that the portion of Ω constrained by $x_1 > x_1^*$, $x_2 = x_2^*$, $\pi < \pi^*$ is completely filled by downward moving vertical trajectories. Along these trajectories money capital alone moves, with real capital held constant, which are situations similar to those in section 5.

The portion of Ω constrained by (62) and $x_2 - x_2^* > 0 > x_1 - x_1^*$, $\pi > \pi^*$ is completely filled by trajectories along which π is rising and the movement of the point (x_1, x_2) is governed by the system of linear differential equations (47), i.e. the system (15) = (16) . The portion of Ω constrained by (62) and $x_1 - x_1^* > 0 > x_2 - x_2^*$, $\pi^* > \pi$ is completely filled by trajectories along which π is falling and the movement of the point (x_1, x_2) is governed by the same system (47).

From inspections of Fig. 13.1b, 1c, 1d and the information above we are sure that no trajectory leads the moving point (x_1, x_2, π) to a critical point as time tends to infinity, and that π goes away from π^* either straightforwardly or eventually. Fig. 13.1e illustrates typical trajectories as a bird's-eye view. The equalization of profit is thereby thoroughly disproved in case (I).

(II) Case of negative Δ. Almost everything is reversed in this case. The lower and upper bounds in (56), (57) have to be interchanged, so that Ω is defined as a region in the space constrained by (58) and

$$a_{21}/[(1 - a_{11})a_{22} + a_{12}a_{21}] > \pi > [a_{11}(1 - a_{22}) + a_{12}a_{21}]/a_{12}. \qquad (64)$$

The counterparts of (I-l), (I-2), (I-3) are:

(II-1)   As functions of π, ϕ_1 is strictly decreasing, and ϕ_2 is strictly increasing, both vanishing at $\pi = \pi^*$.

(II-2)   Both facets of the savings opportunities set are downward sloping, but the facet characterized by equality holding for $i = 2$ in (32) is steeper than the other one characterized by equality holding for $i = 1$ in (32) because the determinant of B is negative.

(II-3)   Same as (I-3).

Phase diagrams are given in Fig. 13.2, the counterpart of Fig. 13.1, drawn likewise with the same legend applied. Fig. 13.2c shows that the portion of Ω constrained by $x_1 = x_1^*$, $x_2 > x_2^*$, $\pi > \pi^*$ is completely filled by vertical trajectories moving downwards toward critical points. Fig. 13.2d shows that the portion of Ω constrained by $x_1 > x_1^*$, $x_2 = x_2^*$, $\pi < \pi^*$ is completely filled by vertical trajectories moving upward toward critical points.

The portion of Ω constrained by (62) and $x_1 - x_1^* > 0 > x_2 - x_2^*$, $\pi > \pi^*$ is completely filled by trajectories along which π is first rising and eventually falling, and the movement of the point (x_1, x_2) is governed by the system of linear differential equations (47), approaching critical points. The portion constrained by (62) and $x_2 - x_2^* > 0 > x_1 - x_1^*$, $\pi^* > \pi$ is completely filled by trajectories along which π is first falling and eventually rising, and the movement of the point (x_1, x_2) is governed by the system of linear differential equations (47), approaching critical points. Other trajectories can never meet any of these four portions, because of uniqueness of solution to a system of differential equations.

From inspection of Fig. 13.2b, 2c, 2d and the information above we see that most trajectories lead the moving point (x_1, x_2, π) to some critical points as time tends to inifinity, letting π converge to π^* either straightforwardly or eventually.

Nonetheless there are other trajectories eventually going toward the boundary away from critical points. As in case I, in the portion of Ω

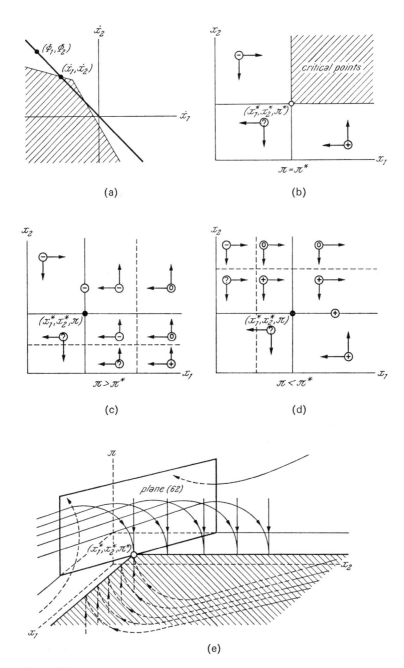

Figure 13.2

constrained by (61) trajectories move farther away from the plane (62) toward the boundary of Ω. Moreover, through each point in the portion of Ω constrained by (62) and $x_2 - x_2^* > 0 > x_1 - x_1^*$, $\pi > \pi^*$ a trajectory penetrates into the region (61) and thereby goes eventually toward the boundary of Ω. In fact, by locating the actual investment point $(\dot{x}_1, \dot{x}_2)$ in Fig. 13.2a corresponding to this situation, we know that

$$p_1^* \dot{x}_1 + p_2^* \dot{x}_2 < 0$$

at this point. The same situation prevails also in the portion of Ω constrained by $x_1 - x_1^* > 0 > x_2 - x_2^*$, $\pi^* > \pi$.

Fig. 13.2e is the bird's-eye view in this case. The set of critical points is situated like a saddle. The equalization of profit rates is therefore not thoroughly ensured in case II. Its validity is conditional on the trajectory.

7   Alternative Modes of Determination of Actual Investment

The process of movement of both money and real capital is a disequilibrium dynamic process in which there are generally discrepancies between intended and actual investment. Its working is conditional on the mode in which actual investment is determined in momentary market disequilibrium.

In the situation considered in section 6 in the aggregate capitalists are not investment-minded, and merely want to reallocate capital in sectors, as is formulated in (45). The markets function so as to determine actual investment by readjusting intended investment subject to the no aggregate net investment constraint (46) as far as possible.

If the market functioning is not so efficient, actual investment may be determined in alternative ways. The following are conceivable alternative modes of determining actual investment:

$$b_{11}\dot{x}_1 + b_{12}\dot{x}_2 = \min\left[b_{11}\phi_1 + b_{12}\phi_2, x_1 - x_1^*\right]$$
$$b_{21}\dot{x}_1 + b_{22}\dot{x}_2 = \min\left[b_{21}\phi_1 + b_{22}\phi_2, x_2 - x_2^*\right] \tag{65}$$

$$a_{11}\dot{x}_1 + a_{12}\dot{x}_2 = \min\left[a_{11}\phi_1 + a_{12}\phi_2, (1 - a_{11})x_1 - a_{12}x_2\right]$$
$$a_{21}\dot{x}_1 + a_{22}\dot{x}_2 = \min\left[a_{21}\phi_1 + a_{22}\phi_2, -a_{21}x_1 + (1 - a_{22})x_2 - c_2\right] \tag{66}$$

$$\dot{x}_1 = \min\left[\phi_1, d_{11}x_1 + d_{12}x_2 - e_1\right]$$
$$\dot{x}_2 = \min\left[\phi_2, d_{21}x_1 + d_{22}x_2 - e_2\right], \tag{67}$$

where

$$\begin{pmatrix} d_{11} & d_{12} \\ d_{21} & d_{22} \end{pmatrix} = A^{-1}(I - A) = B^{-1}$$

$$\begin{pmatrix} e_1 \\ e_2 \end{pmatrix} = A^{-1}\begin{pmatrix} 0 \\ c_2 \end{pmatrix}.$$

Each of (65), (66) and (67) determines levels of actual investment within the savings opportunities (32) and gives a specific instance of (48). Replacement by one of them of the mode of determination of actual investment in the process of capital movement in section 6 gives rise to more complicated time shapes of trajectories, but leads to essentially the same results as to the validity of the conjecture of profit rate equalization. This can be seen by closer inspection of the corresponding similar phase diagrams.

8   The Case where Markets Clear

In this section we will consider a process in which at each moment temporary market clearing equilibrium prices are determinate so as to equate demand to supply in full capacity, making intended investment on real capital always realized.

On the supply side production in full capacity entails net supply of each good (15). On the demand side capitalists are still so simple reproduction minded that they consume all profits, but they want to transfer some amount of capital from the sector yielding a lower profit rate to the other.

The total current profit under full capacity is

$$(p_1 - q_1)x_1 + (p_2 - q_2)x_2, \tag{68}$$

which is by (19) equal to

$$[(1 - a_{11})x_1 - a_{12}x_2]p_1 + [-a_{21}x_1 + (1 - a_{22})x_2]p_2. \tag{69}$$

This is consumed up entirely, so that capitalists' current demand for consumption goods is a function

$$c_2(x_1, x_2, p_1/p_2)$$

$$= [(1 - a_{11})x_1 - a_{12}x_2](p_1/p_2) + [-a_{21}x_1 + (1 - a_{22})x_2]. \tag{70}$$

Capitalists want to transfer capital by realizing the intended net investment $\phi_i(p_1/p_2)$ $(i = 1, 2)$ with the aggregate money value vanishing (45), and ϕ_1 strictly increasing, ϕ_2 strictly decreasing, both vanishing at the prices of production $p_1/p_2 = \pi^*$.

Thus, if at the current levels of output in full capacity x_1, x_2, markets clear so as to determine a *unique* temporary equilibrium relative price p_1/p_2 fulfilling

$$(1 - a_{11})x_1 - a_{12}x_2 = a_{11}\phi_1(p_1/p_2) + a_{12}\phi_2(p_1/p_2) \tag{71}$$

$$- a_{21}x_1 + (1 - a_{22})x_2 = a_{21}\phi_1(p_1/p_2) + a_{22}\phi_2(p_1/p_2)$$

$$+ c_2(x_1, x_2, p_1/p_2), \tag{72}$$

then the intended sectoral net investments are realized

$$\dot{x}_i = \phi_i(p_1/p_2) \quad (i = 1, 2), \tag{73}$$

and movements of capital are generated.

The workability of the dynamic process (71), (72), (73) hinges on the unique determinacy of the relative price p_1/p_2 which, for x_1, x_2, ensures the equality of demand and supply in the markets of both goods (71), (72).

Eqs. (71) and (72) are dependent, since price-weighted sums of both sides of them are equal by (19), (45), (70). Hence, to see the unique determinacy of the equilibrium relative price and its mode of response to output levels, we have only to consider one of (71), (72), say, (71).

The right-hand side of (71), a function of the relative price $p = p_1/p_2$ is expressible as

$$a_{11}\phi_1(p) + a_{12}\phi_2(p) = \Delta\phi_1(p)/(a_{12}p + a_{22}) \tag{74}$$

Δ = determinant of A

because of (19) and (45). The continuous function

$$h(p) = \phi_1(p)/(a_{12}p + a_{22}) \tag{75}$$

vanishes together with $\phi_1(p)$ just once at π^*, prices of production, and is strictly increasing, as p varies from 0 to π^*, since its numerator and denominator are strictly increasing, while $\phi_1(p) < 0$ for $p < \pi^*$. Beyond π^* it is still strictly increasing in an interval, if $\phi_1(p)$ satisfies

$$\phi_1(p') - \phi_1(p) \geqq k(p' - p),$$

k = positive constant

for p', p within a neighborhood of π^*, as is the case when $\phi_1(p)$ has a continuous derivative in the neighborhood of π^*, positive at π^*. For then

$$h(p') - h(p) \geqq [k - a_{12}h(p')](p' - p)/(a_{12}p + a_{22})$$

which is positive for $p' > p$, provided p' is close to π^* enough to make $h(p')$ very small by continuity and hence $k > a_{12}h(p')$. Thus the continuous function $h(p)$ is strictly increasing from $h(0) < 0$ to $h(\pi^* + \varepsilon) > 0$ in an interval $[0, \pi^* + \varepsilon]$, $\varepsilon > 0$ including π^*. Let us make ε as large as possible.

Now, we consider by cases.

(I) Case of positive Δ (74), the right-hand side of (71), which is $\Delta h(p)$, continuously ranges from $\Delta h(0) < 0$ to $\Delta h(\pi^* + \varepsilon) > 0$ in a strictly increasing way, as p varies from 0 to $\pi^* + \varepsilon$. Thus, for any levels of output x_i $(i = 1, 2)$ fulfilling

$$\Delta h(0) \leqq (1 - a_{11})x_1 - a_{12}x_2 \leqq \Delta h(\pi^* + \varepsilon), \tag{76}$$

there is a unique relative price $p = p_1/p_2$ such that

$$(1 - a_{11})x_1 - a_{12}x_2 = \Delta h(p), \tag{77}$$

whence (71) and (72) hold. The system of two differential equations in the two unknowns x_1, x_2, (73) with (71), (72), is well-formulated in the region (76).

Any pair of positive output levels x_1, x_2 fulfilling

$$(1 - a_{11})x_1 - a_{12}x_2 = 0, \tag{78}$$

with π^*, prices of production, as the corresponding unique market clearing relative price, determines a state of simple reproduction with capitalists' consumption $c_2(x_1, x_2, \pi^*)$. Such a pair is a critical point, and the ray (78) is the set of all such critical points.

Off the set of critical points within the region (76) the left-hand side of (77) is not zero. If it is positive, the corresponding unique relative price p determined by (77) is greater than π^*, so that the point (x_1, x_2) moves subject to

$$\dot{x}_1 > 0 > \dot{x}_2 \tag{79}$$

from (73). Such a movement increases the left-hand side of (77) as

$$(1 - a_{11})\dot{x}_1 - a_{12}\dot{x}_2 > 0, \tag{80}$$

and thereby raises the corresponding unique relative price in (77). This implies farther deviation upward of market prices away from prices of production to widen the profit rate differentials and to let the economy leave farther the state of simple reproduction through capital mobility from the second sector to the first. If the left-hand side of (77) is negative, the senses of inequality signs in (79), (80) are reversed, and hence there is farther deviation downward of market prices away from prices of production to widen the profit rate differentials and to let the economy leave farther the state of simple reproduction through capital mobility from the first sector to the second.

(II) Case of negative Δ Since Δ is negative in (77), everything is reversed. (74), the right-hand side of (71), which is $\Delta h(p)$, continuously ranges from $\Delta h(0) > 0$ to $\Delta h(\pi + \varepsilon) < 0$ in a strictly decreasing way, as p varies from 0 to $\pi^* + \varepsilon$. Thus, in the region

$$\Delta h(0) \geqq (1 - a_{11})x_1 - a_{12}x_2 \geqq \Delta h(\pi^* + \varepsilon), \tag{81}$$

the counterpart of (76), the response of the unique relative price to the output levels in (77) is thoroughly opposite to that in case I, so that the deviation of market prices away from prices of production is diminished toward equalization of profit rates, and the economy approaches a state of simple reproduction through capital mobility.

Thus the truth of the conjecture of profit rate equalization is disproved if the capital good sector has a higher organic composition, and proved if it has a lower organic composition.

In this equilibrium dynamic process (73) with (71), (72), only the current relative price p_1/p_2 is determined. The current absolute levels of prices, however, are determined by the level of money capital stock

$$q_1 x_1 + q_2 x_2 = p_1(a_{11}x_1 + a_{12}x_2) + p_2(a_{21}x_1 + a_{22}x_2) = M \tag{82}$$

where M, the total money capital, is the sum of sectoral money capitals

$$M_i = q_i x_i = (a_{1i}p_1 + a_{2i}p_2)x_i \quad (i = 1, 2). \tag{83}$$

If money capital migrates across sectors with its total held constant, p_1 rises and p_2 falls when p_1/p_2 rises, and p_1 falls and p_2 rises when p_1/p_2 falls, as is clear from

$$\dot{p}_1(a_{11}x_1 + a_{12}x_2) + \dot{p}_2(a_{21}x_1 + a_{22}x_2) = 0, \tag{84}$$

which results upon differentiation of (82) in light of (45) and (73).

The intended sectoral investments ψ_i on money capital, which are related to those on real capital by (44), always are unequal to, and deviate by price changes from the actual ones

$$\dot{q}_i x_i + \psi_i = \dot{M}_i \quad (i = 1, 2)$$

except at prices of production, in sharp contrast with the intended sectoral investments on money capital always equal to the actual ones in the disequilibrium dynamic process in the foregoing sections, that leaves prices unchanged when the intended sectoral investments on real capital are realized.

9 Concluding Remarks

By the very definition prices of production are determined exclusively by the society's overall technology, including labor feeding and creation of surplus value and its appropriation by capitalists. They are compatible with any scheme of reproduction, either simple or expanded, whereas their static determination is never affected by the interplay of demand and supply. Nevertheless, the Marxian conjecture asserts a tendency for a centripetal force to attract market prices toward them through capital mobility across sectors in pursuit of higher rates of profit.

In all the situations considered above in order to explore the analytical evidence of the conjecture capital moves across sectors exclusively in pursuit of a higher profit rate without any other motivations, accompanied by necessarily resulting net investments. Net demand originates solely in these net investments and capitalists' and workers' consumption, whereas there is no room for any effects of vulgar subjective utility and marginal productivity. The resulting interplay of demand and supply generates changes in market prices. Our examination has revealed that in the processes of capital mobility motivated solely by higher profit rate seeking the equalization of rates of profit is not a universal tendency, but a phenomenon conditional on such a casual property of technology as the organic composition of capital of the capital good sector relative to that of the consumption good sector. In particular, the nonequalization of profit rates always prevails if the capital good sector has a higher organic composition, the situation which is often presumed in the Marxist view.

Thus the result of our examination seems to suggest that prices of production are not natural prices to which market prices tend to be attracted, but just normative constructions, an attribute of the social relations of production, like labor values.

Notes

This work evolved from its earlier stages done during the author's visit at University of Southern California, 1977–1978, 1981–1982. The helpful comment and suggestions by an anonymous referee is gratefully acknowledged.

1. Okishio (1961a, 1961b, 1965) set up a dynamic adjustment process of prices in which prices are bid down in sectors yielding profit rates higher than the equilibrium uniform profit rate and bid up in the other sectors and proved the convergence of prices toward equalization of profit rates. In his process prices change exclusively and directly in response to profit rate differentials, but not by way of capital mobility. His result thereby proves something else, stability of a cost push price mark-up process, but not equalization of profit rates through capital mobility. He became later self-critical of the result and withdrew it from the revised edition of the book (1965). No other formal work seems to have been done on this thesis in the Marxian economic literature, nor are any related results available in economic dynamics.

2. Cf., for example, Seton 1957 and Morishima 1973.

References

Morishima, M. (1973): *Marx's Economics*, Cambridge: Cambridge University Press.

Okishio, N. (1961a): Stability of Natural Prices (in Japanese), *Kokumin Keizai Zasshi, 104*.

——— (1961b): Existence and Stability of a Uniform Rate of Profit (in Japanese), *Economic Studies Quarterly, 12*,

——— (1965): *Theory of the Capitalist Economy* (in Japanese), Tokyo: Sobunsha.

Seton, F. (1957): The Transformation Problem, *Review of Economic Studies, 24*.

14 Dynamics of Growth and Capital Mobility in Marx's Scheme of Reproduction

1 Introduction

Marx's scheme of reproduction intends to trace how a competitive capitalist economic system evolves over time while reproducing its socioeconomic characteristics. It follows up growth of the relevant magnitudes generated by accumulation of capital through investment of part or all of surplus value. His original analysis, however, was sketchy, though insightful, and did not completely work out the dynamics of the scheme, which later scholars worked out more thoroughly with techniques of modern economic analysis.[1]

The scheme was originally formulated in terms of labor values, and its dynamics has been worked out to get the time path of the relevant magnitudes expressed either in terms of labor values or certain long-run equilibrium prices, the prices of production. These prices are a special set of prices at which rates of profit are equal in all sectors of industry, and toward which market prices are alledged to tend through capital movements across sectors in pursuit of higher profit rates, that result from competition in Marx's conception.

The proposition of profit rate equalization by way of capital mobility to establish the prices of production as long-run equilibrium prices is, however, merely taken granted as a divine law in Marx's theory of competition and his and later scholars' working-out of the scheme. Thus the dynamics of the scheme so functions in their working it out that investment, the driving engine of the scheme, that is, allocation among sectors of the savings from surplus value, takes place either independently of profit rate differentials or on the presumption of perpetual prevalence of the prices of production making capitalists indifferent to sectoral allocation of savings at the uniform rate of profit.

The truth of proposition itself, however, has to be examined in the dynamic process of higher profit rate seeking capital movements across sectors, which is the very evolution process of the economy to be worked out in the scheme but ignored in its working-out so far.[2]

It is therefore worth recasting the scheme with the capital mobility responsive to profit rate differentials incorporated and working out its

From *Zeitschrift für Nationalökonomie* 45, no. 3 (1985): 197–218. © 1985 Springer-Verlag. Reprinted by permission.

dynamics. The scheme so recast generates the growth of real (value) magnitudes, namely, sectoral output levels and fluctuations of market prices and profit rates through their interaction. The solution path thus generated in the scheme will be examined to see how the economy tends to evolve and whether the proposition of profit rate equalization is true. The purpose of this paper is to do this in a simple manner for the general (i.e., extended as well as simple) reproduction scheme.

2   Output, Prices and Profit Rates in the Underlying Economy

In an economy of the Leontief type, which underlies Marx's scheme of reproduction, consisting of two sectors, the first sector producing capital goods and the second producing consumption goods (wage and luxury goods), with no joint products and under constant returns to scale, by using capital goods and labor as inputs, let a_{1j}, l_j be positive amounts of capital goods and labor necessary to produce one unit of output in the jth sector ($j = 1, 2$).

On the basic viability assumption of the economy

$$1 > a_{11} \tag{1}$$

the positive labor values σ_1, σ_2 of the two goods are determined by the equations

$$\sigma_1 = a_{11}\sigma_1 + l_1,$$
$$\sigma_2 = a_{12}\sigma_1 + l_2. \tag{2}$$

The real wage ω is the amount of consumption goods necessary to reproduce one unit of labor power whose value is low enough to allow exploitation

$$\omega\sigma_2 < 1. \tag{3}$$

By introducing the labor feeding input coefficients

$$a_{2j} = \omega l_j \quad (j = 1, 2), \tag{4}$$

(2) can be put in the form

$$\sigma_1 = a_{11}\sigma_1 + a_{21}\sigma_2 + (1 - \omega\sigma_2)l_1,$$
$$\sigma_2 = a_{12}\sigma_1 + a_{22}\sigma_2 + (1 - \omega\sigma_2)l_2, \tag{5}$$

where $a_{1j}\sigma_1$, $a_{2j}\sigma_2$, $(1 - \omega\sigma_2)l_j$ are constant capital, variable capital and surplus value per unit output in the jth sector. The resulting positive matrix

$$A = \begin{pmatrix} a_{11} & a_{12} \\ a_{21} & a_{22} \end{pmatrix}$$

is the economy's basic input coefficients matrix which satisfies the Hawkins–Simon conditions and has a dominant Frobenius eigenvalue less than unity.

At the current prices p_1, p_2 of both goods, the rates of profit

$$r_j = p_j/(a_{1j}p_1 + a_{2j}p_2) - 1 \quad (j = 1, 2) \tag{6}$$

are continuous functions of the relative price p_1/p_2; r_1 monotonically increases from -1 to $1/a_{11} - 1$ and r_2 monotonically decreases from $1/a_{22} - 1$ to -1. Hence r_1 equals r_2 at a unique relative price p_1^*/p_2^* corresponding to the prices of production p_j^* ($j = 1, 2$) which satisfy the equations

$$p_j^* = (1 + r)(a_{1j}p_1^* + a_{2j}p_2^*) \quad (j = 1, 2)$$

with this uniform profit rate r equal to $1/\lambda - 1$, where λ is the dominant Frobenius eigenvalue of A.

On the output side capitalists' share c_1, c_2 in the net products uniquely determines output levels x_1, x_2 through

$$x_i = a_{i1}x_1 + x_{i2}x_2 + c_i \quad (i = 1, 2). \tag{7}$$

The organic composition of capital θ_j of the jth sector is $a_{1j}\sigma_1/a_{2j}\sigma_2$ ($i = 1, 2$), and θ_1 is larger or smaller than θ_2 according as the determinant Δ of A is positive or negative.

3 The Process of Growth and Capital Movement

At each moment of time there is total money capital M, which is divided to sectoral capitals M_j ($j = 1, 2$)

$$M_1 + M_2 = M. \tag{8}$$

M_j is connected to the existing real capital of the jth sector consisting of $a_{1j}\sigma_1 x_j$ units of constant capital and $a_{2j}\sigma_2 x_j$ units of variable capital in value terms at current output level x_j by the relation

$$M_j = q_j x_j \quad (j = 1, 2),$$ (9)

where

$$q_j = a_{1j} p_1 + a_{2j} p_2 \quad (j = 1, 2),$$ (10)

the price of real capital of the jth sector at the current prices p_j ($j = 1, 2$) of both goods.

At the sectoral rate of profit r_j the sectoral money capital M_j earns the profit

$$r_j M_j \quad (j = 1, 2).$$ (11)

The sectoral profits add up to the total profit

$$r_1 M_1 + r_2 M_2,$$ (12)

of which a certain constant percent, $100s$ ($1 \geq s \geq 0$), is saved and the rest is consumed. The savings is invested to increase the money capital at the rate $\dot{M}$, so that

$$s(r_1 M_1 + r_2 M_2) = \dot{M} = \dot{M}_1 + \dot{M}_2.$$ (13)

The allocation of the total investment $\dot{M}$ to the sectoral investments $\dot{M}_j$ ($j = 1, 2$) is responsive to the profit rate differentials and the levels of sectoral profits. Thus $\dot{M}_j$ ($j = 1, 2$) are functions of them

$$\dot{M}_j = f_j(r_1 - r_2, r_1 M_1, r_2 M_2).$$ (14)

From (13) the functions f_j ($j = 1, 2$) fulfill the identity

$$f_1(r_1 - r_2, r_1 M_1, r_2 M_2) + f_2(r_1 - r_2, r_1 M_1, r_2 M_2) = s(r_1 M_1 + r_2 M_2)$$ (15)

When r_1 is larger than r_2, investment allocation is biased to the capital good sector, so that

$$f_1(r_1 - r_2, r_1 M_1, r_2 M_2) > s r_1 M_1,$$

$$f_2(r_1 - r_2, r_1 M_1, r_2 M_2) < s r_2 M_2,$$

and capital moves from the consumption good sector to the capital good sector. When r_1 is smaller than r_2, investment allocation is biased to the consumption good sector, so that

$$f_1(r_1 - r_2, r_1 M_1, r_2 M_2) < s r_1 M_1,$$

$$f_2(r_1 - r_2, r_1 M_1, r_2 M_2) > s r_2 M_2,$$

and capital moves from the capital good sector to the consumption good sector. When r_1 equals r_2, the sectoral profits are invested in the own sectors, respectively, and capital does not move. This capital mobility responsive to profit rate differentials is premised by assuming that the functions

$$\psi_j(r_1 - r_2, r_1 M_1, r_2 M_2) = f_j(r_1 - r_2, r_1 M_1, r_2 M_2) - sr_j M_j \quad (j = 1, 2)$$

(16)

are monotonous with respect to $r_1 - r_2$, ψ_1 increasing and ψ_2 decreasing, and vanish at $r_1 - r_2 = 0$, for all levels of $r_1 M_1$ and $r_2 M_2$, except at $r_1 M_1 = r_2 M_2 = 0$.

With respect to the other two variables $r_1 M_1$, $r_2 M_2$, the functions (16) are assumed to be homogeneous of degree one. They are assumed to be continuous functions of all the variables $r_1 - r_2, r_1 M_1, r_2 M_2$, with continuous partial derivatives. Obviously, (15) implies

$$\psi_1(r_1 - r_2, r_1 M_1, r_2 M_2) + \psi_2(r_1 - r_2, r_1 M_1, r_2 M_2) = 0.$$

(17)

Thus, the investment functions on money capital (14) take the form

$$\dot{M}_j = sr_j M_j + \psi_j(r_1 - r_2, r_1 M_1, r_2 M_2) \quad (j = 1, 2).$$

(18)

On the output side the actual net investments $(a_{1j}\dot{x}_j, a_{2j}\dot{x}_j)$ on sectoral real capitals consisting of $a_{1j}x_j$ units of capital goods and $a_{2j}x_j$ units of consumption goods occur subject to

$$x_1 = a_{11}x_1 + a_{12}x_2 + a_{11}\dot{x}_1 + a_{12}\dot{x}_2$$

$$x_2 = a_{21}x_1 + a_{22}x_2 + a_{21}\dot{x}_1 + a_{22}\dot{x}_2 + (1 - s)(r_1 M_1 + r_2 M_2)/p_2,$$

(19)

that is, they are determined as net savings by which the sectoral levels of output exceed the sum of capital depreciation and capitalists' consumption in both sectors.

The system of the ten Eqs. (18), (19) with (6), (9), (10), which formulates the scheme of reproduction with capital mobility built in, completely determines the time paths of the ten variables, sectoral money capitals M_j ($j = 1, 2$), levels of output x_j ($j = 1, 2$), prices of goods p_j ($j = 1, 2$), prices of sectoral real capitals q_j ($j = 1, 2$) and rates of profit r_j ($j = 1, 2$).

At each moment of time capitalists intend by the investments on money capital $\dot{M}_j$ to carry out the net investment on real capitals in the amount

$$(a_{1j}(\dot{M}_j/q_j), a_{2j}(\dot{M}_j/q_j)),\tag{20}$$

which need not equal the actual investments determined by (19). Generally, the investment on money capital in the jth sector, which is always realized in the intended level, results by the basic relation (9) in the sum effect of the actual net investment on real capital and a change in the price of capital to compensate for the discrepancies between the intended and actual investment on real capital

$$\dot{M}_j = q_j \dot{x}_j + \dot{q}_j x_j \quad (j = 1, 2)\tag{21}$$

Thus the price of capital rises when the intended investment exceeds the actual one, and falls in the opposite situation. It remains to be unchanged when and only when the intended investment is realized. In aggregate prices, however, the actual investment on real capital equals the saved total profits and therefore the intended investment on real capital

$$q_1 \dot{x}_1 + q_2 \dot{x}_2 = s(r_1 M_1 + r_2 M_2) = \dot{M}_1 + \dot{M}_2,\tag{22}$$

as is seen by price-weighted summation of both equations in (19) based on (9), (10). Thence the discrepancies between the intended and actual investments on real capital occur in one sector just in the opposite direction to those in the other sector.

In the good markets there are excess demands for both goods

$$e_1 = a_{11}x_1 + a_{12}x_2 + a_{11}\dot{M}_1/q_1 + a_{12}\dot{M}_2/q_2 - x_1$$

$$e_2 = a_{21}x_1 + a_{22}x_2 + a_{21}\dot{M}_1/q_1 + a_{22}\dot{M}_2/q_2$$

$$+ (1 - s)(r_1 M_1 + r_2 M_2)/p_2 - x_2,$$

which are representable because of (19) as linear functions of the discrepancies between the intended and actual investments on real capital in both sectors

$$e_i = a_{i1}(\dot{M}_1/q_1 - \dot{x}_1) + a_{i2}(\dot{M}_2/q_2 - \dot{x}_2) \quad (i = 1, 2).\tag{23}$$

The price-weighted excess demands add up to zero

$$p_1 e_1 + p_2 e_2 = 0,\tag{24}$$

as is clear from (10), (22). Thence both excess demands are always either of the opposite sign or vanish at the same time.

(23) can be inverted to

$$\dot{M}_1/q_1 - \dot{x}_1 = (\quad a_{22}e_1 - a_{12}e_2)/\Delta, \tag{25}$$

$$\dot{M}_2/q_1 - \dot{x}_2 = (-a_{21}e_1 + a_{11}e_2)/\Delta. \tag{26}$$

The changes $\dot{q}_j$ ($j = 1, 2$) in the prices of capital caused by the discrepancies between the intended and actual investments on real capital induce changes $\dot{p}_j$ ($j = 1, 2$) in the prices of both goods through (10)

$$\dot{p}_1 = (\quad a_{22}\dot{q}_1 - a_{21}\dot{q}_2)/\Delta, \tag{27}$$

$$\dot{p}_2 = (-a_{12}\dot{q}_1 - a_{11}\dot{q}_2)/\Delta. \tag{28}$$

Suppose currently $e_1 > 0 > e_2$. If $\Delta > 0$, then

$$\dot{M}_1/q_1 - \dot{x}_1 > 0 > \dot{M}_2/q_2 - \dot{x}_2 \tag{29}$$

in (25), (26), so that, as was seen,

$$\dot{q}_1 > 0 > \dot{q}_2. \tag{30}$$

Whence

$$\dot{p}_1 > 0 > \dot{p}_2 \tag{31}$$

in (27), (28). If $\Delta < 0$, then the senses of the inequality signs in (29), (30) are reversed, and the same result (31) follows from (27), (28). Likewise $e_1 < 0 < e_2$ implies $\dot{p}_1 < 0 < \dot{p}_2$, and $\dot{p}_1 = \dot{p}_2 = 0$ when and only when $e_1 = e_2 = 0$. Thus the law of demand and supply prevails in the good markets.

The system evolves by growth of output generated through net investment on real capital and changes in prices effected by money capital movements responsive to profit rate differentials across sectors and their interaction. Its solution path will be worked out in the following sections.

4   What Is Going on in Value Terms?

Equation (19), one constituent of the equations formulating the dynamic process of growth and capital mobility, represents in terms of labor values the scheme of reproduction

$$V_1 + S_1 = C_2 + \dot{C}_1 + \dot{C}_2,$$

$$C_2 + S_2 = V_1 + \dot{V}_1 + \dot{V}_2 + \text{capitalists' consumption},$$

which add up to

$$S_1 + S_2 = \dot{C}_1 + \dot{C}_2 + \dot{V}_1 + \dot{V}_2 + \text{capitalists' consumption},$$

where

$C_j = \sigma_1 a_{1j} x_j = $ constant capital of the jth sector,

$V_j = \sigma_2 a_{2j} x_j = $ variable capital of the jth sector,

$S_j = \sigma_j x_j - C_j - V_j = $ surplus value of the jth sector,

$\dot{C}_j = \sigma_1 a_{1j} \dot{x}_j = $ investment in constant capital,

$\dot{V}_j = \sigma_2 a_{2j} \dot{x}_j = $ investment in variable capital.

This scheme just snapshots the sectoral balance of the current levels of the relevant magnitudes in terms of labor values at each moment of time, and the series of these snapshots represents the evolution of the system.

The law which governs the evolution, however, is determined not by these magnitudes in labor value terms alone. Although the total surplus value $S_1 + S_2$ equals the sum of the sectoral investments $\dot{C}_1$, $\dot{V}_1$, $\dot{C}_2$, $\dot{V}_2$ and capitalists' consumption, its allocation to sectors is determined not by the magnitudes in value terms such as $\sigma_j x_j$, C_j, V_j ($j = 1, 2$) alone, but by the current levels of output x_j (equivalently, those in value terms $\sigma_j x_j$) and prices p_j ($j = 1, 2$) and their interaction in the markets where the behaviors of agents, capitalists and workers, who are unaware of values, are motivated by valuation in terms of market prices, which fluctuate over time subject to the law of demand and supply.

In the course of working out of the process the money values of the relevant magnitudes deviate from their values unsystematically. The ratios of the values of aggregate investment and capitalists' consumption to the total surplus value differ in general from those of their money values to the total profits s and $1 - s$. This aspect is typically evidenced in the situation $s = 0$, in which $q_1 \dot{x}_1 + q_2 \dot{x}_2 = 0$ by (22) and the money value of capitalists' consumption equals the total profits, whereas generally $\dot{C}_1$, $\dot{V}_1$, $\dot{C}_2$, $\dot{V}_2$ do not cancel out and the value of capitalists' consumption is unequal to the total surplus value.

5 Long-run Equilibrium

The system has a special solution path, a long-run equilibrium path on which sectoral output levels and money capitals grow steadily at a common rate, and prices are maintained at the prices of production to equalize profit rates to the uniform one.

In fact, at $r_1 = r_2 = r$ the prices of production prevail, so that $r = 1/\lambda - 1$, where λ is the dominant Frobenius eigenvalue of A and

$$q_j = \lambda p_j \quad (j = 1, 2) \tag{32}$$

in (10). Investment in money capital (18) reduces to

$$\dot{M}_j = srM_j \quad (j = 1, 2).$$

implying steady growth of sectoral money capitals at the constant rate sr, which, in conjunction with (9), (21) leads to

$$\dot{q}_j/q_j + \dot{x}_j/x_j = sr \quad (j = 1, 2). \tag{33}$$

As the relative price p_1/p_2 is maintained at a constant level corresponding to the prices of production, $\dot{q}_j/q_j$ ($j = 1, 2$) are equal and have a common value, which will prove to be zero in the sequel. Therefore, $\dot{x}_j/x_j$ ($j = 1, 2$) are equal to a common value ϱ in (33),

$$\dot{x}_j/x_j = \varrho \quad (j = 1, 2). \tag{34}$$

Eliminating $\dot{x}_j$ by (34) and M_j by (9) and taking $r_1 = r_2 = r$ into account in (22), we see $\varrho = sr$. Hence

$$\dot{x}_j/x_j = \dot{M}_j/M_j = sr \quad (j = 1, 2), \tag{35}$$

$$\dot{p}_j/p_j = \dot{q}_j/q_j = 0 \quad (j = 1, 2). \tag{36}$$

On this special solution path prices remain to be unchanged and are maintained at the prices of production with profit rates equalized to the uniform rate r, and sectoral output levels and money capitals grow steadily at the rate sr. The intended net sectoral investments on real capital always equal the actual ones, and the savings from the sectoral profits are ploughed back to the own sectors without any capital movements induced by profit rate differentials, which are nonexistent. This is the only long-run equilibrium state of the system.

6 Dynamics of Certain Ratios

To work out what eventually takes place in the growth process generated by the reproduction scheme, we are concerned with the dynamic behaviors of certain ratios of the relevant variables, rather than their absolute levels. To this end the original system (18), (19) with (6), (9), (10) can be reduced by elimination and simple rearrangements to a system of two differential equations of two variables, the ratio of output levels

$$x = x_1/x_2 \tag{37}$$

and the relative price

$$p = p_1/p_2. \tag{38}$$

In fact, (19) determines simultaneously $\dot{x}_j/x_j$ ($j = 1, 2$) as functions of x and p by (6), (9), (10), so that $\dot{x}/x$ is determined as their difference

$$\dot{x}/x = s(r_1 - r_2) + \{a_{11}p + a_{21} + (a_{12}p + a_{22})/x\}$$

$$[\{1 - (1 + sr_1)a_{11}\}x - (1 + sr_2)a_{12}]/\Delta \tag{39a}$$

1st expression

$$= (a_{22} - a_{11} + a_{21}x - a_{12}/x)/\Delta + (1 - s)(a_{11} + a_{12}/x)$$

$$[\{(1 - a_{11})p - a_{21}\}x + \{-a_{12}p + (1 - a_{22})\}]/\Delta \tag{39b}$$

2nd expression

$$= s(a_{22} - a_{11} + a_{21}x - a_{12}/x)/\Delta + (1 - s)$$

$$\{a_{11}p + a_{21} + (a_{12}p + a_{22})/x\}\{(1 - a_{11})x - a_{12}\}/\Delta \tag{39c}$$

3rd expression

On the other hand, from (18), (21) together with (9) and the homogeneity of degree one of ψ_j in the profits follows

$$\dot{q}/q + \dot{x}/x = s(r_1 - r_2) + \psi_1(r_1 - r_2, r_1, r_2/qx) - \psi_2(r_1 - r_2, r_1 qx, r_2) \tag{40}$$

where

$$q = q_1/q_2. \tag{41}$$

p and q are so related through (10) that

$$q = g(p) = (a_{11}p + a_{21})/(a_{12}p + a_{22}), \tag{42}$$

$$g'(p) = \Delta/(a_{12}p + a_{22})^2, \tag{43}$$

$$\dot{q}/q = \Delta\dot{p}/(a_{11}p + a_{21})(a_{12}p + a_{22}). \tag{44}$$

Hence, (40) and (44) imply in the light of (17)

$$\dot{p} = (a_{11}p + a_{21})(a_{12}p + a_{22})\{s(r_1 - r_2)$$
$$+ (1 + xg(p))\psi_1(r_1 - r_2, r_1, r_2/xg(p)) - \dot{x}/x\}/\Delta. \tag{45}$$

(39) and (45) determine a system of two differential equations of the two variables x and p, which traces the time path of this pair of both ratios generated by those of output levels and prices in the original system.

At the unique critical point (x^*, p^*) of the system (39), (45), which corresponds to the long-run equilibrium in the original system, as given by

$$x^* = (1 + sr)a_{12}/\{1 - (1 + sr)a_{11}\}, \tag{46}$$

$$p^* = a_{21}/(\lambda - a_{11}), \tag{47}$$

the elements of the Jacobian matrix are evaluated as

$$\partial\dot{x}/\partial x = \lambda\{1 - \mu(1 + sr)\}/\Delta,$$

$$\partial\dot{x}/\partial p = a_{12}^2 rs(1 - s)/\Delta\{1 - (1 + sr)a_{11}\}^2,$$

$$\partial\dot{p}/\partial x = -(\lambda^2 p^*/\Delta x^*)\partial\dot{x}/\partial x,$$

$$\partial\dot{p}/\partial p = (\lambda - \mu)\{s + (1 + p^*x^*)\partial\psi_1/\partial(r_1 - r_2)\}/\Delta - (\lambda^2 p^*/\Delta x^*)\partial\dot{x}/\partial p,$$

where μ is the other real eigenvalue of A, less in absolute value than λ. Thus the Jacobian matrix J of the system has at the critical point

Determinant of J

$$= \lambda(\lambda - \mu)\{1 - \mu(1 + sr)\}\{s + (1 + p^*x^*)\partial\psi_1/\partial(r_1 - r_2)\}/\Delta^2 > 0. \tag{48}$$

Trace of J

$$= \lambda\{1 - \mu(1 + sr)\}/\Delta + (\lambda - \mu)\{s + (1 + p^*x^*)\partial\psi_1/\partial(r_1 - r_2)\}/\Delta$$
$$- \lambda^2(\lambda - a_{22})rs(1 - s)/\Delta^2(1 + sr)\{1 - (1 + sr)a_{11}\}. \tag{49}$$

The stability-instability properties of the path are crucially dependent on how both sectors differ in the organic compositions of capital, that is, the sign of the determinant Δ of A. The examination will be done by case in the sequel.

Case I in which Δ is positive, so that the capital good sector has a higher organic composition than the consumption good sector. The first and second terms are positive, but the third term is negative or zero in (49). Nonetheless, if $s(1 - s)$, which is not larger than $1/4$, is small relative to the two preceding terms, e.g. either s is sufficiently small or sufficiently close to 1, the trace of J is positive, and the critical point is locally unstable because of the positive determinant of J in (48). The typical situations are simple reproduction ($s = 0$) and full extended reproduction ($s = 1$), in both of which the third term in (49) vanishes. In each of both situations the critical point is an unstable node, as the locus $\dot{x} = 0$ is a vertical straight line in the phase diagram. In the simple reproduction the locus is $x = a_{12}/(1 - a_{11})$, as seen in (39c), $s = 0$. In the full extended reproduction the locus is $x = a_{12}/(\lambda - a_{11})$, as seen in (39a), $s = 1$, $r_1 = r_2 = r = 1/\lambda - 1$, which is also the positive solution of the equation

$$a_{22} - a_{11} + a_{21}x - a_{12}/x = 0$$

arising in (39b) and (39c), $s = 1$. It carries three trajectories, the critical point and the two rays emanating from it, on which the solution point diverges away from it, as (45) for $\dot{x} = 0$ is positive when p is larger than p^*, negative when p is smaller than p^*.

In the general situation the locus $\dot{x} = 0$ lies in the region bounded by the two straight lines $x = a_{12}/(1 - a_{11})$ and $x = a_{12}/(\lambda - a_{11})$, since $\dot{x}$ is negative if x is less than $a_{12}/(1 - a_{11})$, and positive if x is larger than $a_{12}/(\lambda - a_{11})$ in (39c). Also by the linearity of (39c) in p the locus can be depicted by a single-valued function of x, which is downward sloped at the critical point because of the positivity of both $\partial\dot{x}/\partial x$ and $\partial\dot{x}/\partial p$, but need not be so globally, and which tends to plus infinity as x approaches $a_{12}/(1 - a_{11})$ and takes on a negative value at $a_{12}/(\lambda - a_{11})$. It intersects the straight line $p = p^*$ once at the critical point. Thus the locus looks like as in Fig. 14.1 and 1b.

The locus $\dot{p} = 0$ does not intersect the region above the straight line $p = p^*$ and below the locus $\dot{x} = 0$ and the region below the straight line $p = p^*$ and above the locus $\dot{x} = 0$, in which (45) is positive and negative, respectively. The locus $\dot{p} = 0$ can possibly have several branches, but is either upward sloped or more steeply downward sloped at the critical point than the locus $\dot{x} = 0$, according as $\partial\dot{p}/\partial p$ is positive (Fig. 14.1a) or

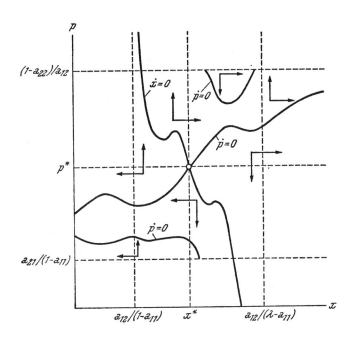

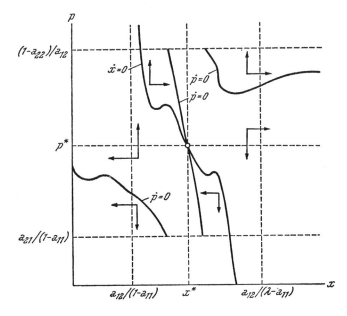

Figure 14.1

nonpositive (Fig. 14.1b), as is seen from the positivity of the Jacobian determinant.

The system is not globally stable, since $\dot{x}$ is negative in the region $x < a_{12}/(1 - a_{11})$ and positive in the region $x > a_{12}/(\lambda - a_{11})$, so that the solution point in these regions never leaves them. Even for the general value of s not close to 0 or 1 the critical point is locally unstable, provided capital mobility is so sensitive to profit rate differentials that $\partial\psi_1/\partial(r_1 - r_2)$ is large enough to make the trace of J in (49) positive, although it can be locally stable for a small value of $\partial\psi_1/\partial(r_1 - r_2)$, as is the case for $s = 1/2$ and

$$A = \begin{pmatrix} 9/10 & 1/20 \\ 17/20 & 1/10 \end{pmatrix}.$$

Case II in which Δ is negative, so that the capital good sector has a lower organic composition than the consumption good sector. The Jacobian determinant is positive as in case I. The trace of the Jacobian matrix is negative, since the first two terms are negative and the last term is negative or zero. Thus the critical point is locally stable regardless of the magnitudes of s and $\partial\psi_1/\partial(r_1 - r_2)$, and always a stable node because of the negativity of all the elements of the Jacobian matrix.

In the extreme special situations of simple reproduction ($s = 0$) and full extended reproduction ($s = 1$), the locus $\dot{x} = 0$ is the straight line $x = a_{12}/(1 - a_{11})$ or the straight line $x = a_{12}/(\lambda - a_{11})$, respectively, as in case I. But $\dot{x}$ is positive on the left-hand side of the locus and negative on the right-hand side of it, while the solution point approaches the critical point on it, as (45) is negative for $\dot{x} = 0$ when p is larger than p^*, positive when p is smaller than p^*.

In the general situation the locus $\dot{x} = 0$ lies between both straight lines $x = a_{12}/(1 - a_{11})$ and $x = a_{12}/(\lambda - a_{11})$ and is depicted by a single-valued function, downward sloped at the critical point, though not so globally, as in case I. But $\dot{x}$ is negative above the locus and positive below it just oppositely to case I because of the negativity of Δ.

The locus $\dot{p} = 0$ does not intersect the region above both of the locus $\dot{x} = 0$ and the straigllt line $p = p^*$ and the region below them, since $\dot{p}$ is negative in the former and positive in the latter. The locus $\dot{p} = 0$, which may consist of several branches, is downward sloped at the critical point because of the negativity of all the elements of the Jacobian matrix, and

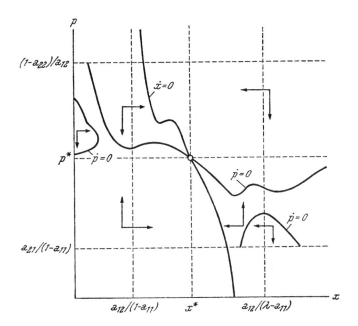

Figure 14.2

less steep than the locus $\dot{x} = 0$ by the positivity of the Jacobian determinant. Thus the phase diagram looks like Fig. 14.2.

Despite the local stability the system need not be globally stable. The shapes and locations of the loci $\dot{x} = 0$ and $\dot{p} = 0$ and the possible presence of branches of $\dot{p} = 0$ may cause some trajectories to approach the boundaries, either $p = a_{21}/(1 - a_{11})$ at which $r_1 = 0$ or $p = (1 - a_{22})/a_{12}$ at which $r_2 = 0$.

7 The Stability-instability Properties of the Path

The stability-instability properties of the paths of x and p in the system (39), (45) clarified above enable us to know those of the ten variables in the original system relative to the long-run equilibrium path.

In the case of positive Δ, where the organic composition of capital of the capital good sector is higher than that of the consumption good sector, the critical point (x^*, p^*) in the system is locally unstable generally, except possibly for an intermediate value of s close to neither 0 nor 1 and capital mobility relatively insensitive to profit rate differentials. The solution point (x, p) never converges to (x^*, p^*) but diverges away from, or fluctuates around, it. Thence in the original system prices p_j, q_j and profit rates r_j $(j = 1, 2)$ diverge away from, or fluctuate around, the prices of production and the uniform rate of profit, while sectoral money capitals M_j and output levels x_j $(j = 1, 2)$, together with their rates of growth $\dot{M}_j/M_j$ and $\dot{x}_j/x_j$ $(j = 1, 2)$ diverge away from, or fluctuate around, those in the long-run equilibrium.

In the case of negative Δ, where the organic composition of capital of the capital good sector is lower than that of the consumption good sector, the critical point (x^*, p^*) in the system is locally stable, and, more specifically, a stable node, at which eigenvectors associated with any of both negative eigenvalues of the Jacobian matrix have nonzero p components.

In a neighborhood of the critical point (x^*, p^*) the solution point (x, p) approaches it with p monotonically converging to p^* eventually because of the directions of the eigenvectors noted above. Suppose that eventually p converges to p^* from below with $\dot{p}$ positive. Then $\dot{p}_1 > 0 > \dot{p}_2$ (31) in the original system and $p_1 < p^* p_2$ eventually, which implies that p_1 is increasing but bounded above and p_2 is decreasing but bounded below. Hence p_1, p_2 converge to some positive p_1^*, p_2^*, respectively, with $p_1^* = p^* p_2^*$ naturally. Likewise supposition of the eventual convergence of p to p^* from above with $\dot{p}$ negative leads to the same result in the limit. Thereby is seen the convergence of good prices p_1, p_2 to p_1^*, p_2^*, the prices of production. Correspondingly, prices of capital q_1, q_2 converge to λp_1^*, λp_2^*. The rates of profit r_1, r_2 converge to the uniform rate r, as p converges to p^*.

If eventually p converges to p^* from below, $\psi_1 < 0 < \psi_2$ in (18) so that

$$\dot{M}_1/M_1 < sr_1 < sr, \tag{50}$$

$$\dot{M}_2/M_2 > sr_2 > sr. \tag{51}$$

Let

$$m_1 = M_1 e^{-srt},$$

$$m_2 = M_2 e^{-srt}.$$

Then

$$\dot{m}_1/m_1 = \dot{M}_1/M_1 - sr < 0 < \dot{M}_2/M_2 - sr = \dot{m}_2/m_2 \tag{52}$$

by (50), (51). Whence m_1 is decreasing and m_2 is increasing, and hence

$$m = m_1/m_2 = M_1/M_2 = qx$$

is converging decreasingly to $m^* = q^*x^* (= p^*x^*)$ from above. Thus $m_1 >$ m^*m_2, implying that m_1 is bounded below and m_2 is bounded above. Therefore m_1, m_2 converge to some positive m_1^*, m_2^* with $m_1^* = m^*m_2^*$ naturally. Likewise supposition of the eventual convergence of p to p^* from above leads to the same result in the limit.

Finally, through the basic relation (9) the convergence of

$$y_j = x_j e^{-srt} = M_j e^{-srt}/q_j \quad (j = 1, 2)$$

to $y_j^* = m_j^*/\lambda p_j^*$ $(j = 1, 2)$ with $y_1^*/y_2^* = x^*$ is ensured by the behaviors of prices and money capitals clarified above.

Thereby is shown that in the original system prices of goods and capital converge to the prices of production with rates of profit tending to the uniform rate, while money capitals and output levels converge relatively to their long-run equilibrium balanced growth paths.

8 The Market-Clearing Process of Growth and Capital Movement

In the process of growth and capital movement the good markets are generally not cleared, with good prices bid up or down in response to excess demand or excess supply, while transactions are carried out at each moment of time. Underlying this market disequilibrium are discrepancies between actual and intended investments on real capital, the former of which is realized as savings from output and the latter of which originates in sectoral investments on money capital always realizing themselves on the intended levels. Prices do not instantly adjust themselves so as to clear the markets at each moment of time, while changing over time to cope with market disequilibrium.

The process is now recast into an alternative process of growth and capital movement in which at each moment of time equality of actual and intended investments on real capital and good-market clearing are attained by instantaneous adjustment of prices, a series of temporary equilibria, to trace evolution of the relevant variables in it.

The intended sectoral investment function on real capital in the jth sector is that on money capital (18) divided by the price of capital

$$\dot{x}_j = \{ sr_j M_j + \psi_j(r_1 - r_2, r_1 M_1, r_2 M_2) \}/q_j, \tag{53}$$

which becomes by virtue of the basic relation (9)

$$\dot{x}_1 = sr_1 x_1 + \psi_1(r_1 - r_2, r_1 x_1, r_2 x_2 q_2/q_1),$$

$$\dot{x}_2 = sr_2 x_2 + \psi_2(r_1 - r_2, r_1 x_1 q_1/q_2, r_2 x_2). \tag{54}$$

The levels of actual sectoral investments are determined by (19), which is substantially by virtue of (9)

$$x_1 = a_{11} x_1 + a_{12} x_2 + a_{11} \dot{x}_1 + a_{12} \dot{x}_2$$

$$x_2 = a_{21} x_1 + a_{22} x_2 + a_{21} \dot{x}_1 + a_{22} \dot{x}_2 + (1 - s)(r_1 q_1 x_1 + r_2 q_2 x_2)/p_2. \tag{55}$$

(54) and (55) with (10) formulate a market-clearing process of growth and capital movement. The process, whose workability will be ensured later, works in the following way. At each moment of time $a_{1j} x_j$ units of constant capital and $a_{2j} x_j$ units of variable capital are existing in the jth sector, with which output levels x_j ($j = 1, 2$) are produced. For these output levels both the intended sectoral investments on real capital determined by (54) and the actual ones determined by (55) depend on the relative price p alone, and are made equal by the adjustment of p so as to determine a temporary equilibrium relative price and the corresponding levels of $\dot{x}_j$ ($j = 1, 2$). The system thereby evolves over time.

In the temporary equilibrium only the relative price is determinate, while absolute levels of prices and sectoral money capitals being indeterminate. Nonetheless, if deflated by the price of consumption goods, the real values of sectoral money capitals

$$N_j = M_j/p_2 = (q_j/p_2) x_j = (a_{1j} p + a_{2j}) x_j \tag{56}$$

are determinate. The actual investments on this real money capital are then

$$\dot{N}_j = (q_j/p_2) \dot{x}_j + (\dot{q}_j/p_2) x_j$$

$$= \dot{M}_j/p_2 + (\dot{q}_j/p_2) x_j \quad (j = 1, 2), \tag{57}$$

in which the first term is the real value of intended sectoral investment on money capital and the second is capital gain or loss. There are generally discrepancies between intended and actual investments on money capital, whereas those on real capital are always equalized, just oppositely to the situation in the original system.

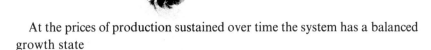
At the prices of production sustained over time the system has a balanced growth state

$$\dot{x}_1/x_1 = \dot{x}_2/x_2 = sr$$

derived from (54) for $r_1 = r_2 = r$, maintaining the ratio of output levels (46) determined in (55), with the sectoral real money capitals growing steadily at the same rate sr. This is the only long-run equilibrium the system has, and substantially the same one to that in the original system.

The workability is ensured when for given output levels x_j ($j = 1, 2$) a unique relative price p and corresponding levels of investments $\dot{x}_j$ ($j = 1, 2$) are determined so as to fulfill (54), (55), (10), thereby getting a system of two differential equations in the two variables x_j ($j = 1, 2$), which governs evolution of output levels.

(54) and (55) are homogeneous of degree one in output levels, and the set of all pairs (x, p) of the ratio of output levels $x = x_1/x_2$ and the relative price $p = p_1/p_2$ fulfilling them together with (10) is nothing but the locus $\dot{p} = 0$ in the system (39), (45) associated with the original system, which is depicted in Fig. 14.1a, 1b and 2, and along which intended sectoral investments on real capital equal the actual ones, and good markets clear. On the locus with an output ratio x is paired a locally unique relative price p. This local correspondence of p with x ensures the workability of the system in question along the locus.

As (x_1, x_2, p) evolves in the process, the pair (x, p) moves along the locus in the direction resonant with the change of x which can be seen by

$$\dot{x}/x = \dot{x}_1/x_1 - \dot{x}_2/x_2 = s(r_1 - r_2) + \psi_1(r_1 - r_2, r_1, r_2 q_2/q_1 x)$$
$$- \psi_2(r_1 - r_2, r_1 q_1 x/q_2, r_2) \qquad (58)$$

derived from (54), which is positive, negative or zero according as p is larger or smaller than or equal to p^*.

Let us examine the stability-instability properties of the path by case according to the direction of difference of the organic compositions of capital of both sectors.

Case I, in which the organic composition of capital of the capital good sector is higher than that of the consumption good sector. Generally (that is, if either s is close to 0 or 1, or capital mobility is sufficiently sensitive to profit rate differentials so as to have $\partial \dot{p}/\partial p$ positive in the Jacobian matrix of the system (39), (45)), the locus $\dot{p} = 0$ is upward sloped in the

neighborhood of the point (x^*, p^*), as in **Fig. 14.1a**. Thence the point (x, p) moves along the locus away from (x^*, p^*), as is seen by the direction of its movement implied by the sign of (58).

Case II, in which the organic composition of capital of the capital good sector is lower than that of the consumption good sector. The branch of the locus $\dot{p} = 0$ passing through the point (x^*, p^*) is downward sloped in its neighborhood and crosses the straight line $p = p^*$ from above to below once at it. Thence the point (x, p) approaches (x^*, p^*) along the branch, as the direction of its movement implied by the sign of (58) tells. Nevertheless movement along other possible branches may send the point (x, p) away from (x^*, p^*) or bring it to a point beyond which the system becomes unworkable.

In the unstable case the solution path of the system (54), (55) with (10) diverges from the long-run equilibrium. In the stable case the solution path converges to the long-run equilibrium path in the sense that $x_j e^{-srt}$ $(j = 1, 2)$ converge to certain constants while p converges to p^*, as can readily be shown likewise as in the foregoing section in the light of the eventual monotonous convergence of x and p to x^* and p^*.

9 Why Does Stability Hinge on Organic Compositions?

In both the non-market-clearing and market-clearing processes the stability of the system and the truth of the profit rate equalization heavily hinge on how both sectors differ in their organic compositions of capital. The logic for this fact is clear in the mathematical proofs in sections 6 and 8, which, however, can not be economically interpreted at every step of them. Nonetheless, the economic implication of the crucial role played by the condition of organic compositions of capital to vitally influence stability in them can be made clear.

The condition regulates the slope of the demand curve for investment, the right-hand side of (40), with respect to the relative price q of capital. The curve is upward sloped with respect to the profit rate differentials, which enlarge with the increase of the relative price p of goods. p and q, which are related by (42), change in the same or opposite direction, and thereby the curve is upward or downward sloped with respect to q at the relative price corresponding to the prices of production according as the capital good sector is higher or lower in organic compositions of capital than the consumption good sector. Thus the positive slope of the curve causes instability, while the negative one ensures stability.

The situation is made more complicated by the shift of the curve with the change of the ratio x of output levels, nonetheless the slope of the curve tends to determine essentially the stability-instability property of the system in the logic for the result.

10   Concluding Remarks

The prices of production, ensuring the uniform rate of profit across all sectors, rectify the unequal opportunities of sectoral capitals to share in surplus value and transform labor values to themselves. They, too, however, are alternative value constructions determined exclusively by the social relations of production, just like labor values, independently of volatile market demand and supply conditions. The relationships between relevant magnitudes in terms of labor values and those in terms of the prices of production, as established in the solutions of the transformation problem, are what naturally exist between the two attributes of the one and the same entity, the social relations of production.

In Marx's theory of competition, however, the prices of production is thought of as special market prices, something more than alternative value constructions, which competition among capitalists brings about through capital mobility across sectors in pursuit of higher rates of profit. Capitals do not instantly move across sectors, but migrate gradually over time through investment of the savings from surplus value in the very midst of the evolution process of the whole capitalist system. In this context Marx and later scholars neither examined this proposition of profit rate equalization through capital mobility nor worked out the dynamics of the evolution of the whole capitalist system.

The process of capital mobility is nothing more or less than the evolution process of the whole capitalist system. The process must involve, together with the evolution of levels of output, formation of current market prices and the corresponding determination of sectoral rates of profit, to which capital mobility is responsive.

In this paper an evolution process of the whole capitalist system in the above sense is formulated by recasting the scheme of reproduction into two alternative processes involving profit rate responsive capital mobility, a non-market-clearing process and a market-clearing process, which are closely related to each other, and their dynamics are worked out.

Both processes have a unique long-run equilibrium in common, in which the prices of production are sustained, keeping the uniform rate of profit, and the output levels and sectoral capitals grow steadily at the common rate equal to the product of the saving ratio and the uniform rate of profit.

In each of the processes the dynamic behavior of the general solution path relative to the long-run equilibrium path crucially depends on how both sectors differ in their organic compositions of capital[3]. If the capital good sector is higher in the composition than the consumption good sector, the path diverges away from the long-run equilibrium path, generally (viz, provided capital mobility is sufficiently sensitive to profit rate differentials), so that the ratio of the output levels deviates from that in the long-run equilibrium, while the market prices diverge away from the prices of production, making the profit rate differentials enlarged. If the compositions are reversed, the path converges relatively to the long-run equilibrium path, within its vicinity, so that the ratio of the output levels converges to that in the long-run equilibrium, while the growth rates of the levels approach to their common steady growth rate in the long-run equilibrium, and the market prices tend to the prices of production, making the profit rates equalized to the uniform profit rate.

Thence the proposition of equalization of profit rates is not universally true, but its truth is conditional on the direction of the difference of sectoral organic compositions of capital. The very difference, which causes the deviation of the prices of production from the labor values of goods, as is well known, confines their establishment in markets through capital mobility resulting from competition among capitals. The prices of production therefore can hardly be considered as market prices beyond their nature of being alternative value constructions attributable to the social relations of production.

Notes

This is a sequel to the author's previous work (1983). Helpful comment and suggestions by anonymous referees are gratefully acknowledged.

1. Cf. for example, Lange 1969, Harris 1972, and Morishima 1973.

2. Nikaido 1983 examines it in the case of simple reproduction.

3. There are apparently similar, but sustantially different two-sector processes of growth and capital mobility in the neoclassical equilibrium dynamics. In all these processes labor as well as capital is kept fully employed in contrast to the scheme of reproduction, in which labor is underemployed, while capital is fully utilized. In Shinkai 1960 sectoral capitals, combined with labor in fixed proportions, are instantly shifted between sectors to attain a temporary equilibrium, and capitals move over time independently of profit rates. In Inada 1966 sectoral capitals are unshiftable instantly, and a temporary equilibrium is attained by allocation of labor in virtue of flexible factor substitution. Capital movement takes place in response to profit rate differentials. The rates of profit, however, are marginal productivities, which diminish with increased capital intensities, and thereby bring the system to a long-run equilibrium, in distinction from the scheme of reproduction in which any nonconstant returns are not operative, and marginal productivities have no bearing on its working.

References

Harris, D. J. (1972): On Marx's Scheme of Reproduction and Accumulation, *Journal of Political Economy*, 80.

Inada, K. (1966): Investment in Fixed Capital and the Stability of Growth Equilibrium, *Review of Economic Studies*, 33.

Lange, O. (1969): *Theory of Reproduction and Accumulation*, New York: Pergamon.

Morishima, M. (1973) *Marx's Economics, A Dual Theory of Value and Growth*. Cambridge: Cambridge University Press.

Nikaido, H. (1983): Marx on Competition, *Zeitschrift für Nationalökonomie*, 43.

Shinkai, Y. (1960): On Equilibrium Growth of Capital and Labor, *International Economic Review*, 1.

Index